# GORBACHEV AND *PERESTROIKA*

# GORBACHEV AND
# *PERESTROIKA*

*Edited by*

## Martin McCauley

*Senior Lecturer in Soviet and East European Studies*
*School of Slavonic and East European Studies*
*University of London*

## St. Martin's Press    New York

All rights reserved. For information, write:
Scholarly and Reference Division,
St. Martin's Press, Inc., 175 Fifth Avenue,
New York, N.Y. 10010

First published in the United States of America in 1990

Printed in Great Britain

ISBN 0–312–04510–7

Library of Congress Cataloging-in-Publication Data
Gorbachev and *Perestroika*/edited by Martin McCauley.
p.   cm.
Includes bibliographical references.
ISBN 0–312–04510–7
1. Soviet Union—Politics and government—1985—Congresses.
2. *Perestroika*—Congress.   I. McCauley, Martin.
DK286.5.G656   1990
947.085'4—dc20                                89–70320
                                                CIP

*In memoriam*

Levenna Anderson McCauley
1 July 1904–26 April 1989

# Contents

# List of Tables

# Preface

At the conclusion of Mikhail Gorbachev's first offical visit to the
United Kingdom on 7 April 1989 he was seen by many as the world's
number one statesman. He brought to a long-suffering world a vision
of hope and of a better tomorrow. He spoke of his dream of a non-
nuclear world by the year 2000 and a common European home. The
transformation of his image and that of the Soviet Union since he
became Communist Party leader in March 1985 was nothing short of
breathtaking. Yet his standing abroad was in sharp contrast to his
position at home. After four years, *perestroika* had failed to produce
a tangible improvement in Soviet living standards. The old problems
of food and housing continued to dominate most people's minds.
Opposition to restructuring surfaced among those who judged that
Gorbachev's radical revolution could cost them dear: middle- and
lower-level bureaucrats, workers, Russian nationalists and those who
wanted a quiet life.

Most of the chapters in this book consider the first four years of
*perestroika*. However, this survey does not claim to be comprehensive; nevertheless it should provide the reader with an in-depth
analysis of the most stunning political, economic and social experiment in the Soviet Union since 1929. It is still too early to judge
whether the great experiment has succeeded or failed. What is
striking is the gulf which has emerged between foreign and domestic
achievements. Whatever the outcome, the Soviet Union will never
again revert to its pre-1985 condition, and some of the attempts to
move towards a more democratic political culture have put down
permanent roots. Gorbachev has perceived that unless restructuring
succeeds, the Communist Party will gradually lose control of the
country. Everyone, within the Soviet Union and outside it, will be
touched by the outcome of the epic struggle now under way.

Most of the chapters were originally delivered at a conference on
7–8 July 1988 at the School of Slavonic and East European Studies,
University of London. They have been updated to take into consideration later events. Other chapters were specially commissioned for
the book. Professor R. W. Davies's chapter originally appeared in

his own *Soviet History in the Gorbachev Revolution*, published in 1989.

Special thanks are due to those who presented papers at the conference, but also to those who contributed from the floor to make it such a rewarding and stimulating experience. Warm thanks are also due to Professor M. A. Branch, Director of the School, and his administrative staff, especially Philip Robinson. Jacek Rostowski's helpful comments on a preliminary draft of the Introduction are also appreciated.

Finally, gratitude is due to the Ford and Nuffield Foundations without whose generous financial support the conference could not have taken place.

MARTIN MCCAULEY

# Notes on the Contributors

**Stephen Dalziel** works for the Research Department of the BBC World Service, and previously was at the Soviet Studies Centre, Royal Military Academy, Sandhurst.

**R. W. Davies** is Emeritus Professor of Soviet Economic Studies at the University of Birmingham. He is the author of many works on Soviet history and his most recent book is *Soviet History in the Gorbachev Revolution*.

**Julian Graffy** is Lecturer in Russian Language and Literature at the School of Slavonic and East European Studies, University of London. He is co-editor of *Culture and the Media in the USSR Today*.

**Philip Hanson** is Professor of Soviet Economics at the University of Birmingham, and the author of many books and articles, including *Trade and Technology in Soviet–Western Relations*.

**Michael Kaser** is a Professorial Fellow of St Antony's College, Oxford. He is the author of many books and articles on Soviet and East European economics.

**Nick Lampert** is Lecturer in Sociology at the University of Birmingham. Among his recent publications is *Whistleblowing in the Soviet Union: Complaints and Abuse under State Socialism*.

**Margot Light** is Lecturer in International Relations at the London School of Economics and Political Science. She has written widely on Soviet foreign policy and among her books is *The Soviet Theory of International Politics*.

**Alastair McAuley** is Senior Lecturer in Economics at the University of Essex. Among his publications is *Women's Work and Wages in the Soviet Union*.

**Martin McCauley** is Senior Lecturer in Soviet and East European Studies at the School of Slavonic and East European Studies, University of London. Among his recent publications is *The Soviet Union under Gorbachev*, which he edited.

**Michael Maltby** is on the staff of Barclay's Bank, and was formerly a research student at St Antony's College, Oxford.

**Bohdan Nahaylo** is senior research analyst on the staff of Radio Liberty, Munich. He is co-author of *Soviet Disunion: A History of the Nationalities Problem in the USSR*.

**Elizabeth Teague** is on the staff of Radio Free Europe/Radio Liberty, Munich. She is the author of *Solidarity and the Soviet Worker*.

**Karl-Eugen Wädekin** is Professor Emeritus of Soviet, East European and International Agrarian Policy at the University of Giessen, West Germany. His many publications include *Agrarian Policies in Communist Europe*.

# Introduction

## MARTIN McCAULEY

The four years under Gorbachev (1985–9) have seen the most radical attempt to restructure the Soviet political, economic and social system since 1929. Gorbachev has sought to redistribute power and privilege in the Soviet Union. He has been trying to effect a revolution from above and below. His main target has been the state and Party bureaucracy. By reducing its decision-making functions, enterprises and cooperatives and individual producers gain greater control over their activities. Radical legislation has been promulgated effecting this transfer of power, but the bureaucracy has fought back. In a speech to Moscow industrial workers (*Pravda*, 16 January 1989) Gorbachev revealed the pressure he was under. He was very critical of the Party apparat. *Perestroika* was becoming bogged down because central decisions were being transformed 'somewhere on the way to the work collective in such a way that they are frequently drained of their lifeblood'. He also conceded that restructuring was being hindered 'to a considerable extent by opposition from specialists and managers'. He then referred to exchanges he had had with workers. 'I think the fact that you today subjected us to sharp criticism shows that your patience has reached its limit because we show excessive tolerance'. Gorbachev thus had to admit that, after four years, restructuring had not brought any tangible improvements. How long could the great experiment last before patience was exhausted? Aleksandr Yakovlev, regarded as an ardent supporter of renewal, revealed in a speech in Perm (*Zvezda*, 17 December 1988) how tense the situation was:

> We probably have no more than two or three years to demonstrate to ourselves and others that socialism in its Leninist version is not utopia. . . . If we get cold feet when faced with the difficulties of *perestroika*, then destructive tendencies in the economic and moral-political sphere may acquire irreversible characteristics. Then we may be threatened not simply with a return to the situation we had before, to stagnant thinking, but by an aggressive and vengeful conservatism revelling in its victory.

1

By 1989 the battle for *perestroika* had reached a critical point. The left, led by Gorbachev, was ahead of the right, under Ligachev, but only on points. Four years of restructuring had wrought many personnel changes at the top but old attitudes still persisted at middle and lower levels of the bureaucracy and society. The 'human factor', on which Gorbachev laid so much store, had still to play an important role. *Homo perestroicus* had clearly not yet emerged.

Gorbachev speaks of revolutionary *perestroika*. Will this involve the breakup of the present system? Is Gorbachev capable of getting rid of 'real, existing socialism' or will real, existing socialism get rid of him? Will real, existing bureaucracy devour him as it has devoured all previous reformers? And what is meant by the term bureaucracy in the Soviet context?

Max Weber has greatly influenced Western thinking on the subject of bureaucracy, which is normally viewed as an apparatus of professional officials guided by hierarchical principles and governed by rules, regulations and conventions. A bureaucracy is necessary for the functioning of a modern state. The Soviets, however, have never developed a theory of bureaucracy. When they use the word it usually denotes 'defects of the mechanism', failures which have occurred due to the misdemeanours of officials. The implication always is that if party and state officials carried out their duties conscientiously the system would function perfectly. No model of this perfect, rationally functioning, system has ever been published.

Remoulding the administration is an immense task, but Gorbachev is quite determined to press ahead because potential gains are very considerable. In late 1987, in Murmansk, he had the following to say (*Pravda*, 2 October 1987):

Since the administration of the economy and society over a period of many decades was based on centralisation and command–administrative methods, this resulted in a great expansion of the administrative apparatus, state as well as economic. Also the apparatus of social organisations and to a certain extent the Party apparatus. There are now about 18 million persons employed in administration, of whom 2.5 million are in the apparatus of various administrative organs and 15 million run associations, enterprises and organisations. They make up 15 per cent of all workers and employees.... [The administrative apparatus] costs us about 40 billion rubles a year but the increase in national income over past years was about 20 billion rubles.

The bloated administrative apparatus is to be reduced by 40 per cent by 1991. This, based on Gorbachev's figure would result in 7–8 million civil servants losing their jobs. When families are considered, this reform would affect about 10 per cent of the Soviet population. The 18 million quoted by Gorbachev appears to include only regional and municipal administrators and the state economic bureaucracy. However, there are also the social and other organisations: the Party, Komsomol, trade unions, kolkhozes and so on. The Party apparatus may employ as many as 500 000. The total involved in running the Soviet state and socialist economy may be as high as 25–30 million (Jozsa 1989). The astonishing fact emerges that, if families are taken into account, about one-third of the population directly or indirectly runs the Soviet state.

Sergei Andreev, a biologist working in the oil research institute in Tyumen, Siberia, set out to discover the size of the economic bureaucracy, since he regards it as a 'new socio-political class' (Andreev 1989).

In 1979 he counted 615 all-Union, Union-republican and republican ministries. The economic bureaucracy consisted of 17.718 million persons. Of these 11.5 million worked in enterprises and organisations and 3 million were engineers. The elite were the 1.604 million employed in ministries and departments. However, cutting down the size of the elite will not solve the problem. Andreev cites an example taken from *Izvestiya*. The Ukrainian Ministry of Coal was ordered to shed 744 jobs; 255 of these became the staff of a newly-created production association. A few went into production and a quarter were pensioned off. The rest, the majority, found other administrative jobs. It is clear that bureaucrats will always find jobs for sacked bureaucrats!

A raion agroprom in Chita oblast employed 530 persons with wages coming to 1 675 100 rubles. This despite the fact that there are barely ten kolkhozes in the raion. After restructuring, the wage bill came to 1 504 00 rubles – a saving of 2.1 per cent! (*Argumenty i fakty*, no. 10/1988).

Gorbachev reveals, from to time, that his understanding of reality is defective. A case in point was his discovery of the queue. The queue is a fundamental part of Soviet life with something like 65 billion man, or more correctly, woman hours being devoted to it annually. He announced his discovery at the Central Committee (CC) plenum in July 1988 and was very annoyed at this waste of time. He then concluded: 'And this was in Moscow, comrades, where everything is available!' This compounded his error and revealed how ill-informed he and the leadership were about everyday life in Moscow. Did he never look out of his official car in the capital and ask himself why so many people were hanging around, apparently with nothing to do? Insight had not come through observation. A woman worker at a factory he had been visiting had brought home the truth to him in no uncertain terms.

His frustration at the slow pace of *perestroika* has produced some memorable metaphors. For example, when addressing Moscow communists (*Pravda*, 10 January 1989), he lamented that some people regarded *perestroika* as 'manna from heaven, an omelette which someone serves up [every] morning on a pan or a plate'. This is a reference to the food which the Jews, led by Moses, in the Old Testament, picked every morning in the desert during their long trek from Egypt to the Promised Land, Israel. It would appear that many Soviet citizens regard Gorbachev as their Moses and expect him to work miracles every day. He makes the sacrifices and they reap the benefits! No wonder this latter-day Moses vents his spleen from to time on the lethargic and lazy. However, he must discover a recipe to inspire them to follow him into the Promised Land, a restructured Soviet Union.

Gradually Gorbachev has become more radical. Is this growing radicalism the result of frustration at the limited impact of *perestroika* or is it part and parcel of an overall plan for the renaissance of the Soviet economy and society? A striking fact about the reforms and initiatives which have so far been launched is that they have not been sufficiently thought through. They are clearly the result of rapid decision-making, and economic reform has outpaced political reform. Some fundamental reforms, such as the reform of prices, have been put off. One explanation for the inconsistency of the reforms would be that Gorbachev has become more radical as his political authority has grown. Reforms are introduced as a consequence of winning political battles. This school of thought would argue that he is a revolutionary but has not been able to show his full hand. As his political authority grows so one can expect more and more far-reaching reforms. The other way of looking at his performance to date would be to regard his innovations as the result of increasing frustration at the poor record of *perestroika* so far. The worse the situation becomes, the more radical will be the solutions adopted by Gorbachev. This would seem to explain why restructuring over time has appeared to be uncoordinated and hasty. Another explanation for the hastiness would be that Gorbachev and his supporters are aware of the strength of opposition to reform. If a reform were to go through a lengthy process of debate and be introduced gradually, the reform would most likely fail. The thinking might be that a short, sharp, very radical move is capable of succeeding. Once this initiative had been blunted by bureaucratic obstruction, introduce another radical change. Reform becomes an iterative process.

The decision to convene a USSR Congress of People's Deputies in March 1989 in order to elect a new USSR Supreme Soviet which will function as a parliament is an example of a very radical move which was introduced peremptorily. Most Party first secretaries are expected to become chairmen of their local soviets. Gorbachev argues that this will make these officials more accountable to the local population. However, this fusion of Party and soviets already exists in Romania. No one could claim that Romanian experience offers much hope for optimism. As Academician Andrei Sakharov has pointed out, the new office of President represents a dangerous concentration of power in a one-party system. If a conservative replaced Gorbachev he would have the levers to set aspects of *perestroika* into reverse. A multi-party system is needed to cope with this problem. Why should the USSR Congress of People's Deputies be directly elected but the parliament be indirectly elected? If multi-candidate elections are being encouraged, why is there only one candidate, Gorbachev, for the post of President?

While Gorbachev argues that the people are behind him, other voices concede that opposition reaches down to the common man and woman. For example, Valentin Falin, head of the International Department of the CPSU Central Committee, divides the opponents of *perestroika* into three groups. The first group comprises ordinary people who in the past suffered disappointment after disappointment: this made them distrustful of innovation and official promises. Their attitude was to wait for evidence that *perestroika* was working before they would believe in it. The second group consisted of the 'guardians of instructions' in the ministries. They possessed 'enormous power' and they reaped 'considerable profits' from the present state of affairs. *Perestroika* could cost them dearly. The third group were the 'dogmatists' who rejected democratisation and the introduction of market elements. These represented a 'return to the past' from their point of view (*Suddeutsche Zeitung*, 19 June 1987).

G. Lisichkin thinks the core of opposition to *perestroika* is to be found among the unqualified in the administration, the economy and science. They have a powerful interest in mobilising opinion against the introduction of market mechanisms which are designed to promote efficiency. Their natural allies are the dogmatic philosophers and economists who propagate 'eternal' laws of socialism. The market has no place in their perception of socialism (*Lit. Gaz.*, 24 June 1987).

Fedor Burlatsky, a leading political scientist and commentator in *Literaturnaya Gazeta* and a passionate supporter of *perestroika*, put his finger on some of the contradictions, in *Pravda* on 18 July 1987. He conceded that many were misusing change to enrich themselves. Others were indulging in chauvinism, anti-Semitism and localism. The haste with which legislation on enterprises, cooperatives, individual labour and non-labour incomes had been introduced has made it possible for local officials to disrupt its implementation. He was critical of Nikolai Shmelev, a radical economist, for his acceptance of unemployment under socialism, but conceded that there were enterprise directors who were ready to dismiss a quarter or a third of their labour force so as to increase profits. If this happened on a national scale the results would be disastrous. Turning to the bureaucracy Burlatsky envisaged cutting it by half. But what was to become of the nine million sacked bureaucrats and their families, not to mention the army of unemployed workers? Burlatsky offered no solution except to recommend that some national body retrain and relocate the unemployed (Jozsa 1988).

Elizabeth Teague points out that the Party is now at a crossroads. *Izvestiya* has conceded that there now exists a 'crisis of confidence in the Party'. Party membership has begun to fall in areas as far apart as Moscow and Yakutia in Siberia. Komsomol membership is also down. She poses the crucial question. Is it possible for the Soviet leadership to manage change so skilfully that democracy can eventually evolve?

*Glasnost* has loosened the tongues of witnesses to the past. The immense suffering and, indeed heroism, of the Soviet people are now finding expression. As R. W. Davies points out, the full horror of the Stalin era is being relived in many novels and plays. A biography of Stalin by General Volkogonov has appeared. It has begun the process of reassessing much more objectively the role of Stalin and the circumstances which permitted Stalinism to flourish. Gorbachev changed his views on the value of critically reevaluating the past as obstacles to *perestroika* mounted. Journalists have been in the forefront of historical writing while the historical profession has been much slower to take up the challenge.

Philip Hanson believes that the drive for reform from above is 'supported by a substantial group of the more socially active members of the population'. However, the fate of *perestroika* will depend on the following: are the 'group of active, reform-minded officials and others in reasonable agreement about what should be changed and how'; and, if they 'are in reasonable agreement, are there enough of them to provide a critical mass of support for radical political and social reforms; and not just for promulgating such reforms but for carrying them through?

One sector of the economy where urgent improvements are necessary is housing. Even the high-priority military sector has fared badly. In Moscow alone over 7000 officers and their families are awaiting accommodation. Even in the prestigious General Staff, over a thousand officers have not been allocated housing. Meanwhile, they are having to spend one-third of their pay on temporary accommodation (*Pravda*, 12 February 1989). The USSR Ministry of Defence has decided that self-help is the only solution and is setting up its own construction department. A key question will be access to building materials.

Agriculture will have a major influence on whether *perestroika* achieves its goals. The 1988 harvest of 195 million tonnes was under the level of the two previous years and over 30 million tonnes short of target. Gorbachev has lamented the fact that about 20 per cent of agricultural output is lost between production and consumption. The four stages – production, storage, transport and trade – are under the authority of a multitude of authorities. But how are all these stages to be coordinated? The body running agriculture, between 1985 and 1989, USSR Gosagroprom, was a Leviathan. Another bureaucratic nightmare is the State Committee for Supply (Gossnab). It is proving too much for even Gorbachev. At a conference which he chaired in the CC, devoted to agriculture, he said: 'Doing battle with Gossnab – that's a job! As they say, you'll rupture yourself doing that!' He also broke the convention that a member of the Politburo does not directly criticise another in public. 'Yesterday I asked comrades Ligachev, Nikonov and Murakhovsky (chairman of USSR Gosagroprom) two questions, and that's where we remained, with these questions.' Ligachev and Nikonov are full members of the Politburo. Gorbachev's tetchiness was excised from the version of the speech which appeared in *Pravda* on 15 January 1989, as was the swipe at Gossnab. The speech was broadcast on Moscow Radio (BBC, SWB SU/0359, 16 January 1989). There appears to be an air of despondency at the highest levels. Prime Minister Nikolai Ryzhkov, at a USSR Council of Ministers' meeting on fruit and vegetable production, could only say (*Pravda*, 15 January 1989):

> Let us, comrades, once again instruct USSR Gosagroprom and the State Committee for Prices to look again soberly at this problem, to analyse where we are going.

Tass reported on 21 January 1989 that gross agricultural output for 1988 was only 0.7 per cent up on the previous year. Thus it was below the rate of growth of the population. Fruit production in the previous 15 years had declined nationally by 30 per cent, but in Moscow oblast it had fallen by 80 per cent. The drift from the countryside continued. During 1986 and 1987 over one million persons left rural areas in the Russian Federation and the Ukraine. It came as no surprise when USSR Gosaproprom was abolished in March 1989. Karl-Eugen Wädekin notes an overall quantitative improvement in crop production under Gorbachev. There have been some spectacular increases in hectare yields of grain, sunflower and sugar beet. In animal husbandry qualitative improvements have been more marked than in crop production. It is very difficult to measure just what impact Gorbachev has had on agricultural performance so far. However, he is committed to helping the private or individual producer and the *podryad*. If this continues, agricultural output should grow.

Michael Kaser and Michael Maltby point out that Gorbachev's 'domestic restructuring, both economic and political, would be much easier if the USSR were earning the huge profits on energy and gold' which Brezhnev enjoyed in the1970s. Gorbachev stated at the CC plenum in February 1988 that the increase in national income over twenty years was attributable to sales of energy and vodka. Changed foreign trade conditions and the need to import about 30 million tonnes of grain annually have resulted in a worsening of the USSR's external balance under Gorbachev.

Soviet authorities have taken only the first tentative steps towards providing a system of financial support for those declared redundant, states Alastair McAuley. Legislation, however, only provides for redundancy pay equivalent to one month's wages! In certain cases it will be possible to get three months' wages. After that there is nothing. Hence Gorbachev is 'likely to encounter political opposition from the traditional working class. As in Hungary in the early 1970s, this may make it easier for opponents of reform to mount an effective resistance campaign by appealing to ideologically potent symbols'.

Unemployment is, in fact, becoming a sensitive issue. A special conference at the All-Union Central Council of Trade Unions heard some disturbing facts (*Trud*, 20 January 1989). Decisions to terminate employment were often taken in secrecy and in great haste. Often it was not the unproductive who went, but the troublemakers. Other groups who felt they were being unjustly treated were women with children, and labour veterans. Restructuring has also been used to lower the grades of some specialists, in effect depriving them of their jobs. During 1988 about a million jobs were lost and it is expected that this process will accelerate. What facilities are available for retraining? Who is responsible for providing redundant workers with new skills? The trade union conference did not know. There are plenty of jobs in some areas, such as Siberia, but housing and social conditions there are held to be worse than in the European part of the country. Hence the incentive to move is very low. *Trud* concluded the report with a warning: The 'situation regarding our labour resources is fraught with the most serious social consequences if we underestimate it. And time is not on our side in this matter'.

Bohdan Nahaylo argues that in 'no other area has the impact of *glasnost* and democratisation been so dramatic as in the nationality sphere'. When Gorbachev took over as Party leader, problems appeared to be well under control. However, in 1989 they had forced their way to near the top of the policy agenda. He has conceded that the success or failure of *perestroika* will 'depend to a decisive extent' on how this burning issue is handled. Nick Lampert reveals that the concept of the socialist legal state has emerged as a central theme of Gorbachev's reforms. It signals the 'search for greater predictability and central control over unruly officials and wayward citizens'. However, it is also a precondition for the evolution of a democratic political order and the protection of the citizen against arbitrary power. Battle has now been joined by those reformers who borrow 'uninhibitedly from a liberal-democratic tradition' and those who stay within the socialist legal tradition. The debate on the socialist legal state owes its genesis to the 'crisis of political authority and is part of a wider effort to strengthen the legitimacy of the Soviet state'. Stephen Dalziel examines *perestroika* in the armed forces and reveals the contradictory nature of the process. The new policy has seen the military lose some influence in top councils. The Party leadership has also begun to seek civilian advice on military questions. The advent

of a new Minister of Defence, a new Chief of the General staff, and a
new Commander-in-Chief of the Warsaw Pact forces, testifies to a
radical rethinking of the role of the military in Soviet society. The
policy of defensive defence has caused considerable disquiet in some
military circles. General Aleksei Lizichev, Chief of the Main Political
Administration of the Soviet Army and Navy, has revealed that there
are two main approaches to reforming the military at present
(*Krasnaya Zvezda*, 4 February 1989). One is to improve and refine
the present system without introducing fundamental change. The
other would be to make the armed forces a professional body. This
would mean the end of conscription. Every man or woman serving
would be a volunteer. The professional army could either be based on
the 'territorial militia principle or each Union republic could have its
own army, its own national formation'. A purely professional army
would afford military officers more authority. As a result political
officers would find their role and functions diminished. Gorbachev's
announcement of a reduction of 500 000 in Soviet military personnel
at the United Nations in New York on 7 December 1989 and the
completion of the withdrawal of Soviet troops from Afghanistan,
estimated at 115 000, on 15 February 1989, have provided the
opportunity for a radical reassessment of Soviet military priorities.
Margot Light points out that Soviet foreign policy, before 1985, was
simply too expensive. The political or economic returns on Soviet
diplomatic investment, and on economic and military aid, were too
small. The new political thinking had transformed Soviet foreign
policy but it is still too soon to judge whether the changes are
irreversible. Does the Brezhnev doctrine still apply to Eastern
Europe? What would happen if an East European leader declared he
was taking his country out of the Warsaw Pact? Verification is seen as
a major breakthrough. The Soviet discussion of it led to a consideration of trust in international relations. The Soviets now admit to some
responsibility for past events and perceive that their rhetoric can have
a negative effect on their competitors. The West can contribute
positively to the process of restructuring in the Soviet Union.
However, at the end of the day it is the success or failure of domestic
*perestroika* which will determine whether the new foreign policy can
continue.

Julian Graffy sees the world of literature, cinema, theatre and
painting in the Soviet Union enlivened to a degree unhoped for in the
course of the last four years. *Glasnost* can indeed be viewed as the
aphrodisiac of the intelligentsia. The official face of Soviet culture has

been transformed. A striking phenomenon of the Gorbachev years is the growth of informal groups. There are now thousands of them, pursuing political, ecological and other goals. This has permitted many groups and individuals who had been existing underground to surface and become a 'parallel culture'. Rock music has broken through the bonds of official disapproval. The hegemony of the state version of Soviet culture appears to be breaking down and the country is returning to the diversity of the 1920s.

However, the battle for diversity has not yet been won. A powerful voice in favour of more discipline within the Party and society is General Viktor Chebrikov, former head of the KGB and at present chairman of the CC commission on legal reform. As such he is responsible for elaborating a legal framework for the new society emerging. This will include deciding, for instance, how far workers' control can go. He complained that the tolerance extended under *glasnost* had produced a situation where 'some people felt that everything was permissable and nothing was punishable' (*Pravda*, 11 February 1989). A special target were the 'so-called informal associations':

> Coming under the influence of extremist leaders, they embark on a path of anti-social and illegal activity. While demagogically declaring their support for *perestroika*, they hinder it by their actions. There are also frankly anti-socialist elements which are attempting to create political structures opposed to the CPSU.... We must deal a resolute and public rebuff, from a Marxist-Leninist position, to the leaders of those formations which seek to push the masses on to a path of anarchy and lawlessness, on to a path of destabilising the situation, on to a path of creating legal and illegal structures in opposition to the Party.

After four years *perestroika* appears to be irreversible. However, it has become quite clear that restructuring will be a much longer, more complicated task than ever the Gorbachev leadership imagined. He now speaks of no tangible rise in living standards for three to four years, and this will probably lengthen in the near future. When he came to power Gorbachev spoke of inheriting a 'pre-crisis situation'. In 1989 the country is acknowledged as being 'in deep crisis'. Gorbachev has demonstrated on many occasions that he is the most skilful, fleet-footed politician in the Soviet Union, but he is not the most popular. That accolade falls on the shoulders of Boris Eltsin, the 'tribune of the people'. However, Eltsin is a poor political tactician and does not offer tangible solutions to the present economic malaise. Gorbachev has consolidated his position politically and only ill-health or an unfortunate combination of circumstances could bring him down.

The burden of office has aged hm by almost a decade over the last four years and future battles will be tough and gruelling. Ethnic tensions have regularly spilled over into violence, and the scheduled CC plenum on nationality affairs has been postponed time after time. This testifies to the fact that no solution proposed by Moscow is acceptable to all non-Russians. Economic reasons have fuelled ethnic strife, as minorities have become the scapegoat for high prices and poor supplies. Economic advance would ease many of Gorbachev's problems but this is not in sight in 1989.

Economic and social tensions, ethnic strife, mass strikes and a collapse of Party authority could all produce a situation favouring a return to more central, autocratic Party rule. Military and KGB support would be needed for a conservative Party leader to replace Gorbachev.

Gorbachev is politically in a powerful position but economically in a weak position. He has been quietly laying the institutional foundations of *perestroika* but is faced with a sceptical population. Like Stolypin, who tried to reform agriculture in the years before 1914, Gorbachev needs time and world peace. Stolypin failed because both were denied him. Gorbachev may be more fortunate.

# 1 *Perestroika* and the Party*

## ELIZABETH TEAGUE

Mikhail Gorbachev has taken up arms against the Communist Party bureaucracy. He holds the Party's full-time, paid officials largely to blame for the economic slowdown and social malaise from which the Soviet Union is suffering. He accuses them of usurping the powers and functions of state and government bodies, stifling the initiative of ordinary people and rank-and-file Party members, and snarling up the country in red tape and corruption. In short, Gorbachev sees the Party bureaucracy as a major obstacle in his attempts to modernise and revitalise Soviet society.

Gorbachev rose to power through the Party hierarchy and the position he assumed in March 1985 – that of General Secretary of the Central Committee of the Communist Party of the Soviet Union (CPSU) – has since Stalin's day wielded the greatest political power of any in the Soviet system. But, even though he owes his job to the CPSU, Gorbachev's efforts to reform Soviet society also entail a *perestroika* (restructuring) of the Party. In fact, the changes Gorbachev is trying to make are likely to have a greater impact on the Party than on any other Soviet political institution. With Hungary announcing its intention of moving toward a multi-party system, the long-term ability of the CPSU to retain its monopoly on power is coming into question. Gorbachev has warned the Party that it is losing authority among the population and that, unless it is prepared to reform itself, it may not survive as a ruling body. The problem, as Gorbachev sees it, is that too much power is concentrated in the hands of Party officials. He wants to slim the bureaucracy down, reduce its powers of appointment, cut back its privileges, and end its tradition of jobs for life. Under the system Gorbachev has inherited,

*Thanks are due to Philip Hanson and Peter Reddaway for comments on an early draft and to Alexander Rahr for help compiling data on personnel appointments.

13

all matters of any importance (to say nothing of countless extraordinarily trivial ones) are referred to Party officials for decision.
Gorbachev has called on the Party to relinquish some of its all-
embracing functions to the soviets (local government councils) and
to concentrate instead on the formulation of policy, leaving the
implementation of that policy to state and government bodies.

Gorbachev does not for a moment intend the Communist Party to
relinquish its commanding role in setting national policy; he is
committed to maintaining the Party's monopoly on political power;
and he dismisses as 'nonsense' any idea of a multi-party system for
the USSR (Soviet television, 15 February 1989). At the same time,
Gorbachev believes the CPSU must become more open to new
opinions and fresh faces. He wishes to promote to key posts a new
generation of leaders loyal to himself. Above all, he wants an
obedient Party that will help rather than hinder the realisation of his
policies.

Gorbachev's reforms have run into stiff resistance from functionaries worried about loss of status and privilege. In an effort to outflank
this opposition, Gorbachev has launched a far-reaching reorganisation of the political system. He has established the Soviet Union's
first standing parliament and a powerful new executive presidency,
and assumed the post of President himself. He has introduced
multi-candidate secret balloting instead of the former practice whereby all candidates for office were elected by a unanimous show of
hands from lists drawn up privately by Party bosses; he has ruled that
no one will be permitted to occupy an official post for longer than two
successive five-year terms; and he has advanced a controversial
proposal whereby Party bosses will be required to secure a popular
mandate by running in local government elections.

Possession of the new post of executive president promises
Gorbachev the leeway, if he chooses to use it, to operate more or less
independently of the Party bureaucracy. In setting up a standing
parliament, Gorbachev has created an alternative power structure
that parallels the Party and may even, in time, come to rival it. He
himself occupies a unique position as head of both structures and is
now, as a result, politically almost invulnerable: the Party cannot
remove him from the post of President, while the parliament is
unable to remove him from the Party leadership.

Even Gorbachev's supporters have expressed concern that the new
post concentrates too much power in the hands of one man and would
be dangerously open to abuse should Gorbachev leave the scene.

Alarmed by the baleful precedent of the monopoly on power accumulated in the 1920s and 1930s by Josef Stalin, they have warned that Soviet society is still not politically mature enough to counter the threat of tyranny. The physicist and human-rights activist Andrei Sakharov, for example, has argued that to appoint a president 'with such powers in a country that does not have a multi-party system is just insanity. This is practically boundless power. Today it is Gorbachev, but tomorrow it could be somebody else. There are no guarantees that some Stalinist will not succeed him' (*Washington Post*, 2 November 1988). The legal expert Boris Kurashvili has also warned of the dangers involved in creating so powerful an office in a single-party system. An executive presidency, Kurashvili has argued, requires effective parliamentary control and that, in turn, presupposes the existence of a multi-party system and a parliamentary opposition (*Izvestiya*, 15 November 1988).

Gorbachev's answer to such apprehensions is that the old system has had its day and drastic measures are needed to restore dynamism and purpose to Soviet society. The most serious problem from Moscow's point of view is the loss of central control. The 19-million-member CPSU is hierarchically structured. In theory, orders pass down from the centre for implementation at the base, while information flows in the opposite direction, from the grassroots to the centre. Ossification and bureaucratisation led, during the long years of the Brezhnev leadership, to an almost total breakdown of this two-way system. The opinions of rank-and-file Party members were ignored by officials, while powerful regional Party bosses cultivated fiefdoms best likened to feudal baronies. Reliable information ceased to be ferried upward; commands issued by the centre were ignored in the provinces; abuse of power flourished at every level. Soviet society became, in certain respects, virtually ungovernable. This led, according to the government newspaper, to 'a crisis of confidence in the party' (*Izvestiya*, 22 March 1988).

Soviet citizens displayed their anger and frustration with their rulers by their rejection of many Party-backed candidates in the general elections of March 1989. In the Soviet Union's second largest city, Leningrad, not one top leader received the 50 per cent of votes needed to win election to the Soviet parliament. Echoing *Izvestiya*, a meeting of Leningrad Party leaders held after the event spoke again of 'a clear crisis of confidence' (*Sovetskaya Rossiya*, 6 April 1989). A further symptom of this crisis is the fact that, since some time in the autumn of 1988, Party membership has begun to fall. The rate of recruitment of new members has slowed down; a smaller proportion of candidate members is proceeding to full membership at the close of their probationary period; and full members are opting in increasing numbers to leave the Party (*Izvestiya TsK KPSS*, Nos 1 and 2, 1989; Hanson and Teague 1989). In the Baltic states of Estonia and Lithuania, there has been a rash of Communists turning in their Party cards; the fall in Party numbers is also marked in Armenia. Membership of the Party's youth arm, the Komsomol, dropped from 42 million in 1986 to 36 million in 1988 and is still falling (*Komsomolskaya pravda*, 19 November 1988).

Replacement of the single-party system by some kind of multi-party system is not on the Party's agenda, but it is an option that ordinary Soviet people are increasingly beginning to discuss. This can be seen from the letters members of the public are writing to the newspapers and the questions they are posing to phone-in programmes on Soviet television. Moreover, a number of small, unofficial political parties has recently sprung up in the Soviet Union. National independence parties were, for example, established in 1988 in Estonia and Georgia. The outlawed Karabakh Committee, set up to campaign for the transfer of the Armenian enclave of Nagorno-Karabakh from Azerbaidzhan to Armenia, was operating virtually as an alternative government in Armenia until its leaders were detained by the authorities in December 1988 and January 1989 (*Le Monde*, 16 December 1988; *Komsomolskaya pravda*, 7 January 1989).

The Democratic Union has been much in the public eye; it is a loose association of dissidents and human-rights activists which held its founding conference in Moscow in May 1988. Created specifically as a political party in opposition to the CPSU, the Democratic Union is dedicated to fight for a multi-party system, a free press, and independent trade unions (for the group's platform, see Radio Liberty *Samizdat Archive*, No. 6217). Its members describe themselves as the 'children of the Prague Spring' – those who were in their teens and twenties when, in 1968, they saw Czechoslovakia's attempt to build 'socialism with a human face' crushed by Soviet tanks. The Democratic Union claims 2000 members nationwide, and hardly a week has passed since its foundation without its staging a public demonstration of some sort. These have been declared illegal by the authorities, their leaders have been harassed and imprisoned, and the official Soviet press has condemned the fledgling party as anti-Soviet, yet the Democratic Union has maintained its precarious existence. Indeed, the new party is only one of thousands of 'informal groups'

– grassroots associations formed mainly of young people – that have blossomed all over the USSR since Gorbachev was appointed Party General Secretary.

The Popular Fronts that sprang up in the spring and summer of 1988 in the Baltic Republics of Estonia, Lithuania and Latvia were an entirely new phenomenon for the USSR. All three insist that they wholeheartedly support Gorbachev's reforms, are not political parties, and have no pretensions to that status. However, their massive popular support clearly holds the potential for their metamorphosis into independent political parties at some future date. Even before that stage is reached, the Popular Fronts in the Baltic states have had an enormous impact on developments in their respective republics and, in particular, on the ruling Communist Parties. Estonia's reformist Prime Minister, Indrek Toome, has asserted that, in tolerating the rise of the Popular Front in Estonia, the Estonian Communist Party has 'given up its claim to a monopoly over the formulation of policy' (*Dagens Nyheter*, 1 October 1988). Latvian Party leader Janis Vagris, on the other hand, has complained that conflicting loyalties to the republic's Popular Front, whose membership is predominantly Latvian, and to its rival, the International Front, which is dominated by Russians living in Latvia, have split the Latvian Communist Party into two competing factions (Tass, 7 January 1989).

There have been moves to set up Popular Fronts in other Soviet republics too (Azerbaidzhan, Belorussia, Georgia, among others) as well as in several big cities (Moscow, Leningrad, Lvov), but none has yet mustered the huge popular support evoked by the Baltic movements. According to Radio Free Europe's analyst Saulius Girnius, 'Within a month [of the creation of Lithuania's Popular Front] its spokesmen, rather than the Central Committee of the Lithuanian Communist Party, were setting the tenor of public life, and the Party was forced to make a number of significant concessions on Lithuanian national and religious questions' (Girnius 1988).

Gorbachev regards the fact that 'Soviet people have changed' as *perestroika*'s main achievement to date. 'The whole country', he asserted in an interview with American journalists, 'is now an enormous debating society' (*International Herald Tribune*, 23 May 1988). There is indeed evidence that, under the impact of Gorbachev's policy of *glasnost* (openness), there are appearing in the USSR the first shoots of a 'civil society' – that is, a situation where society controls the state instead of vice versa (Scanlan 1988, p. 41)

– and that Soviet people are acquiring those habits of self-organisation that once it appeared they might never learn at all. Gorbachev's assertion seems nonetheless slightly exaggerated: the impact of *glasnost* has been dramatic, particularly in the Western borderlands, but resistance to his social and economic reforms is still immense. This resistance should not be seen merely in terms of individual opposition: the idea of a Gorbachev-led reformist wing of the Politburo doing battle with a conservative wing led by Egor Ligachev is an oversimplification. Opposition to *perestroika* goes much deeper. Entire social groups – including not only the 18 million-strong bureaucracy, but also large sectors of the industrial working class – are deeply alarmed by the pace and scope of the changes Gorbachev is trying to make. It was to outflank the opposition that, after four years in power, the General Secretary shifted the USSR to a presidential style of government.

Gorbachev unveiled his reform blueprint at the XIX Party Conference, held in Moscow in June 1988 (for Gorbachev's speech, see *Pravda*, 29 June 1988; for evaluations of the conference, see Mann 1988; Tatu 1988). Gorbachev's proposals were formally adopted in December 1988 (for the relevant constitutional amendments, see *Pravda*, 3 December 1988). In March–May 1989, general elections were held for the Soviet Union's new 'supreme organ of state power' – the USSR Congress of People's Deputies. This reform has profound implications for the role of the CPSU.

The Congress is composed of 2250 members. One-third (750) of the deputies were appointed on a corporatist basis: that is, they were nominated by specific bodies such as the CPSU (with a block of 100 seats) and other Party-dominated 'social organisations' such as the Komsomol, the trade unions, women's councils and veterans' associations. (This arrangement was criticised by some Soviet citizens on the grounds that it gave members of such organisations a double vote and was therefore undemocratic. Moreover, the vast majority of the Soviet Union's new independent movements, including the Popular Fronts of the Baltic states and the anti-Stalinist 'Memorial' society, did not qualify for representation.)

The remaining two-thirds (1500) of the Congress deputies were elected by the general public in mainly multi-candidate elections held in March–May 1989 (with one-third representing territorial districts and one-third representing national–territorial constituencies). Multi-candidate voting was itself an innovation for the USSR, where uncontested elections were previously the norm. The results came as a surprise to all those who had written the Soviet population off as apathetic, cynical, and apolitical. Turnout was high (80–85 per cent) and, contrary to Gorbachev's subsequent claim that the results proved the people's support for the Party and for *perestroika* (Tass, 30 March 1989; see also Mann, 1989), many members of the electorate seized the opportunity to cast a vote of no confidence in their rulers. Senior Party and government officials – including one candidate Politburo member – were defeated in Moscow, Leningrad and Kiev. In the Baltic states, resounding victories were won by candidates backed by the Popular Fronts and demanding regional autonomy. In the USSR overall, some 20 per cent of the powerful regional Party bosses failed to win election. Where voters had a choice between a Party-backed candidate and an independent, they tended to choose the independent. Where a candidate ran unopposed and the voters were denied the choice they had been promised, they simply crossed the name of the single candidate off the ballot paper. The most stunning result was in Moscow where Boris Eltsin received 89.4 per cent of the vote with Evgeny Brakov, the official candidate, only winning 6.9 per cent.

The result was not of course a total defeat for the Party. Thanks to an elaborate pre-election vetting process, 85 per ent of all candidates were Party members and efforts were made (though not always successfully) to exclude candidates unacceptable to local Party organisations. Moreover, the fact that one-third of the deputies were selected by Party-dominated organisations assured the Party a built-in majority in the Congress. But the sense of purpose with which many voters turned out to cast a negative vote against candidates they saw as Party hacks was striking. The poet Andrei Voznesensky rejoiced at the results, saying, 'We intellectuals always saw ourselves as the symbol of democracy but we thought the people weren't ready for it. The joyful thing about all this is that in many ways we have been proved wrong' (*Washington Post*, 29 March 1989).

With its 2250 members, the USSR Congress of People's Deputies is a large and unwieldy body which participates in policy formation on a largely ceremonial basis, for it meets only briefly, once a year. It has two main tasks. First, it elects, from among its members, a streamlined, bicameral legislature, called the USSR Supreme Soviet and consisting of a Council of the Union and a Council of Nationalities. The Supreme Soviet, which has 542 members, is a standing legislative, administrative and supervisory body. The first permanent parliament in Soviet history, it meets for two sessions of three-to-four months each in the spring and autumn of every year. (In the past, the Soviet parliament met only for one- or two-day sessions two or three times a year.)

As a standing parliament, the Supreme Soviet has at least the potential to grow into more than the rubber-stamp it has replaced. Attached to it will be a number of permanent legislative commissions overseeing, among other important areas of national life, the army, the uniformed police, and the KGB, though how much power these commissions will have remains to be seen. The former Moscow Party leader, Boris Eltsin has spoken of his desire to organise a 'left revolutionary bloc' in the new Supreme Soviet (*Christian Science Monitor*, 21 February 1989). Whether such a development will be possible, and whether the Supreme Soviet will wield real political influence, will depend on whether its members are able to become permanent 'politicians' in the Western sense, or are merely seconded from full-time jobs in other parts of the country.

The second task of the Congress of People's Deputies is to elect an executive president, whose formal title is Chairman of the USSR Supreme Soviet. This is the position Gorbachev holds. (Some Soviet citizens have criticised this arrangement on the grounds that the President should be directly elected by universal suffrage, rather than indirectly by the Congress.) The President is elected for a five-year term, for not more than two terms in succession. Gorbachev will therefore be required to stand down in 1999, at the age of 68. If he does so, he will be the first Soviet leader to leave office voluntarily. Lenin, Stalin, Brezhnev, Andropov and Chernenko all died in office; Khrushchev was ousted by his colleagues.

The powers of the new President are considerable. Described in the amended constitution as 'the highest official of the Soviet state', the chairman of the USSR Supreme Soviet has the authority to determine domestic, foreign and security policy, negotiate state treaties, nominate the Prime Minister and other leading officials, and issue legislative orders. He oversees the KGB and chairs the Defence Council – the USSR's highest military decision-making body in wartime – a post previously held by the Party General Secretary. To be sure, there are some checks on the President's powers. Thus, the constitution specifies that he is accountable to both the USSR Supreme Soviet and the USSR Congress of People's Deputies; he can be recalled 'at any time' by secret ballot of the USSR Congress of People's Deputies; and presidential orders may be repealed by the

USSR Supreme Soviet. It is as yet too soon to tell, however, how these controls will operate in practice.

Gorbachev seems to have constructed this new presidential post in a deliberate move to avoid the trap into which his predecessor, Nikita Khrushchev, fell. The policies of the reformist Khrushchev alienated many sections of Soviet society but, according to his former colleague Andrei Gromyko, it was his attempt to divide the CPSU into two separate organisations that was the last straw (interviewed in *The Observer*, 2 April 1989). Although Khrushchev took the precaution of having himself appointed Prime Minister as well as Party leader, he made a fatal error in antagonising the Party apparatus when he had no effective power base outside it. He was unceremoniously ousted from both his posts in a Kremlin coup in 1964.

Having taken steps to make himself invulnerable to attack, Gorbachev turned in earnest to the question of Party reform. His aim was to resolve the problem of *podmena* or 'substitution' that is, the tendency of Party officials to usurp the rights and functions of state and government bodies. The problem is as old as the Soviet system itself. The Party's role is supposed to be confined to the political sphere: it should *guide* but not *run* society and the economy. In the words of Leonard Schapiro, the Party 'should always be ready to tell other people how to do the job, but should not attempt to do the job itself' (Schapiro 1961, p. 111). In reality, all decisions of any importance are referred to Party bodies, which duplicate state and government bodies at every level of the hierarchy. This 'substitution' deprives state and government bodies of power and initiative. Because it overloads the Party with pettifogging, time-consuming responsibilities, it is extremely inefficient. Finally, it leads to a situation where the public blames the Party for anything and everything that goes wrong (Yasmann 1988). For all these reasons, Gorbachev's aim has been to remove the Party, once and for all, from day-to-day involvement in the management of society and the economy.

At first, after his election as general secretary in 1985, Gorbachev tried to bully, cajole, and exhort the Party into behaving as he wanted. He made impassioned pleas for tighter discipline among members; Party leaders of the old generation were pilloried in the press and sacked from their posts amid charges of nepotism, corruption and general lack of concern for the welfare of ordinary people; Gorbachev protégés stepped into their places; new Party rules were adopted; threats of a Party purge were voiced. And, at a plenum of the CPSU Central Committee in January 1987, Gorbachev made what was at that time the sensational proposal of multi-candidate, secret balloting for Party posts (*Pravda*, 28 January 1987).

These measures had little or no effect. Party bosses paid lip-service to Gorbachev's proposals but in practice they ignored them. Gradually, as his efforts met with failure, Gorbachev underwent a process of radicalisation. He told the XIX Party Conference that the problems faced by the USSR had turned out to be a good deal more serious than he and his colleagues thought when they first came to power and their solution far harder than appeared at first sight (*Pravda*, 29 June 1988). Gorbachev's closest Politburo ally, Aleksandr Yakovlev, put it this way: 'the accumulation of conservatism turned out to be stronger than we had thought and the hunger for democracy turned out to be less than we thought' (interview with *The New York Times*, 28 October 1988).

At the Party conference, Gorbachev resorted to drastic methods to separate the functions of the Party from those of the state. He announced the abolition at all levels of the Party hierarchy of the industrial departments (*otraslevye otdely*) set up by Stalin in the 1920s to oversee branches of the economy such as machine-building, construction, and transport. Gorbachev's aim was to force individual enterprises and local soviets to make the decisions that had until then been made for them by Party officials. This measure, Gorbachev warned, would lead to sweeping staff-cuts. In September 1988 the first reductions were made in the Central Committee apparatus (the Party's Moscow-based 'civil service' or permanent staff).

The number of departments of the CPSU Central Committee in Moscow was reduced from 20 to nine and their staffs cut by 40 per cent. Six of these departments are now subordinated to six newly-established Central Committee commissions, namely: the Agrarian Commission, the Ideology Commission, the Commission for International Policy, the Commission for Legal Affairs, the Commission for Party Organisation and Personnel Policy, and the Commission for Social and Economic Policy. (The three remaining departments are the General Department and the Administration of Affairs, which do staff work for the Party leadership and whose status appears unchanged, and a Defence Department whose status is unclear). The commissions – each of which is headed by a Central Committee Secretary – are policy-setting bodies; their task is to elaborate options for submission to the Politburo.

The creation of the new commissions, announced at an emergency plenum of the CPSU Central Committee in September 1988, was heralded as a major departure from the way the CPSU had traditionally operated, since commission members were to include rank-and-file members of the CPSU Central Committee instead of full-time employees of the central Party apparatus. It remains to be seen how active a role these members will play, since all have full-time jobs of their own, but the purpose of their inclusion, according to the Soviet journalist Mikhail Poltoranin, was to enhance the policy-making role of the Central Committee. In the past, Poltoranin noted, decisions adopted in the name of the Committee were in fact drawn up, without consultation, by the Secretariat and the apparatus, and 'most Central Committee members learned about the decisions adopted in their names from the newspapers' (*Novosti*, 6 October 1988).

So far, the Central Committee commissions have maintained a remarkably low profile. How they are to interact with the new standing commissions of the revamped USSR Supreme Soviet is not yet known. Since Gorbachev first mapped out his proposals in June 1988, the Soviet system has been in a process of transition, the final goal of which has not been revealed. It is still not clear, in particular, how the CPSU is to interact with the USSR Supreme Soviet. Improbable though it may seem in light of the dominant role the Party has played in the past, the possibility cannot be ruled out that the Central Committee commissions may eventually take a back seat to those of the USSR Supreme Soviet.

Gorbachev's reorganisation of the apparatus and his creation of the six new Central Committee commissions had an immediate impact on the Party Secretariat. Regarded until 1988 as second in power only to the Politburo, the Secretariat was disbanded in September 1988 (Rahr 1988 and 1989). The reorganised Central Committee departments report to their respective commissions, which in turn report not, as the old Central Committee departments did, to the Secretariat, but to the Politburo (headed, of course, by Gorbachev). When the role of the Secretariat vanished, so too did the traditional role of the CPSU's unofficial 'second secretary'.

Two factors seem to have been at work here. First, by abolishing the Secretariat as an effective decision-making body, Gorbachev was able to dislodge his conservative rival, Egor Ligachev, from his influential post as 'second secretary' with oversight of the activities of all the Central Committee departments. Second, the Politburo was, under the impact of Gorbachev's assertive leadership, reclaiming decision-making prerogatives relinquished to the Secretariat and its apparat during the inertia of Brezhnev's last years. Politburo member Lev Zaikov told journalists early in 1988 that the weekly Politburo meetings, which used to last 'an hour or two' under Brezhnev, went on late into the night now that they were chaired by Gorbachev (*Newsweek*, 4 April 1988). This suggested that debates had become fiercer and more decisions were having to be referred to the Politburo for resolution than had been the case under Gorbachev's predecessor.

At the Party conference in June 1988, Gorbachev made one very puzzling proposal. Even while calling on the CPSU to stop interfering in the work of the local soviets – and taking concrete organisational steps to ensure that this happened – Gorbachev suggested that local Party bosses should stand for election as chairmen of the soviet at the corresponding level. Gorbachev's suggestion took many conference delegates by surprise. Some went to the rostrum to argue that such a step would, far from separating the functions of state and Party, confuse them even more hopelessly than before, and concentrate too much power in the hands of single individuals. Gorbachev riposted that, after 70 years' passivity, the soviets were hardly likely to start flexing their muscles overnight, and that they would find it particularly hard to assert themselves against the all-powerful Moscow ministries, accustomed to acting as a law unto themselves in matters notionally controlled by the soviets. He argued that combining the post of Party secretary with that of chairman of the local soviet would strengthen the authority of the soviets over the ministries; the point, he told the conference, was to increase the sovereignty of the soviets by the authority of the Party'. Meanwhile, the soviets were given more teeth with the promise that they would, for the first time, be granted funds to dispose of at their own discretion.

Even among Gorbachev's supporters, many were unconvinced by this argument. Aleksandr Yakovlev gave the game away when he told a meeting in Lithuania that only by promising Party leaders they could chair the beefed-up soviets had it been possible to persuade them to give up some of the Party's prerogatives (*Komsomolskaya pravda* [Vilnius], 18 August 1988). Some Soviet reformers comforted themselves with the thought that, with this plan, Gorbachev was introducing through the back door an element of popular control into the selection of Party leaders (Gavriil Popov in *Moscow News*, No. 32, 1988, p. 13). They argued that requiring an official to stand first in a contested election for the post of Party secretary, second for a seat on the local soviet, and third in a secret ballot for ratification as soviet chairman, would, if implemented fairly and honestly, subject Party officials to a threefold screening and introduce at least an element, if only indirect and *ex post facto*, of public control into the selection of Party personnel. If the Party boss failed to win election as soviet chairman, Gorbachev implied at the Party conference, he might well lose his Party post as well.

It is also possible that, as multi-candidate elections become the norm, informal groups and Popular Fronts will, by making their preference for a specific candidate known prior to the election, acquire some power to influence the outcome. (In some areas, informal groups acted in precisely this way during elections of delegates to the Party conference in the summer of 1988 and during the general elections of March 1989.) Gorbachev's proposal was approved by the Party conference but with clear misgivings on the part of a number of delegates. It is as yet too early to say how the system will work in practice; elections to the soviets at local level are not due until the spring of 1990.

Charges of footdragging in the Party have already been heard. A Central Committee official complained early in 1989 that lower-level Party organisations were 'in no hurry' to reform themselves, that rank-and-file Party members were passive and apathetic and that, as a result, the CPSU was lagging seriously behind the rest of society in the process of democratisation and *perestroika* (*Pravda*, 2 January 1989). It is fair to say, too, that Gorbachev's almost total failure so far to stop the Moscow branch ministries meddling in the affairs of individual firms and factories does not augur well for his attempts to prevent similar interference by equally powerful Party bodies.

Many people, both inside and outside the Soviet Union, sympathise with Gorbachev and with the ends he is trying to achieve – the modernisation and liberalisation of his society. Some have misvigings, however, about the means he has chosen to achieve those aims. They note that Gorbachev has often resorted to intrigue to get his own way and that, when it has suited him, he has not hesitated to double-cross colleagues who helped him to power, such as former foreign minister Gromyko. For example, the reshuffle of the Politburo and the dissolution of the Secretariat which Gorbachev conducted at the hastily convened Central Committee plenum in September 1988 bore all the marks of a palace coup, while it took a session of the old, rubber-stamp Supreme Soviet, summoned a few days later, a bare 40 minutes to give unanimous approval to his personnel changes.

Others ask whether, after four years in power, Gorbachev is not beginning to run up against the limits of the Soviet system. In order to circumvent the opposition mounted by the Party and government apparatus to his reforms, the General Secretary has sought to draw the general population into the political process; to counteract the entrenched bureaucracy, he has gone outside the Party organisation and set up an alternative political structure. Gorbachev must ensure that this new parliamentary system is strong enough to prod the arthritic Party apparatus into action; eventually, the new USSR Supreme Soviet may come to counteract the Party, to compete with it, and even, perhaps, to supplant it. Dismantling the Party's monopoly on power was not Gorbachev's intention when he came to power in 1985 but, four years later, the possibility that it may prove the final outcome of his reforms cannot be ruled out.

The situation is vastly complicated by the fact that the USSR is the world's last multi-national empire. The recent manifestations of ethnic tension in the Western borderlands and the Transcaucasus suggest that popular participation cannot be taken very far for very long in such a society without the generation of explosive demands for national independence. How will Gorbachev and the CPSU respond to such challenges to their rule? Is the encouragement of independent grassroots organisations – perhaps even the toleration of opposition parties – not the only effective means of ensuring the expression and mediation of conflicting social and national aspirations? Is that not the logical outcome of 'pluralism' – even the 'socialist pluralism' that Gorbachev professes?

The self-proclaimed 'leading role' of the Communist Party remains at the heart of the question. Gorbachev told the Party conference that, unless the CPSU was prepared to share some of its power, it could lose it altogether. From the Party's point of view the danger is that, if it relinquishes even a few of its prerogatives, its claim to an exclusive right to rule will almost certainly come under challenge. Gorbachev has fewer inhibitions; during his four years in power he has proved himself a skilled and pragmatic politician who will, if need be, find ways to rule without the Party. If the existing system proves inadequate to the tasks he has set it, he will seek other means to attain them. The bureaucracy will not give up without a fight: resistance to Gorbachev's policies is to be found at every level of Soviet society but it is the Communist Party apparatus that stands to lose the most from the changes he is seeking to make. The jury is still out on the question with which Geoffrey Hosking concluded his 1988 Reith Lecture (*The Listener*, 15 December 1988, p. 7). Without the wrenching upheavals of internal collapse, revolution and civil war, 'can a totalitarian system evolve straight towards democracy?'

## APPENDIX: PERSONNEL TURNOVER UNDER GORBACHEV

Mikhail Gorbachev has made sweeping changes in the leadership of his country. Officials of the Brezhnev generation have been unceremoniously retired and their places awarded to younger, predominantly technocratic appointees in the Gorbachev mould. Thus, of the nine men who held full (voting) membership of the Politburo on Gorbachev's appointment as General Secretary in March 1985, only three (Gorbachev himself, Ukrainian Party leader Vladimir Shcherbitsky, and Russian Federation President Vitaly Vorotnikov) were still members of the Party's supreme decision-making body in October 1988. [Further personnel changes had not been made in the Politburo at the time this chapter was written.]

It was in October 1988 that Gorbachev assumed, in addition to his post as Party General Secretary, the title of Chairman of the Presidium of the USSR Supreme Soviet (a ceremonial post not to be confused with the post of executive president, formally entitled Chairman of the USSR Supreme Soviet, to which he was elected in spring 1989). Gorbachev added the state post to his Party post following an emergency plenum of the CPSU Central Committee, held at the end of September 1988, at which he engineered the effective demotion of a number of his conservative Politburo colleagues in the biggest shake-up in the senior ranks of the Party leadership since his ascent to power. Gorbachev emerged, as a result of these changes, in an extremely strong personal position in the Kremlin leadership. His assumption of the post of executive president in the spring of 1989 strengthened his personal position still further.

As for the candidate (non-voting) members of the Politburo, not one of those who held that rank in March 1985 was still in office in October 1988 while, of the eight men who were members of the Central Committee Secretariat at the time of Gorbachev's appointment as General Secretary, only two (Gorbachev and Egor Ligachev) still held seats in October 1988.

All but two of the Party leaders of the Soviet Union's fifteen constituent republics (those in the western border republics of

Ukraine and Moldavia) were replaced during this period. Of the 118 men and one woman who in October 1988 made up the Soviet goverment, all but 26 had been appointed to their posts since Gorbachev's appointment as General Secretary in March 1985. Over 70 per cent of the Soviet Union's powerful regional Party leaders (*obkom* and *kraikom* first secretaries) were also replaced during Gorbachev's first three-and-a-half years in power.

As for the members of the Party's leading body, Gorbachev succeeded at the XXVII Party Congress, in the spring of 1986, in replacing only 41 per cent (125 of 307) of the full members of the Central Committee. This relatively low turnover meant that many old Brezhnevites retained their membership. By the end of 1988, however, about 25 per cent of the full members of the Central Committee had come to qualify for the description of 'dead souls', that is, they had died, retired, or been ousted from the posts that had in 1986 won them full Central Committee membership.

There were significant changes lower down the hierarchy, too. In the Far Eastern region of Krasnoyarsk, for example, 40 per cent of the secretaries of the grassroots primary Party organisations – the lowest level in the Party hierarchy – were replaced in routine Party elections held throughout the USSR in the autumn and winter of 1988 (*Radio Moscow*, 15 September 1988). In Sverdlovsk oblast in the Urals, overall turnover of Party functionaries was also 40 per cent (*Sotsialisticheskaya industriya*, 27 December 1988).

New blood was injected into the leadership in the spring of 1989 when the Soviet public elected the members of the new USSR Congress of People's Deputies. In three-quarters of the 1500 territorial and national-territorial constituencies, voters were offered not a single name but a choice of two or more competing candidates. Although Party stalwarts won a majority of seats, hard-fought elections resulted in a number of cases in the defeat of Party-backed candidates and the election of independent candidates, such as Boris Eltsin, armed with their own distinctive political platforms.

The most extensive purge of the Central Committee (CC) since the death of Stalin took place at a CC plenum on 26 April 1989. One hundred and ten full and candidate members 'resigned'. Among those departing were Andrei Gromyko, Mikhail Solomentsev, Nikolai Tikhonov and Boris Ponomarev. All these men were close associates of the late Leonid Brezhnev. The military also suffered casualties. Marshal Nikolai Ogarkov, Chief of Staff until he was demoted in 1984; Marshal Viktor Kulikov, a former commander-in-chief of the

Warsaw Pact forces; and Marshal Sergei Sokolov, dismissed as Defence Minister in 1987, all left the CC. As many as 83 of those who departed had lost the posts which had qualified them for membership of the CC, elected at the XXVII Party Congress in 1986. Twenty-four candidate members were promoted to full membership. They included Evgeny Velikhov, Vice-President of the USSR Academy of Sciences and Valentin Falin, head of the International Department of the CC Secretariat. However, many of those promoted under Gorbachev still remain outside the CC, since members can only be added at Party Congresses. The next Party Congress is due in 1991.

Besides reducing the size of the CC, the purge made it much more difficult for the conservative reformers in the Politburo (Chebrikov, Ligachev and Shcherbitsky, for example) to find supporters in the CC. Hence it was a considerable coup for Gorbachev and made it more likely that radical reforms would be acceptable to the CC. Gorbachev again revealed himself as a master political tactician, and thereby enhanced his power and authority.

# 2 The Politics of Soviet History, 1985–8

## R. W. DAVIES

### THE MENTAL REVOLUTION

In the eighteen months preceding the XIX Party Conference in June 1988 the Soviet press, television, cinema and theatre were engaged in a vast reconsideration of the Soviet past.

The first major event was the publication within the Soviet Union at the end of 1986 of the novel *Novoe naznachenie* (New Appointment), written in the early 1960s by the veteran industrial journalist Aleksandr Bek, and already published abroad in 1969. This fictionalised biography of the prominent Soviet industrial manager Tevosyan offers a searching critical assessment of the Soviet planning system and its effect on conscientious administrators.

In January 1987 Abuladze's bitter allegorical satire on Stalinist and other tyrannies, the film *Pokayanie* (Repentance), was released and shown to mass audiences, first in Moscow and then throughout the Soviet Union.

In the next few months the literary journals published a scintillating array of previously banned novels. Mozhaev's *Muzhi i babi* depicted the collectivisation of agriculture in the early 1930s as an unmitigated disaster. Antonov's *Vaska* displayed both the inhumanity of dekulakisation and the waste as well as the heroism involved in the building of the Moscow Metro in the 1930s. The greatest literary sensation of 1987 was Rybakov's *Deti Arbata* (Children of the Arbat). This novel depicted how a sickly-suspicious and increasingly tyrannical Stalin came to plan the murder of Kirov in the months before December 1934. It also described quite fully the milder processes of arrest, questioning and exile, and the pernicious use of informers by the OGPU. On the postwar Stalin regime Dudintsev, who wrote *Not by Bread Alone*, the outstanding novel of the Khrushchev thaw, and had been almost silent for two decades, now

30

returned to print with the long novel *Belye odezhdy* (Robed in White). The title refers both to the white coats of scientists and to those 'who have passed through the great ordeal', the 'robed in white' of the Apocalypse; the novel depicts the persecution of honest scientists in the years of Lysenko, and concludes that Soviet socialism must be rethought fundamentally – a one-sided concept of socialism has prevailed ever since the revolution. (Fuller discussion of these publications will be found in Hosking 1987, Barber 1988, Davies 1988).

The flood of novels, films, plays and television presentations continued unabated in the first six months of 1988. Two novels already long-published in English translation outside the USSR were made available to Soviet readers for the first time: Pasternak's *Doctor Zhivago*, which presents the years of revolution through the eyes of an intellectual who stood quite outside Bolshevism, and Grossman's immense and tragic *Zhizn i sudba* (Life and Fate), which displays the Second World War as a struggle between state coercion (both Stalinist and Nazi) and the spirit of human freedom liberated by the patriotic defence of the Soviet Union. This novel also presents the full horror of the Nazi extermination of the Jews to a Soviet mass audience for the first time in many years.

The greatest controversy in 1988 was produced by Shatrov's *Dalshe...dalshe...dalshe!* (Onward...Onward...Onward!), the latest of his numerous plays about Lenin. This discusses the history of the Soviet regime, from the Bolshevik Revolution to Lenin's death, in the form of a complex series of arguments among Bolsheviks of different views, including Lenin, Stalin, Trotsky and Bukharin, and their opponents, ranging from Rosa Luxemburg to Martov, Spiridonova and Kerensky. The play reaches broadly Leninist conclusions; but the alternative views are presented with unprecedented honesty. (See Shapiro 1988).

These works vary considerably in their artistic merit. But they all engage in a quite profound debate about the Soviet past, and there is no doubt that this debate has engaged the attention of many millions of Soviet citizens. This was dramatically demonstrated at the beginning of the year with the announcement of the 1988 print runs for Soviet journals; the number of copies printed is increased in accordance with the increase in the number of advance subscriptions. *Novyi mir*, the principal critical literary journal, increased its circulation from 495 000 to 1 150 000; *Druzhba narodov* (which published Rybakov's novel) from 150 000 to 800 00; and *Znamya* from 277 000 to 500 000. These are all thick monthlies of a couple of hundred pages of text, with few or no illustrations; and the more sensational numbers are passed from hand to hand among many readers. The circulation of the more conservative journals increased much more slowly.

The rethinking of Soviet history in works of imagination was accompanied by an equally probing discussion in the general press by journalists, economists and scientists, and even by a few historians. Virtually no issue relating to the Stalin period was passed over. At first, specific cases of the suffering caused by collectivisation and the Stalinist repressions were described, but no attempt to assess their extent was published. But in the months before the XIX Party conference the scale of both the 1932–3 famine and the 1936–8 repressions was frankly discussed, and guesses about the number of victims appeared (some greatly exaggerated). Another remarkable feature of the discussion in the months before the Party conference was that assessments of major past events were published which directly contradicted recent official Party statements. This broke a firm convention which had been imposed on public discourse ever since the end of the 1920s. Thus one hard-hitting article condemned the whole process of collectivisation and dekulakisation (G. I. Shmelev, in *Oktyabr*, no.2/1988 pp. 3–26), while another, by the famous anti-fascist journalist Ernst Henri, condemned the Soviet–German pact of 1939 (*Moskovskaya pravda*, 18–19 May 1988). These opinions contradicted the specific conclusions of Gorbachev in his major report of 2 November on the occasion of the 70th anniversary of the revolution (of which more below).

The extraordinarily frank publication of facts and judgements was accompanied by almost equally frank analysis. On the eve of the XIX Party conference, the dominant view in the central press and the media was that the New Economic Policy should not have been brought to an end. Collectivisation, and still more the mass expulsion of 'kulaks' and recalcitrant peasants, were disasters which should never have occurred. Bukharin and the Rightists were correct. This view was advocated without challenge, for example, in *Protsess*, the major television programme about the Stalin period first shown in May 1988.

A major theme of the discussions was the nature of the Stalinist system. No one assessment predominated. Much attention was devoted to the personal responsibility of Stalin. But hardly anybody now accepts the Khrushchev view that it was merely or even primarily a matter of Stalin's personality. Even the formerly quite conservative D. A. Volkogonov, until recently deputy head of the Main Political Administration of the Soviet Army, who has completed an important biography of Stalin, conceded that a 'deficit of popular power (*narodovlastie*) developed after the death of Lenin', so that there were insufficient 'democratic attributes for social defence from accidents' (*Lit. Gaz.*, 9 December 1987).

The whole gamut of rival Western theories about Stalinism was presented – or has been rediscovered. The totalitarian hypothesis was put forward by N. A. Popov, of the USA and Canada Institute:

> *Stalin destroyed millions of the best, most enterprising and talented (we have yet to learn the true number of our losses). But the main thing is that he created an ideal totalitarian state, in which his personal power extended to everything – economics and science, literature and art* (*Sovetskaya kultura*, 26 April 1988).

Other contributors took the view that the central feature of Stalinism, and of Soviet society up to 1985, was that power had been usurped by the bureaucracy as a social group, and that Stalin's personal power was erected on the political power of the bureaucracy. S. Dzarasov argued that a pyramid of bureaucratic power had emerged in which every group of officials had a boss (*nachalnik*). The structure was logically completed by the 'boss of the bosses'. 'The old system was born out of bureaucratism and itself gave birth to and "multiplied" bureaucrats; it corresponds fully to their interests and is the main basis of their power.' (*Moskovskaya pravda*, 31 January 1988). Dzarasov is a person of some influence; this article was distributed by the official press agency APN and he played a prominent part in the television film *Protsess*. Even V. V. Zhuravlev, the principal historian in the Institute of Marxism-Leninism (see below), while insisting that socialist property relations continued under Stalin, acknowledged that Stalin and the bureaucracy may have usurped political power, occupying a relationship to the working class and socialised peasantry similar to that discerned by Marx between Napoleon III, his bureaucracy, and the French peasantry (*Voprosy istorii KPSS* no. 2/1988 pp. 132–3; Marx, *Eighteenth Brumaire*). Dzarasov's approach was not dissimilar to that of Djilas with his 'new class', while Zhuravlev's resembled Trotsky's in *Revolution Betrayed* (if we strip away from Trotsky his outmoded political conclusions). Trotsky is almost always treated with near-contempt in Soviet publications but his approach to the problem of Stalinism cannot be avoided by Marxists.

Discussion of the years 1917 to 1924, when Lenin was at the helm, was much less open. This reluctance to criticise Lenin was negotiated by emphasising the unsolved problems at the end of Lenin's life. The Lenin of the Soviet reformers is Lenin after the Civil War, undogmatically seeking new ways forward. As one more orthodox writer complained, the Lenin we are offered is often more like Chekhov than Lenin. And many writers frankly stated that the revolution and Civil War swept away important values which were emerging during the last decades of tsarism. *Perestroika* was thus presented as an endeavour to change the whole course of socialism since the revolution, not just since Stalin rose to power (see for example Granin on the extinction of mercy after the revolution, in *Lit. Gaz.*, 18 March 1987, and Vaksberg on the jury system, ibid., 8 June 1988). But objective reassessment of the Soviet past was crabbed and confined by the impossibility of frankly discussing Lenin's ideas and political conduct.

## THE POLITBURO AND SOVIET HISTORY

In the first eighteen months after Gorbachev's appointment the Politburo seemed to take a cautious or even conservative attitude to Soviet history. In his speech on the occasion of the fortieth anniversary of victory in the Second World War, Gorbachev proclaimed that the 'gigantic work at the front and in the rear was led by the Party, its Central Committee, and the State Committee of Defence headed by the General Secretary of the CC CPSU(b) Iosif Vissarionovich Stalin', and this statement was greeted with prolonged applause (*Pravda*, 9 May 1985). Four months later he unstintingly praised Stakhanovism at the meeting celebrating the fiftieth anniversary of Stakhanov's record shift (*Izvestiya*, 21 September 1985). At the XXVII Party congress in February–March 1986, Gorbachev briefly remarked about the history of the Soviet period that 'mistakes in policy were not avoided, and various kinds of subjective distortions (*otkloneniya*)'. This is extremely bland by the standards of 1988. At the XXVII Congress Gorbachev's one remarkable reference to history was his statement that what was needed in Soviet agriculture was the 'creative utilisation of the Leninist tax in kind in application to present conditions' (a reference to the crucial step towards the New Economic Policy in March 1921). According to an unofficial report, in June 1986 he is reported to have told a group of Soviet writers:

> If we start trying to deal with the past, we'll lose all our energy. It would be like hitting the people over the head. And we have to go forward. We'll sort out the past. We'll put everything in its place. But right now we have to direct our energy forward' (*Radio Liberty Research*, 399/86, a document first obtained by *L'Unità* and *La Repubblica*).

A month later, in July 1986, Molotov was restored to his rights as a Party member, an event which seemed to confirm the unwillingness of the Politburo to reconsider Stalinism (see Wheatcroft 1987 (1), p. 103).

Behind the scenes, however, some important changes had already taken place. In 1985 the Party Control Commission began to investigate the cases of some former Party members who had not been rehabilitated in the Khrushchev period, including at least one former Trotskyist, N. I. Muralov; Muralov was rehabilitated without publicity as early as April 1986 (see *ibid.* p. 131). These investigations must have required approval at Politburo level.

The approach to Soviet history changed sharply towards the end of 1986. At the time of the USSR Writers' Congress in June 1986 it was unofficially announced that the powers of the state censorship were to be greatly reduced. During the last few months of the year new reform-minded editors were appointed to major literary journals such as *Novyi mir* (Zalygin) and *Znamya* (Baklanov), and to certain newspapers, including *Moscow News* (E. Yakovlev). At this time Yu. Afanasev was appointed Rector (Vice-Chancellor) of the Moscow Historical-Archive Institute, which trains archivists, and proved to be a vigorous and even intemperate advocate of the reconsideration of the past. The end of 1986 saw the beginning of the flood of publications about Stalinism described above.

The appointments of the editors, and the mass showing of *Repentance* early in 1987, must have been authorised by someone very high in the party apparat, perhaps Gorbachev himself. In February 1987, at a meeting with editors and other leading media figures, Gorbachev publicly reversed the attitude he had previously taken to the role of history in *perestroika*, making his famous declaration that 'there should not be any blank pages in either our history or our literature' (*Pravda*, 14 February 1987).

In the course of 1987 Gorbachev made a number of public statements about the Soviet past. His views were quite consistent, and could be summed up in the cliché 'Triumph and Tragedy'. He told the meeting of editors in February 1987 that 'history has to be seen as it is; there was everything; there were mistakes, it was hard, but the country moved forward'. His book about *perestroika*, written during his famous 52 days' leave in the summer of 1987, praised industrialisation and declared of collectivsation that 'it proceeded painfully, not without serious excesses and blunders in methods and pace, but further progress in our country would have been impossible without it'. The first edition even added that 'if it had not been for collectivisation, we could have died from hunger in the war', but this sentence was omitted in the paperback edition (see Harrison 1988, p. 28).

His major report for the seventieth anniversary of the October revolution took the same general line. It declared that 'Bukharin and his supporters underestimated in practice the importance of the factor of time in the construction of socialism in the thirties'. But it also strongly condemned the repressions of the 1930s (though timorously referring merely to 'many thousands' of people being involved). Moreover, while praising industrialisation, and, with reservations, the collectivisation of agriculture, it placed them in the context of the emergence of the 'administrative-command system of Party-state management of the country'. According to Gorbachev, this system had restrained the progress of socialist democracy and provided the context for the arbitrariness and repressions of the 1930s. Such a framework of analysis for the Stalin period had never previously been presented by a Soviet leader.

Lenin once remarked that there is no such thing as a 'sincero-meter' by which the sincerity of a politician can be measured. Did Gorbachev already have a very critical view of the Stalin period when he took office, or did his views evolve under the pressure of events and of the views of his supporters? We do not know. But it does seem clear that he changed his mind about the political importance of a radical re-evaluation of the past as the difficulties in the way of *perestroika* became more obvious. By the time of the Central Committee plenum in February 1988 he was openly stressing the intimate connection between history and *perestroika*:

Comrades, I want to stress once again that close attention to our history is brought about not simply by interest in the past. It is

urgently necessary for our present work, for resolving the problems
of *perestroika*. We have issued the slogan 'More socialism!' – and
we must establish which values and principles should be considered
really socialist (*Pravda*, 19 February 1988).

Even more bluntly, Gorbachev's close associate Razumovsky explained in his Lenin anniversary speech:

> The Party has initiated a sober examination of the post-October
> history of the country not least because many of our present
> troubles have their origins in yesterday's departures from the
> political, economic and moral principles of socialism. Learning the
> truth about history is difficult work, it stings many people to the
> quick. And some people generally did not want an honest dis-
> cussion of the past. We are learning to see achievements and
> failures in a correct light, to evaluate objectively the contribution
> of all Soviet generations to the birth of Soviet society. . . .
>    This work helps to clean the path to the future. The CPSU
> [Communist Party of the Soviet Union] intends to continue it,
> keeping silent about nothing, not sweetening the truth, however
> bitter it may be (*Pravda*, 23 April 1988).

In general Gorbachev and his close associates, confronted with
obstacles to wider *glasnost* and to the continuation of *perestroika*,
have so far generally followed the famous Stalinist principle of
'widening the bottleneck' rather than 'planning on the bottleneck'.
Gorbachev is well aware that previous attempts at economic and
political reform have foundered on inertia from the past. This has
also been his stance in international affairs, where he has made offer
after offer and even concession after concession in order to keep the
momentum of the negotiations going. It is in this context that
Gorbachev has moved to a firmer insistence on the public expression
of a plurality of views, and tried (within certain limits) to prevent the
re-emergence of what he called the 'practice of bans characteristic of
the period of stagnation'. With fits and starts, between the end of
1986 and the summer of 1988 the boundaries of historical discussion
continuously widened.

   These policies met with strong opposition at every level. Prominent
writers and important literary journals resisted the renunciation of so
much of the past, and many members of the public have backed them
up. In the summer of 1987 two leading members of the Politburo,

Ligachev and the head of the KGB Chebrikov, openly expressed disquiet. Ligachev, who had at first called for greater frankness about the past (see Wheatcroft 1987 (1), pp. 94–6), condemned the 'one-sided' treatment of the past by the newspaper *Sovetskaya kultura* and others (*Sovetskaya kultura* 7 July 1987; *Pravda*; 17 September 1987). And Gorbachev ominously warned that 'imperialist special services' were encouraging some writers to 'blacken certain stages of the historical development of our country' (*Pravda*, 11 September 1987).

In this atmosphere of intense disagreement it is not surprising that Gorbachev's November report gives the impression of an amalgam drafted by several different hands, and it is significant that two months later he publicly referred to its provisional nature:

the understanding of our history which we achieved in preparing for the 70th anniversary of October is not something frozen, and given once and for all. It will be deepened and developed in the course of further research (*Pravda*, 13 January 1988).

In 1988 the conflict became even sharper. On 13 March the newspaper *Sovetskaya Rossiya* published the remarkable full-page letter 'I Cannot Give Up My Principles', by Nina Andreeva, a Leningrad chemistry lecturer. The letter strongly supported the historians who had criticised Shatrov's new play (they included Zhuravlev, mentioned above) and went on to defend Stalin and his policies. It even claimed that current attacks on the dictatorship of the proletariat and on former political leaders must owe their origin to a variety of anti-Soviet sources: to professional anti-communists in the West; to the remnants of the defeated classes within the USSR, including Nepmen, basmachi (Central Asian anti-Bolshevik insur-gents) and kulaks; and to the spiritual successors both of the Mensheviks Dan and Martov, and of Trotsky and the secret-police chief Yagoda. The tone of the argument was nationalist and anti-Semitic (Dan, Martov, Trotsky and Yagoda were all Jews).

Andreeva's letter was generally regarded as highly authoritative. Usually reliable Western reports claimed that its publication was authorised by Ligachev (e.g. *The Sunday Times*, 10 April 1988; and see the remarkable account in *L'Unità* (23 May 1988), reported in *Radio Liberty Research*, 215/88). While there was much objection to the letter behind the scenes, no national newspaper (except the small-circulation *Moscow News*) dared to publish any criticism of it. Three weeks later, however, on 5 April, *Pravda* published a counterblast, which also occupied a full page, and was unsigned, indicating that it carried particular authority (later rumours claimed that it was approved by the Politburo, with two dissentients).

Following this rebuff to the conservatives, in the remaining months before the XIX Conference an even greater number of articles about the Stalinist past appeared in the press, written with an even greater degree of frankness. On 23 May, a Central Committee plenum approved theses for the conference which called for the avoidance of 'political confrontation', but insisted that the discussion of the Soviet past must continue:

> The Party will systematically carry out a policy of frankness and openness, of free discussion of problems of past and present, because only such a policy will assist the moral health of Soviet society, the liberation of it from everything alien to its humanist nature.
>
> We are far from indifferent to the question not only of the goals and values of socialism but also of the means of achieving them, the price which must be paid for them. It is our Party and civic duty to rehabilitate those who became victims in the past of unjustified political accusations and lawlessness (*Pravda*, 27 May 1988).

## *PERESTROIKA* AND THE HISTORIANS

Decision-making about Soviet history is influenced by at least five major centres of authority:

(1) The Department for Science and Education Establishments of the Central Committee overlooks history on behalf of the Party.

(2) The Institute of Marxism-Leninism, the main Party research establishment, has a substantial sector for Party history, and supervises similar republican and local institutes; it is also responsible for the all-important central Party archives. It is associated with the Party Academy of Social Sciences which may also carry out substantial research on Party history, but with very little publicity.

(3) The History Division of the Academy of Sciences of the USSR, itself part of the Social Sciences Sector of the Academy, manages historical research within the Academy. The History Division of the Academy contains all those full and corresponding members of the Academy who are historians; these gentlemen exercise considerable

personal influence on decisions about historical research, particularly that conducted within the Academy. The major Academy research institute concerned with pre-revolutionary and Soviet history is the prestigious Institute of the History of the USSR.

(4) The state archives (quite separate from the Party archives) are the responsibility of the State Archive Administration of the USSR (GAU), the head of which is a non-voting member of the Council of Ministers of the USSR.

(5) The mass of practising historians themselves play a varying but considerable part in the decisions about their own activities. This was true even in the days of Brezhnev (and to some extent even in the days of Stalin). Historians of high intellectual quality and achievement who are well-regarded by their Western colleagues have high prestige in the USSR, and are often taken seriously even by bureaucrats.

As far as the study of twentieth century history is concerned, all five 'centres of authority' were demoralised, ossified, or even actively reactionary in the decade before 1985. In 1965 S. P. Trapeznikov was appointed head of the Central Committee Science and Education Department, and remained in this post for over fifteen years. Trapeznikov was politically an extremely 'orthodox' historian who was at the same time quite unscrupulous with the facts. The role of his Department was bluntly described by Yu.Afanasev:

> The campaign to stop scientific initiative in historical science was headed in the early 70s by S. P. Trapeznikov, who used unlimited authority (*neogranichennaya vsedozvolennost*) in the leadership of science to appoint to almost every post people who were dependent on him and on that basis held together by 'business' connections (*Sovetskaya kultura*, 21 March 1987).

This is not the whole story. Trapeznikov was supported in the campaign by Brezhnev and the Politburo and by the History Division of the Academy. More orthodox or more opportunist historians, particularly from the Institute of Marxism-Leninism, actively assisted this campaign, which eventually secured the acquiescence of historians generally.

'Purge' might be a better word than 'campaign'. A series of major cases involving the demotion and silencing of creative historians disfigured these years. Two notorious examples will illustrate this process. In the course of 1964–9 it was decided not to publish a critical book on the collectivisation of agriculture edited by V. P. Danilov, following fierce attacks on Danilov's approach to Soviet history by F. M. Vaganov and other historians from the Institute of Marxism-Leninism (e.g. in *Kommunist*, no. 3/1966). Danilov was removed from his position as head of the Soviet peasant sector of the Institute of History and as secretary of the Party group of the entire Institute. And in 1967 S. P. Trapeznikov published his own history of the Soviet peasantry, which dealt with collectivisation – and peasant history generally – in an extremely traditional way. In 1972, in an equally notorious case, the distinguished historian P. V. Volobuev was condemned for his interpretation of the 1905 and 1917 revolutions, and forced to resign from his post as Director of the Institute of the History of the USSR.

The new orthodoxy was imposed throughout the media by a variety of formal and informal channels. We have recently learned from Shatrov that on 27 January 1982 the director of the Institute of Marxism-Leninism, Academician A. Egorov, wrote to Andropov in the latter's capacity as head of the KGB (!), complaining that Shatrov's play *This is How We Conquer*, then showing at the Moscow Arts Theatre, idealised the New Economic Policy. Egorov recommended to Andropov that it should be quietly removed from the repertoire of the theatre, and that the Ministries concerned should establish 'firm obstacles' against future plays of this kind (*Lit. Gaz.*, 18 May 1988).

In the 1970s, in a further blow at serious historical research, the access of historians to archives relating to the Soviet period was considerably restricted, and their access to higher Party and government archives virtually ceased altogether. In 1982 F. M. Vaganov, who was the author of a well-known strongly anti-Bukharinist history of the Right deviation, was appointed head of the State Archives Administration (it should be noted, however, that several years before March 1985 a marked improvement took place in the access of foreign historians to archives of the Soviet period with Vaganov's active support).

In all these circumstances it is not surprising that Soviet historians lagged far behind the novelists, the journalists and the film-makers in the re-evaluation of Soviet history. Independent-minded historians were in low spirits. Few changes occurred in the historical establishment: at the end of 1986, as we have seen, Afanasev was appointed Rector of the Historical Archive Institute, but at that time this was a relatively minor teaching establishment.

The first major change came early in January 1987 with the appointment of G. L. Smirnov as Director of the Institute of Marxism-Leninism, and then of V. V. Zhuravlev as a deputy director responsible for history. In the spring of 1987, the History Sector of this Institute was for a time in the forefront of cautious moves to greater openness among professional historians. On 29 April 1987, Afanasev, Volobuev and Danilov took part in a 'round table' at the Institute; the participation of these three heretics at the Institute's invitation was in itself a remarkable event. Zhuravlev, in the chair, while warning against too sweeping a rejection of the past, called for a 'profound examination' of the 1930s, and a fresh approach to the 'cult of personality' different from that of the Khrushchev period (*Voprosy istorii KPSS*, no. 7/1987, pp. 137–52). A similar line was taken by V. A. Grigorev, the new head of the influential Department of Science and Education Establishments of the Central Committee. At this time Zhuravlev also sought to attract progressive historians to his staff from other institutes, and gave the impression to foreign visitors that he was an enthusiastic reformer.

But the efforts of the Institute to spearhead the drive for *glasnost* in Soviet history were, it is said, met unsympathetically by Ligachev. And at the beginning of 1988 Zhuravlev and one of his colleagues published a most intemperate criticism of Shatrov's *Dalshe. . . dalshe. . . dalshe!* (*Pravda*, 28 January 1988). Thus there were strict limits to the *glasnost* advocated by Zhuravlev and his Sector (the potential of some of the younger historians in the Institute, however, has been praised by Shatrov – see Shapiro 1988, p. 8).

Meanwhile the academic establishment in history remained unreformed. Academician Fedoseev, veteran head of the Social Services Sector of the Academy, Academician Tikhvinsky, head of the History Division, Dr S. S. Khromov, Director of the Institute of History, a former Party official, and the editors of the major historical journals, remained in post. And the election of six full and ten corresponding members to the History Division of the Academy of Sciences in December 1987 resulted in the consolidation of the conservative bloc. Members of the Academy are elected in the first instance by the appropriate Division of the Academy, subject to confirmation by the general meeting of all Academicians. Outstanding candidates specialising in twentieth century history who failed to be elected included Volobuev and Polyakov, candidates for full membership, and Arutunyan, Danilov, Drobizhev and Shkaratan, candidates for corresponding membership. On the other hand, several far less well-qualified historians of the Soviet period were elected: thus Kukushkin (long-standing Dean of the History Faculty of Moscow University) became a full member, and Kasyanenko (editor of *Voprosy istorii KPSS*) a corresponding member. (For the candidates see *Vestnik Akademii Nauk*, no. 11/1987; for those elected see *Izvestiya*, 25 December 1987). Kukushkin and Kasyanenko have quite good reputations as administrators, but their writings on Soviet history are orthodox and without originality. Some Soviet historians have unkindly joked that the old Academicians elected such a feeble cluster of new Academicians so that there would be someone worse than they were who would be thrown out when *perestroika* eventually reached the Academy.

But, a little late in the season, the ice was now beginning to crack. In the autumn of 1987 Danilov was elected head of the Soviet peasantry sector of the Institute of the History of the USSR, the post which he had been forced to relinquish at the end of the 1960s. And in mid-winter came an unexpected thaw. On 7 January 1988, a meeting of the bureau of the History Division of the Academy discussed a report from Khromov about the progress of *perestroika* in the Institute of the History of the USSR. This was an 'extended sitting' of the bureau, attended by historians of various viewpoints, and by the new deputy head of the Science and Educational Department of the Central committee, V. V. Ryabov. Ryabov was particularly critical of Khromov's report:

> This report contains more data about plans for the future in connection with *perestroika* than about real achievements at the present day. It remains unclear why historical science permits itself a substantial lag ... and why the Institute does not cultivate the development of scientific schools and approaches which differ from each other in their creative approach, while being unified in their Marxist-Leninist methodology. Historical science owes a large debt to the Soviet public (*Voprosy istorii*, no. 3/1988, pp. 130–31).

On the following day, 8 January, a round table of leading historians under the auspices of *Voprosy istorii* discussed the future of Soviet history. Strong criticisms were made of scholars who had established a monopoly or near-monopoly control of branches of history. The published version of the round table reported fierce attacks on the medieval historian Academician Rybakov (*Voprosy istorii*, no. 3/1988, pp. 28–30). Apparently Academician Kukushkin was also strongly criticised.

Two weeks later on 21 January, what was described as a 'general meeting' of the History Division also heard Khromov's report. In a long resolution it criticised the backwardness of the Institute of the History of the USSR, and blamed the 'management of the Council' of the Academic Institute for failing to encourage new research and new approaches. The resolution confirmed an earlier decision that the famous banned book on collectivisation should be revised as a two-volume work for publication in 1990 and 1991 by the five original authors under Danilov's editorship. It also called for the reexamination of the '"portfolio" of completed works by researchers in the Institute which were rejected in their day for reasons not related to their scientific level'. (The resolution is in *Istorii SSSR*, no. 3/1988, pp. 207–10; see also the interview with Danilov in *The Times Higher Education Supplement*, 1 April, 1988).

By now a revolutionary *perestroika* was under way. The old editor of the principal history journal, *Voprosy istorii*, had resigned in the summer of 1987, but his post was vacant for some months. By January 1988 A. A. Iskenderov, a respected and reform-minded historian of pre-revolutionary Russia, had been appointed editor (*Voprosy istorii*, 3/1988, p. 3). The new editorial board of 23 persons contains only five names from the old board (see *Voprosy istorii*, nos. 1 and 2/1988), and is fairly reform-orientated. New members of the board include Volobuev and Danilov.

By the beginning of 1988 Khromov, Director of the Institute, had reached retirement age, and was not allowed to stay on. Following the new principles of democratisation, the History Division of the Academy balloted the staff of the Institute about the two candidates, Novoseltsev and Sherstobitov. Both candidates promised to identify themselves with the interests of the collective. Novoseltsev, a distinguished historian of ancient Rus, who had no connection with the existing establishment of the Institute, received the majority of votes. Under the new as under the old Academy rules, the History Division of the Academy (i.e. its conservative-minded Academicians) has the ultimate right to appoint the Directors of its institutes, much to the indignation of many research workers (see E. Dabagyan and A. Karavaev in *Lit. Gaz.*, 8 June 1988). But it evidently thought it prudent to accept the democratic vote.

Further remarkable changes followed. Perhaps the most notable event before the Party conference was the publication in *Voprosy istorii* of a six-page letter from Danilov entitled 'The Discussion in the Western Press on the Famine of 1932–1933 and the "Demographic

Catastrophe" of the 30s and 40s in the USSR (no. 3/1988, pp. 116–21). This reviewed the whole discussion of the famine in the Western literature, including the estimates of Conquest and Rosefielde as well as Wheatcroft, Anderson and Silver. It firmly rejected Conquest's estimate that 7 million died of starvation in 1932–3, and cautiously favoured an estimate that three million died. But Danilov frankly admitted that his view must be provisional because Soviet scholars have not worked on the demographic problems of the 1930s and 1940s; he commented bitterly that in consequence of such scandalous omissions Soviet history has a 'deservedly low' reputation both in the USSR and abroad. When this research was at last undertaken by Soviet historians, Danilov argued, the 'experience and results of the research carried out by our colleagues and our opponents abroad must be taken into account and utilised'. He also envisaged the prospect of 'joint scientific discussion and joint search for truth between historians of different schools (*napravleniya*) even in such a sensitive and political matter'.

In spite of such developments, a great deal has yet to be done to complete the *perestroika* of the history profession. All the conservative Academicians, and the editors of all the other historical journals, remain in place. And there is a great shortage of trained young historians of the Soviet period: in the 1970s independent-minded students went into other disciplines, or at best into other periods. The general problems facing *perestroika* in the Soviet Union are particularly sharply reflected in the Soviet history profession.

Perhaps the greatest obstacle to serious research on the 'blank places of Soviet history' is that the most important archives have not yet been opened. Some improvements in access to materials have occurred. In the libraries the state censorship organisation Glavlit has already moved over half the books in the 'special reserves' (*spetsfondy*) into general library stores; this includes the writings of Kerensky, Milyukov, Bukharin and Rykov (but apparently not of Trotsky); and henceforth all Ph.Ds have the right to work in the special reserves (*Sovetskaya kultura*, 22 March 1988). Some documents in the central state archives have been removed from restricted access (*Voprosy istorii*, no. 2/1987, pp. 128–9). The detailed records of the suppressed population census of 1937 and the party-published census of 1939 are also being made available. And records of the secret trials and interrogations of persons arrested in the 1930s and 1940s have been made available to the special Party commission investigating the repressions. But in the state archives the all-important records of the

Council of People's Commissars and its commissions apparently remain closed; in the Party archives the records of the Politburo and other leading Party bodies remain inaccessible; and such important government departments as the People's Commissariat of Foreign Affairs and the OGPU also keep their archives firmly barred, even to senior historians (see B. Ilizarov in *Lit. Gaz.*, 1 June 1988). The popular journal *Ogonek* pointed out that it had to confine itself to publishing reminiscences from survivors of the repressions because the answers to the important questions 'are so far still gathering dust in interdicted archives' (8/1988, p. 28). Here is a strange paradox of *glasnost*. Both Gorbachev and the more conservative members of the Politburo frequently call for a careful, detailed and objective study of the 1930s and 1940s, avoiding sensationalism. But without the archives this is impossible.

## THE XIX PARTY CONFERENCE, JUNE–JULY 1988

The reassessment of the Soviet past was the most contentious issue at the Party conference. (For the conference proceedings cited below, see *Pravda*, 29 June–4 July 1988). In his opening report, Gorbachev had nothing to say about the serious challenges which had appeared in the press to his quite favourable assessment of industrialisation and collectivisation in November 1987. Instead, he frequently referred his listeners back to 'Leninist norms' as both the inspiration and a yardstick for *perestroika*. He claimed that, in the present economic reform, 'we have attached the significance and role to cooperation which was ascribed to it by V. I. Lenin'. And in proposing to reform the soviets and increase their role, Gorbachev drew on the immediate post-1917 experience. According to Gorbachev, the Congress of Soviets was 'powerful' and the Central Executive Committee to which it delegated authority between sessions was 'very powerful'. He also called for a system of supervision which would 'revive the fine tradition of the Workers' and Peasants' Inspectorate of Lenin's time'.

Gorbachev's 'Leninist norms' have a substantial mythical content: the weaknesses of the Central Executive Committee and the arbitrariness of the Workers' and Peasants' Inspectorate played their part in the emergence of the Stalinist political system (see Rigby, 1979 *passim*, and Rees 1987, chs 1–2). But Gorbachev made it abundantly clear that his primary purpose was to bring about a complete break with the Stalinist political system:

With the consolidation of the command–administrative system the atmosphere of Party comradeship gradually gave way to relations based on orders and their execution, on the division of Party members into bosses and subordinates, on the violation of the principle of the equality of communists. Although from time to time it was recognised that this situation was intolerable, in practice everything remained as it was (*Pravda*, 30 June 1988).

But many, perhaps most, of the delegates at the conference were extremely hostile to the hard-hitting and uncompromising condemnation of the whole Stalinist system which predominated in the most popular journals in the weeks before the conference. The attitude of the more orthodox delegates found a powerful voice in the popular writer Yuri Bondarev, who ferociously condemned 'nihilist criticism', and claimed that 'it is becoming or has already become a dominant force in the press'. Several other speakers took a similar line; and Gorbachev himself, while never departing from his insistence on 'pluralism of opinions' and the right to speak out, criticised in moderate terms the attempt to 'replace one monopoly by another, one half-truth by another half-truth'. Baklanov, editor of the strongly anti-Stalinist journal *Znamya*, met with such hostility from the audience that Gorbachev had to intervene on his behalf. Finally, on the last day of the conference, Ligachev expressed his own opposition to the 'complete distortion of the truth' which was appearing in some publications:

> Soviet people – and this is in our own press publications – are presented as slaves, and I am almost quoting, who were supposedly fed only by lies and demagogy, the whole people being subject to the cruellest exploitation.

Ligachev almost threateningly demanded that 'the Central Committee and the editorial staffs must draw the proper conclusions'.

Other delegates, including the first secretary of the Georgian Party, were much more critical of the Stalinist past. And in his concluding speech Gorbachev made no concessions to these calls for restrictions on *glasnost*, and instead pushed *glasnost* further:

> It is our political and moral duty to restore justice to the victims of lawlessness. Let us carry this out by erecting a monument in Moscow. I am convinced that this step will be supported by the whole Soviet people (*Applause*).

The erection of a monument to the victims of repression was one of the foremost demands of the informal political groups in the weeks leading to the conference, and a petition to this effect from a group called 'Memorial', signed by 46 000 people, was presented to the conference (*Lit. Gaz.*, 6 July 1988). This proposal could hardly be resisted by Ligachev, who reported to the conference that his own relatives had been victims of the repressions, but it had the effect of ensuring that the anti-Stalin campaign would continue to be at the centre of public attention. A significant further step towards frankness about the past was the recommendation of the conference, in its resolution 'On *glasnost*', 'to enable access to all library stocks, and to regularise the use of archival materials by legislation'.

While the conference was in progress, the issue of *Literaturnaya gazeta* which printed Gorbachev's report to the conference also announced the rehabilitation of Ryutin and his anti-Stalinist group of 1932, and published extracts from the famous 'Ryutin platform'. This has never before been available, and proved to be much more critical of the Stalin system than the rumours of the past 55 years have suggested. (See A. Vaksberg in *Lit. Gaz.*, 29 June 1988). Nine days after the conclusion of the conference, the long-awaited announcement appeared in the Soviet press that Party membership had been posthumously restored to the Right-wing leaders Bukharin, Rykov and Tomsky – and also to Trotsky's close associate Rakovsky (*Pravda*, 10 July 1988). The reconsideration of Soviet history continues apace.

# 3  Industry

## PHILIP HANSON

### INTRODUCTION

The basic impulse behind *perestroika* comes from the Gorbachev leadership's desire to make sure that the Soviet Union remains a superpower and, what is more, a superpower they can be proud of: not merely a partially-developed and socially unattractive country that somehow maintains the military strength to match NATO.

So far as the economy is concerned, the reasons for dissatisfaction and even shame about the state of affairs in the early 1980s can be listed under four headings: slow growth; technical backwardness; stagnating or near-stagnant levels of household consumption and signs of a worsening social environment.

### Slow Growth

Official Soviet estimates have shown the Soviet national income (net material product) stuck at 66–7 per cent of the equivalent US figure since 1974. (*Narodnoe Khozyaistvo SSSR*, various years. The Institute of World Economy and International Relations (IMEMO) has produced alternative estimates which are less favourable to the USSR in comparison with the US than those of the State Statistics Committee: for instance, 1986 industrial output at 66, not 80 per cent of US (*MEMO* 1988, pp. 11–12). At a time when the Western superpower has experienced a productivity slowdown, the historic Soviet project of 'catching up and overtaking' has been failing.

### Technical Backwardness

The official Soviet claim is that the USSR accounts for about a fifth of world industrial output. Western estimates (which are lower than Soviet claims but comparable with Western data) put the number of Soviet scientists and engineers engaged in research and development

(R & D) around 1980 some 50 per cent above that of the US. Yet the Soviet Union has been able to win only a tiny (about 0.5 per cent) and declining (since the mid-1960s) market share in total OECD imports of manufactures and only 1 per cent of all patents registered abroad in the world; only 1–2 per cent of the weight of its engineering output is made up of materials other than iron and steel, against 15–20 per cent for the US, and leading Soviet scientists are now beginning to refer publicly to a 'crisis' in fundamental research – where both Soviet official claims and Western conventional wisdom have hitherto credited Soviet research with considerable strength (see Hanson and Pavitt 1987; 'TPP SSSR: partner na vneshem rynke', *Ekonomicheskaya Gazeta*, no. 16/1988, p. 23; B. Konovalov, 'Ne stalyu edinoi', *Izvestiya*, 22 April, 1988, p. 2; R. Sagdeev, 'Gde my poteryali temp', *Izvestiya*, 28 April 1988, p. 3).

## Consumption Levels

Food rationing had been introduced in a number of Soviet provincial cities by the early 1980s, and Brezhnev spoke in 1982 of the food problem as critical in both a political and an economic sense. The weakness of agriculture and the food supply system has become a fundamental structural problem. Food output growth had slowed to about the rate of growth of the population. Retail food prices were set far below both average costs and market equilibrium levels, creating shortages and a severe burden on the state budget. Around one-tenth of the population's calorie intake in 1983 was derived from imports of food and food materials from non-socialist countries (Hanson in Gelman 1985, pp. 29–51).

## Social Environment

The evidence of increasing infant mortality rates and falling average life expectancy was the most dramatic indicator of social malaise. In addition there was a widespread belief that corruption, unjustifiable material privilege and cynicism were more widespread by the end of the 1970s than they had been ten or twenty years earlier.

In other words, the leadership in the early 1980s should have been worried about the Soviet future. There were powerful reasons for worrying about the country's ability to remain a military superpower for more than another decade. There were also grounds – though how strong they were is unknowable – for the leaders to fear that the population might rebel. Andropov was sufficiently far-sighted and determined to address the problems; Gorbachev picked up where Andropov left off, and has since gone much further.

## GORBACHEV'S ECONOMIC POLICIES

It is a mistake to think of Gorbachev's policies on the economy as amounting simply and exclusively to economic reform. The usual definition of economic reform, so far as centrally administered economies are concerned, is changes in economic institutions and standard operating procedures that tend to replace central administration with market dealings. Reforms in this sense are central to Gorbachev's policies as they had evolved by late 1988, but there are other important ingredients. Current Soviet economic policy is in fact a blend of tradition and novelty. The novelty lies in the reforms and the attempt to link the economy more closely to the outside world. The traditional elements are to do with personnel, priorities and pressure from above.

On the personnel ('cadres') front there has been a spring-cleaning: a removal of demonstrably ineffective or corrupt officials and managers. There has also (one suspects) been an extremely traditional tactic of removing even effective managers if they were closely identified with Brezhnev (Dzherman Gvishiani and Vladimir Dolgikh, for example). In general, however, the personnel changes seem to be more than just a changing of the guard. It is beginning to look like an ending of sinecures; the subsequent demotion of some of Gorbachev's early appointees such as Nikolai Talyzin suggests this. No doubt this can make people try harder (and increases X-efficiency, in economic jargon). It also runs the risk of creating a panic-stricken paralysis. It has been backed up by a more general discipline campaign, in which the anti-alcohol drive is conspicuous.

The anti-alcohol drive was not accompanied by offsetting measures to increase the supply of non-alcoholic consumer goods or to reduce the money in the hands of the population that could no longer be spent on alcohol. (It is assumed that illicit alcohol supplies did not increase enough to absorb all this extra purchasing power.) Therefore consumer shortages have worsened, though there may have been improvements (as is officially claimed) in health and mortality rates as a result of the anti-alcohol campaign. In 1987–8 the campaign levelled out; first-quarter 1988 official alcohol sales were the same as first-quarter 1987 (*Izvestiya*, 29 April 1988). By 1987, however, official sales of alcohol were down dramatically: from 8.7 litres of absolute alcohol per person per year in 1984 (about the same as the British level) to 3.3 in 1987 (*Argumenty i fakty* no. 22, 1988).

In 1985–6 priorities, as reflected in the 1986–90 plan, shifted as follows (the changes are relative, so the 'losers' need not suffer absolute reductions): from household consumption towards investment, including some kinds of social infrastructure investment (health services, housing construction); from investment in agriculture and a number of other branches towards investment in food distribution and the engineering sector: from the 'older' kinds of engineering-sector investment towards information-technology investment, and into research and development. In 1988 there were signs of a mid-plan shift of priorities back towards consumption. There was a flurry of decrees on the consumer sector, with targets for that sector increased (*Izvestiya*, 21, 23, and 24 August, 1988).

Whether there has been a shift of resource-allocation priority either to or from defence as an end-use as against consumption and investment cannot be reliably determined. Nor is it clear whether there has been a shift within investment from or to defence production capabilities as against the build-up of capacities to produce civilian items. It is possible that there has been a shift of investment priorities away from the creation and replacement of capacities for the final-stage assembly of military systems towards a build-up of capacities to produce information-technology components and subsystems that could be incorporated in either civilian or military final products. (See European Strategy Group. *The Gorbachev Challenge and European Security*, forthcoming.)

There has probably also been some dilution of defence priorities, not demonstrably by way of shifts in the allocation of labour and capital as usually measured but by pressure on the military production sector, to produce more for civilian customers (Gorbachev's Krasnodar speech of 18 September 1986, BBC SWB SU/8371/C/9–11; the transfer of some civilian engineering plants to military management, *Izvestiya*, 22 February 1988, p. 1; N. V. Emelina's speech at the Party Conference, *Izvestiya*, 2 July 1988, pp. 6–7; the group of consumerist decrees of August 1988, mentioned above). In these cases, the idea seems to be that the skills and time of military-sector managers, though not necessarily their military-production capacities, will benefit the consumer sector; this is a kind of priority dilution.

The effort to upgrade a dual-use, high-technology sector (electronics, computing, telecommunications and new materials) has been conducted mainly on traditional lines. One indication of this is the old-fashioned exertion of pressure from above by setting very high targets: an increase in the output of machining centres, for example, from 2500 in 1985 to 10 700 in 1990, and a growth of capital spending for 'science' (roughly, research and development, including pilot-plant facilities) of over 11 per cent a year in 1986–90 (*Izvestiya*, 19 June 1986 pp. 2–5).

While the approach to other aspects of economic policy has become more radical, Gorbachev's own treatment of industrial modernisation has remained largely traditional. In early 1988, for example, he said that Soviet output of electronic equipment needed to increase tenfold by the year 2000 (*Izvestiya*, 10 April, 1988); in other words, the emphasis was still on quantitative targets. In the June 1988 Party Conference speech (BBC SWB SU/0191 C/1-32 of 29 June 1988) there was an example of equally unreconstructed old thinking in his criticism of top-level bodies which he held responsible for continued slow innovation: the USSR Council of Ministers' Machine-Building Bureau, the State Committee for Science and Technology, and senior branch officials. Implicit in this criticism is the assumption that responsibility is carried by bodies at the top of the hierarchy. That means in practice that those bodies will feel obliged to interfere in the details of their 'subordinates' activities, which undermines the campaign to endow the latter with autonomy and elicit initiative from them.

In general, the Party-state leadership shows no sign of even attempting to stand back and refrain from transmitting orders that can only end up, down the hierarchy, as micro-economic 'interference'. Witness, even in 1988, the meetings in the Central Committee to discuss the problems of particular industries: the supply of power-station equipment (*Izvestiya*, 17 April 1988, p. 2), the chemicals sector (*Izvestiya*, 23 May 1988, p 3) and a number of industries in the course of an apparently routine meeting of the USSR Council of Ministers, according to a remarkable, blow-by-blow description by V. Arkhangelskii (*Izvestiya*, 15 May 1988, p. 3). On each of these occasions branch ministers were criticised by the Central Committee secretariat or the Prime Minister and given instructions – treated, in other words, as having operational responsibility for product-mix, capacity expansion, the fulfilling of contracts, etc., in their industries. It is hard to see any cure for this short of the abolition of branch ministries.

The favourite factory manager of the reformist press, Kabaidze, at least raised the question at the Party Conference. He said that he did not need his ministry. But even he went on to say that he was not proposing the abolition of all 'coordinating centres'. If a minister could 'catch mice' for him (Kabaidze), Kabaidze would be prepared to contribute to the minister's maintenance (*Izvestiya*, 1 July 1988, p. 5). Meanwhile the problem remains that reliance on a hierarchical structure of responsiblity is incompatible with a shift to relying on horizontal, market relations between enterprises. Nonetheless, at the same time there is a serious attempt at reform under way.

## THE REFORM PROCESS AND REFORM MEASURES

The reform process consists of debate (not all of which is public), bargaining amongst policy-makers, the promulgation of reform measures (laws and decrees) and the implementation of those measures. 'Implementation' here is itself a process, taking time and incorporating resistance as well as faithful carrying-out, and its outcome is uncertain. This transitional process will have effects on economic performance that are different from the effects of the reform measures once implemented. Economists have only limited understanding of the side-effects of the transition or attempted transition from one system to another. If reform measures are more or less faithfully carried out (a big 'if'), the consequences for economic performance will themselves take time to appear. We have a rather better understanding of what they should be than we have of transitional effects, but even here our power to predict is quite limited. In short, predicting the outcome of Gorbachev's economic reforms is a mug's game. What is reasonably safe to say is that long-term effects on Soviet economic performance will not be clear before about 1995.

The debate has become more open than at any time since the 1920s. Issues of ownership and of the role of the Party in the economy, which were only touched on during the Khrushchev era, have been not only discussed in public but are already being addressed in legislation. In addition some Soviet specialists have publicly discussed, and criticised, the bargaining process within the policymaking apparatus over reforms; in other words, the politics of reform discussion has itself been discussed. (For example, by

B. P. Kurashvili, who has said that he was excluded from testifying to the Gosplan economic reform commission after he had addressed them on what he calls the 'conservative–bureaucratic trap' in the preparation of reform measures, 'Bolshe sotsializma!' (round-table discussion), *Ogonek*, no. 12/1988, pp. 4–21).

The reform measures so far are of two kinds: those intended to decentralise the state sector and those intended to expand the legal non-state (private and cooperative) sector. The former consist of the Law on the State Enterprise of July 1987 and associated decrees redefining the responsibilities of ministries and central planning agencies and outlining planned changes in the system of pricing, finance and supply. The latter consist primarily of the 1986 Law on Individual Labour Activity and the 1988 Draft Law on Cooperatives. Loosely related to both these kinds of reform is the attempt to link the economy more closely with international markets, an attempt so far reflected mainly in a cluster of decrees announced in 1986–8.

**Decentralising the State Sector** [1]

The approach underlying the measures in this sphere seems to come mainly from the tradition of the Soviet 'optimal planning' school of mathematical economists. This is not a tradition that wholeheartedly embraces the market. Instead, its adherents mostly envisage the continuation of an overall hierarchy for managing the economy, with branch ministries subordinate to central policymakers and enterprises subordinate to branch ministries. The main difference from the traditional system is that the enterprise is supposed to be given greatly extended rights and responsibilities, while the powers of the branch ministries to 'interfere' in enterprise decisions are supposed to be severly circumscribed.

Within what remains a hierarchical framework, the centre controls 'structure-determining' investments and 'key' prices while the ministries are responsible only for broad guidance of enterprises and do not issue detailed instructions to them. Correspondingly, the enterprises determine some prices and some investments and have considerable freedom to choose suppliers and seek customers at their own discretion: in other words, they can engage in market transactions with other enterprises, but in a heavily guided market.

The measures of 1987 envisage a price reform coming mainly in 1990, a transition from centralised supply allocation to market allocation of material inputs that will not be complete before 1992

and – apparently – no abandonment of the branch-ministry structure
or even its modification into a small number of 'superministries'.
They also envisage the following: enterprises are to pay their own
way from their own sales revenue, covering a large part of their
investment as well as current expenditure; coefficients fixed for five
years at a time (and potentially equivalent to a profits tax) will
determine enterprise payments to the budget; the state is to steer
production by means of state [commercial] orders for 'important'
items, which may be bid-for competitively; some continued central
allocation of perhaps 400 'key' items will remain.

The aim of industrial modernisation is an aim that is being pursued
by mainly traditional means. Even in this sphere, however, there
have been some reform measures that could alter the traditional
Soviet rules of the game.

There are now, for example, no centrally-set guidelines regulating
contract prices for the supply of research services by R & D organisations to industry. The prices are simply to be negotiated – an
arrangement apparently reflecting the preferences of the much-
maligned State Committee for Science and Technology (*Ekon. Gaz.*,
no. 19/1988, p. 5 and no. 24/1988, p. 12).

Secondly, a new law on inventors' rights and rewards is at last close
to final drafting, though there is still controversy over its content.
There are signs that it may be appropriate for a market environment:
S. N. Fedorov of the Research Institute of Micro-surgery of the Eye
argues that the new law will only make sense when there is a real
market for inventions (*Izvestiya*, 20 June 1988, p. 2). The consensus
of inventors invited by the Council of Ministers to discuss the new
draft law (the third draft in 18 months) was reported to be that
inventions should become commodities (*tovary*); that is, that they
should indeed be traded on a market (*Ekon. Gaz.*, no. 26/1988, p. 4).

The crucial long-run requirement is precisely for the development
of a buyers' market in research services and new equipment. That
would simply be one aspect of a general development of a 'market
mechanism' in the economy as a whole. To be effective, it requires
that 'self-financed' state and non-state enterprises be left to sink or
swim according to their success in generating income in a broadly
competitive environment.

In the state sector as a whole, there had by the end of 1988 been no
progress towards a competitive environment. At the Party Conference in June, Gorbachev complained of a lack of progress. His
speeches at the conference were concerned mainly with political

reform, but he also made it clear that at least some of the weaknesses of the economic reform in the state sector had been perceived by the Politburo, and that efforts would be made to correct them.

The first of these weaknesses is to do with the state orders (*goszakazy*). These are supposed to be purchase contracts placed by the central authorities with production units, covering only part of production and replacing directive targets. In practice, they have immediately turned into the old, comprehensive directive targets under a new name. So long as nearly all output (intermediate as well as final) was the subject of these state orders, there was no scope for market relations to replace centralised supply allocation. The Soviet leader promised measures to correct this.

There duly followed a temporary statute on the setting of *goszakazy* for 1989 and 1990 (*Ekon. Gaz.*, no. 31/1988, pp. 18–20). It restricts the coverage of *goszakazy* to certain kinds of goods. What is odd, from the point of view of a market reformer, is that state orders are still meant to cover most of the output of whatever is deemed to be 'high priority'. This applies to anything connected with 'key' innovation programmes, to fuel and energy products (although they are intermediates) and to most food and consumer durables (although these are precisely the final products where decentralised responses to consumer demand would be most appropriate). In short, the deeply-ingrained perception still dominates: if something is in particularly short supply or is currently treated by the political leaders as 'important', its supply has to be centrally controlled. The upshot is, however, an apparent opening for wholesale trade in several product groups (for example, only 25 per cent of [civilian] engineering output is to be covered by state orders in the 1989 plan). And the 1989 plan is supposed to deal with substantial segments of production in terms only of so-called control figures that are supposed to be purely indicative, not imperative, plans when disaggregated to enterprise level (interview with Gosplan deputy chairman L. B. Vid, *Ekon Gaz.*, no. 36/1988, pp. 1, 2, 4).

In his Party Conference speech Gorbachev also made it clear that there would be an attack on two of the damaging delays built into the original design of the reform programme. First, the transition from centralised supply allocation to wholesale trade in producer goods would be completed by 1990 instead of 1992. Second, price reform, including the reform of retail prices, would be tackled soon – he implied, sooner than previously laid down.

The leadership has apparently grasped a basic point that has been propounded by many economists: that 'self-financing' of enterprises will do little to promote efficiency if prices continue to send misleading signals and enterprises have little choice of suppliers and inputs.

Some other, and perhaps more fundamental, problems about the reform of the state sector may not have been grasped by the Soviet leaders and their senior advisers. Or rather, if they have been, there is no publicly available evidence of it. The conflict between high plan targets and radical reform is one such problem. Another is the conflict, already described, between the preservation of a hierarchy – however streamlined – and the stimulation of initiative from below. Of the two available forms of 'self-finance' for state enterprises, it is said that hardly any have adopted the riskier version in which both wage-bill and bonuses are residual incomes dependent on net revenue. In mid-1988 all but 172 of the 44 000-odd state industrial enterprises had opted for the safe variant in which only bonuses become a residual; but this makes the incentive effect of 'self-finance' weaker (*Ekon. Gaz.* no. 32/1988, pp. 4–5).

There remains a fundamental doubt about state-sector reforms. If a thorough market-socialist reform were in fact carried through – and the Soviet Union is still a long way from that – there is a question mark against the ability of even a market-like system to generate high product quality and dynamic technological change, so long as capital assets remain state-owned. This point will be taken up later. What is striking is that Soviet policymakers have shown a readiness to tackle the ownership issue, despite its ideological sensitivity.

### Extending the Non-state Sector[2]

The provisions so far for so-called 'individual labour activity' are severely limited. Individuals engaging in private enterprise under this rubric cannot employ anyone outside their immediate family, and nobody who is able-bodied and of working age can engage in such activity full-time. Thus small-scale catering and other service ventures seem to be what is mainly envisaged for these small family firms. One particular variant may be of special importance in the long run: the individual or family contract within state and collective farms. This could, if fully implemented, amount to a limited recreation of small-scale peasant farming based on a *de facto* leasing of land and equipment to households by the farms, with sales of output back to the latter on a negotiated, contractual basis. The distinction between these arrangements and the more traditional household plots could, in the long run, dwindle to a mere formality.

The law on cooperation (*Izvestiya*, 8 June 1988, pp. 1–4), is broader in scope. It is also remarkably radical: in several ways more radical than equivalent legislation even in Hungary. It contains the following provisions: no ceiling on size of cooperatives or on the earnings of their members; the possibility for cooperative members to employ non-members (without a ceiling on the numbers employed); no apparent restriction on who joins or works for cooperatives or on their broad field of activity; the possibility of issuing shares and of engaging directly in foreign trade; declared equality of status with state enterprises; and the assumption by the collective farms of the rights of producer cooperatives as set out in the law, so that they, too, could engage in any legal activity, issue shares and so on.

Two other developments affecting property rights are of some importance. One is the encouragement of the leasing from the state (in practice from the 'superior' ministry) of a state enterprise by its workforce. Official guidelines for this have been set out (*Ekon. Gaz.*, no. 36/1988, p. 17). The idea is that the leased enterprise is no longer dependent on its ministry, has a predetermined rent to pay to it for perhaps 8–15 years, and must on that basis fend for itself. Its staff should in principle face both greater risks and greater prospective rewards; but it should also have greater security from arbitrary redeployment of its funds by its ministry. The second development is permission for state enterprises as well as cooperatives to issue shares. These are normally saleable only to employees of the enterprise concerned.

So far, the legal non-state sector is still tiny. If the collective farms are excluded, the total numbers engaged in it are over 700 000 out of a labour force of over 130 million, and presumably many of the 700 000 so engaged are only part-time. Potentially, however, the new type of cooperatives could operate as *de facto* private partnerships, outside direct state control (though of course taxed and licensed and required to operate within the law), and necessarily acting on a purely market basis. In particular, they ought not to be subject either to administrative direction or to bailing out by a higher authority if they get into difficulties. They would therefore be subject to competitive pressures with respect to market entry and market exit – which will not be the case for state enterprises. Average size of cooperative workforces was said to be 14 by mid-1988; members' incomes are said to be 50–100 per cent above wages in comparable state employment, and one engineering cooperative with a workforce of 1000 has been mentioned in the press (*Ekon. Gaz.*, no. 34/1988, p. 12; *Moscow News*, no. 31/1988, p. 12).

Some state enterprises have already issued shares or fixed-interest bonds. The restriction of share ownership to employees limits the development of a capital market and therefore of the basis for a market valuation of capital assets and a market allocation of investment funds between different activities. (The Adagi argibusiness firm in Latvia has been reported as selling shares to all comers [*Moscow News*, no. 34/1988, p. 11] but this report may not be correct). The 'shares' are usually short of being normal equities: generally they seem to be redeemable at a fixed face-value but the annual return to shareholders varies with profits.

As with the other innovations, the leasing of state enterprises has been made the subject of the usual, tediously enthusiastic, Soviet press campaign. It appears that both weak, loss-making enterprises and a few favoured high-performers (notably Svyatoslav Fedorov's Institute of Micro-Surgery of the Eye) have been allowed or pushed into leasing (Federov in *Izvestiya*, 14 June 1988, p. 1; V. Rutgaizer in *Izvestiya*, 17 May 1988, p. 2).

In Hungary and China, where such measures have been in place for some time, the logic of the reform process has led to tentative discussion of the creation of a capital market. Soviet movement in that direction, though it takes a leap of the imagination for any battle-scarred sovietologist to imagine it, cannot be ruled out as a long-run possibility. Recent developments, therefore, constitute a redefinition of socialism in the USSR. So far that redefinition is to be found chiefly in the implicit logic of recent legislation, rather than in practice. It is still remarkable. If Hungarian and Chinese experience is any guide, this more or less veiled privatisation could yield greater gains than the more orthodox state-sector reforms.

The obstacles to extensive privatisation in practice are huge. They can be divided thus:

1. Difficulties arising out of the continued central administration of the state sector (making input supplies for non-state firms problematic).
2. Restrictions apparently imposed on the non-state sector by deliberate policy: such as the reaffirmation of the 'predominant' role of the state sector in the law on cooperation, alongside the proclamation of equality of esteem for cooperatives; also the

restrictions on the sale of shares to employees, perhaps out of a fear of the emergence of a *rentier* class: the lack of a capital market will blunt both the positive and the negative stimuli to enterprise.

3. The hostility of many, probably most, local and branch-ministry officials. The explanation that is most commonly given by reformers is that state officials and managers are determined to avoid having their own inefficiency shown up by a better-motivated competitor.

4. The resentment against entrepreneurs on the part of many ordinary people who prefer material security albeit at a low level; are annoyed by changes in customary differentials and in general want to see their neighbours kept in their place. This obstacle and the resistance of officials have been amply illustrated in the press, for example in a saga about the trials of a food-wholesaling cooperative that had its registration delayed, was denied co-operation by state wholesale organisations and had its truck deliveries harassed by bribe-seeking highway police (V. Tolstov in *Izvestiya*, 13 August 1988, p. 2). Also by the sad story of the award-winning milkmaid who was pressured (!) by her farm manager into setting up a family-contract operation and then ostracised by neighbours for making money (N. Matukovskii in *Izvestiya*, 8 August 1988, p. 2).

These impediments reinforce one another. If the fear of officials and the envy of many ordinary people restrict the growth of cooperatives, while the state company remains riddled with shortages, it is only to be expected that the independent non-state businesses will take their profit where they can, exploiting the prevailing excess demand. If their own costs are inflated by (for instance) bribe-hungry officials, they may not even be able to offer more attractive prices. Above all, they will tend to restrict themselves to low-investment, quick-return activities so long as doubts remain about the duration of the current liberal policy on the non-state sector. How credible is the green light?

## CLOSER LINKS WITH THE WORLD ECONOMY

The foreign-trade reforms are basically a matter of following changes introduced in the 1970s in Eastern Europe: allowing some production

ministries and enterprises to engage directly in buying and selling
abroad, and thus diluting the monopoly of the Ministry of Foreign
Trade (the latter now merged with the body responsible for military
and technical aid and re-labelled the Ministry for External Economic
Relations), and legislating for the creation of equity joint ventures on
Soviet territory, including joint ventures in which a Western partner
can have an equity stake up to 49 per cent. These institutional
changes are associated with a declared policy of seeking closer
relations with international economic organisations such as the
General Agreement on Tariffs and Trade (GATT) and the European
Community, and aiming to make the ruble externally convertible by
the late 1990s.

Soviet exchanges with the West tended in fact to fall in real terms
in 1985–7 (though there was some recovery in early 1988). This, and
the lack of real novelty in the Soviet measures, might suggest that
changes on this front are not significant. That conclusion, however,
would be unfair. For the time being at least, the fall in the earning-
power of Soviet staple exports, combined with continued caution
about borrowing, has produced cutbacks in imports from the West.
(Indeed Soviet trade with Eastern Europe has also stagnated.) The
changing of Soviet institutions so as to allow a closer integration with
the world economy amounts to a considerable departure from the
traditional Soviet view of the outside world. But it is a long-run
objective that can only be reached if the reforms of the domestic
economy go far enough to take the Soviet Union across the threshold
of a market system. Then the ruble could be given non-resident
convertibility.


POLICY AND PERFORMANCE

Table 3.1 shows Western and Soviet official figures for Soviet
economic growth from 1965 to 1988. Obviously, growth has not
surged since 1984–5. Indeed aggregate performance in 1987 was
weak. (Joint CIA/DIA assessments, spring 1988). In 1988 growth
picked up again after the slowdown of 1987. Still the statistical picture
is not one of a radiant transformation.

It would be odd, however, if radical policy changes brought instant
improvement in aggregate growth rates. In the long run a reform that
forced Soviet producers to compete in order to survive should bring
faster productivity growth through faster introduction of new products

TABLE 3.1  *Soviet economic growth since 1965: Sectors, inputs and outputs (% p.a. growth rates)*

**A  Soviet official measures**

|  | 1966–70 | 1971–75 | 1976–80 | 1981–85 | 1986(a) | 1987 | 1988 |
|---|---|---|---|---|---|---|---|
| NMP produced | 7.7 | 5.7 | 4.2 | 3.5 | 4.1 | 2.3 | 4.4 |
| NMP utilised | 7.1 | 5.1 | 3.9 | 3.2 | 3.6 | 1.5 | 3.9 |
| gross industrial output | 8.5 | 7.4 | 4.4 | 3.6 | 4.9 | 3.9 | 3.9 |
| gross agricultural output (b) | 3.9 | 2.4 | 1.7 | 1.1 | 5.1 | −0.6 | 0.7 |
| investment (b) | 7.4 | 7.2 | 5.0 | 3.3 | 8.3 | 5.7 | 4.8 |
| capital stock | 7.5 | 7.9 | 6.8 | 6.0 | 5.3 | 5.3 |  |
| electric power | 7.9 | 7.0 | 4.5 | 3.6 | 3.6 | 4.1 | 2.4 |
| three main fuels (c) | 5.2 | 5.4 | 4.2 | 2.5 | 4.6 | 3.1 | 2.6 |

**B  CIA estimates (d)**

|  | 1966–70 | 1971–75 | 1976–80 | 1981–85 | 1986(a) | 1987 | 1988 |
|---|---|---|---|---|---|---|---|
| GNP | 5.1 | 3.0 | 2.3 | 1.9 | 3.8 | 0.5 |  |
| industrial output | 6.4 | 5.5 | 2.7 | 1.9 | 2.5 | 1.5 |  |
| agricultural output | 3.6 | −0.6 | 0.8 | 1.2 | 8.2 | −3.1 |  |
| investment | 5.5 | 4.3 | 4.3 | 3.5 | 6.0 | 4.7 |  |
| capital stock | 7.4 | 8.0 | 6.9 | 6.2 | 5.5 | 5.3 |  |
| labour (man-hours) | 2.0 | 1.7 | 1.2 | 0.7 | 0.4 | 0.4 |  |
| per capita cons. | 5.3 | 2.8 | 1.9 | 0.5 | −2.0 | 0.7 |  |

*Notes:*  General: All output series and the investment and capital-stock series are, in principle, in constant prices, i.e. denote 'real' changes. The Soviet official series, however, are known to contain an element of hidden inflation and therefore to be upward-biased. See also note a.
(a) Soviet reported growth rates for 1985 and 1986 are more than usually upward-biased.
(b) For five-year periods, the growth rates shown are those between the total for the period and the total for the preceding five-year period.
(c) Oil + gas + coal; author's estimates in terms of standard coal fuel units.
(d) At 1982 ruble factor cost. 1987 figures are preliminary.

*Sources:*  *Narodnoe khozyaistvo SSSR* (various years); *Pravda*, 22 January 1989; CIA, *Handbook of Economic Statistics 1986*; Laurie Kurtzweg, 'Trends in Soviet Gross National Product,' in US Congress Joint Economic Committee, *Gorbachev's Economic Plans*, Washington DC, US Government Printing Office, 1987, Vol. 1, pp. 126–66; CIA/DIA, Gorbachev's Economic Program: Problems Emerge, report to the Subcommittee on National Security Economics of the US Congress Joint Economic Committee, 13 April 1988.

and processes. But that is a very long-run prospect indeed. On the way to it one might expect cuts in total output, as poor-quality production was reduced and resources were shifted out of activities where they were wastefully used. Meanwhile, no radical reforms have been extensively implemented, so not even the initial health-giving wounds should be expected.

Some disruption might, however, result from transitional events: the turmoil created by massive personnel changes, for example, or by uncertainty about the survival of major institutions. (It is said that in early 1987 many industrial branch ministries almost ceased to function because there were rumours that they would be abolished). When the rules of the planning game change, as they did in 1986–7 and probably will in 1989, there could be similar disruption even though the changes may not be steps along the road to radical reorganisation.

The traditional, non-reform policies affecting personnel, priorities and pressure from above might meanwhile produce some positive effects. The shift of priorities towards the information-technology sector, for example, or simply the reduction in wasteful spending on agriculture. And in the farm sector, to judge from Chinese experience, a large and rapid response to privatisation is possible. At the moment, however, it is hard to see clear evidence of such changes. (It should, however, be said that the lack of obvious improvement in food supplies in the shops does not reflect stagnation in output; farm output has grown rather better since 1985, but food imports have been cut for balance-of-payments reasons).

## OBSTACLES TO PROGRESS

So far, very little has changed in the actual working of the Soviet economy. This is not simply because implementation of decrees and new laws take time. There are flaws in the design and planning of the changes. So far as the state sector is concerned, there are five crucial defects.

First, the branch-ministries, though they are supposed to be trimmed in size, are still there and still responsible to central policymakers for the performance of 'their' branches. So long as branch-ministries exist and are held responsible for the production of 'their' industries, those ministries have in practice no alternative but to intervene continually in the decisions of their enterprises. This undermines the whole attempt to alter motivation at the enterprise level. At present there is a deeply-ingrained expectation that if you increase profits you will have a larger share of them deducted by your 'higher authority', and that if you make losses that same higher authority will bail you out. This expectation undermines incentives to save on inputs, increase productivity, raise quality and introduce new products and processes. But if the branch-ministry continues to be held responsible for the sum of 'its' enterprises' performance, its inability to judge accurately the exact potential of each of those enterprises will force it to intervene continually in this and other ways, reallocating resources and targets amongst the enterpries for which it is responsible.

Second, price reform is to follow after other changes, so that for the time being any increase in enterprise autonomy is as likely as not to have perverse effects; profits are not a good guide to resource allocation as things stand. That reinforces the pressures to intervene from above.

Third, and closely related to the price-reform issue, is the murky subject of inflationary pressure – murky because the information about it is so poor. It deserves a brief digression.

In his speech at the XIX Party Conference, Gorbachev described the Soviet budget deficit as creating inflationary pressure. This is odd, because no budget deficit has been reported for years. A regular, small surplus of revenue over expenditure had been reported in the most boringly smug fashion, year in, year out.

Then, in October 1988, the Finance Minister, Boris Gostev, announced a planned budget deficit for 1989 of 35 billion rubles (*Pravda*, 28 October 1988). His report also included a budget revenue item described as 'resources of the all-government loan fund' (see Table 3.2). The latter appears to be borrowing from the banks, while the former is simply printing money. A recent article describes the situation as follows: unable to match expenditure rises from the existing rates and structures of taxation, the government has tended to increase transfers from enterprise gross profits to the budget by borrowing them as well as taxing the so-called 'free residual' of profit, and has even tapped enterprise amortisation funds. The result is a Soviet-style crowding-out. To compensate for these transfers, enterprises have borrowed more from the banks, increasing money supply faster than the volume of transactions – probably faster, indeed, than the money value of transactions, and therefore showing up in increased shortages. No measure of transactions that includes both

TABLE 3.2  *Price distortions and money supply pressures in the USSR:*
*some numbers*
(Plan 1989, bn. r., current prices and percentage of national income)

| | | |
|---|---|---|
| NMP produced (est., approx) | 660 | 100 |
| subsidies from state budget | 103 | 15.6 |
| of which, on food | 88 | 13.3 |
| turnover tax | 104 | 15.8 |
| budget income and exp. arising from differences between Soviet & world prices, given the official exchange rate:* | | |
|   income | 60 | 9.1 |
|   expenditure | 29 | 4.4 |
|   net budget income | 31 | 4.7 |
| declared budget deficit | 35 | 5.3 |
| 'resources of govt. loan fund' | 63 | 9.5 |
| hence, apparent total govt. borrowing | 98 | 14.8 |

*income = (?) $Q_m(P_m - RP_{wm})$ (?) excl. intra-FTO offsetting
expenditure = (?) $Q_x(RP_{wx} - P_x)$ excl. intra-FTO offsetting (usually negative)
*Source* (for numbers):   derived from Gostev budget speech, Maslyukov plan speech and final USSR Supreme Soviet amendments, *Pravda*, 28 and 29 October 1988.

intermediate sales and the service sector has been spotted, but one such account compares growth in Soviet-definition nominal income produced (4.6 per cent a year in 1981–5) with growth in bank credits over the same period (8.7 per cent a year) (B. Pavlov, *Ekon. Gaz.*, no. 14, 1988, pp. 6–7).

Part of the growth in budget spending has been in subsidies of all kinds – not just food subsidies. According to Pavlov, subsidies were equal in 1986 to 12 per cent of national income. Gostev's report gives a planned 1989 figure equivalent to 15 per cent (Table 3.2). The reduction in revenue from alcohol has made the problem worse (though Pavlov notes that bank credit was reduced in 1986). It may also be that gains in the so-called 'special earnings of foreign trade' are treated as budget revenue even when they do not correspond to any increases in resources available: notably, when they arise from changes in the official ruble exchange rate.[3] Clearly adjustment in these confused circumstances is exceptionally difficult. The deficit planned for 1989 appears to amount to about 15 per cent of Soviet-style national income (Table 3.2), or about 11 per cent of Gross National Product.

The fourth obstacle to reform in the state sector is that the reform process has been accompanied by high targets and increased pressure on many branches of the economy (for example, very high targets for investment in high-technology industries). That has helped to keep the setting of output targets and the allocation of inputs by the centre very much in place. The margin of enterprise autonomy and therefore of market relations, remains tiny and cannot easily be increased.

Fifth, the state enterprise would probably remain dependent on the central authorities even if most of the above defects were rectified. Hungarian experience suggests that this is very hard to avoid so long as the traditional form of state ownership is maintained and the enterprise director continues to be beholden to the Party-state authorities for his career. As a result, conventional market-socialist reforms, even if they are more wholehearted in design than the Soviet measures, may well be ineffective in creating powerful incentives to improve quality, adapt product-mix to the market and introduce new technology. The threat of bankruptcy or takeover probably cannot be simulated in a market socialist system, so budget constraints remain soft, and managerial behaviour remains unenterprising. That is the lesson of the Hungarian reform process so far.

The non-state sector is in some ways more promising, but there are severe limits to its development so long as the dominant state sector remains effectively unreconstructed. The non-state sector needs an environment of market prices and market allocation of materials and equipment if it is to function as more than a small fringe of unplanned economic activity.

By the same token, the foreign-trade reforms are limited in their potential effects. Joint ventures will develop much better in a market environment and with a convertible currency than in the present Soviet economic environment. Soviet enterprises will be similarly inhibited in their direct links with the outside world. Some benefits in the acquisition of management skills and new technology may flow from the foreign-trade reforms, because Western partners familiar with the traditional system can find ways of making particular joint-venture or other deals work; but extensive integration with the world economy depends ultimately on the progress of domestic economic reform. It is hard to see the Soviet Union becoming a dynamic exporter of manufactures without radical domestic reform, whatever the innovations in the foreign-trade machinery.

To sum up: an unexpectedly bold attempt at changing the system is underway; but, like any radical political initiative, it is full of internal inconsistencies and up against horrendous obstacles.

## POSSIBLE WAYS AHEAD

The ways in which progress might be made are more or less deducible from the description of the obstacles. One encouraging sign is the readiness of top policymakers to adopt increasingly radical initiatives on ownership and to make the state-sector reforms more radical.

At the Party conference, Gorbachev indicated once more that radical changes in resources ownership are part of his vision of economic reform. Speaking of his long-run aims, he referred to a socialist economy 'based on varied forms of public and personal property'. He also gave two particular examples of this approach. He said that a widespread introduction of rental and other contracts (between farms and households), together with various kinds of cooperatives, was the quickest and surest way to solve the food problem. And he observed that private and cooperative housing construction should increase and that 'numerous proposals' to sell state apartments to their tenants made sense – the Soviet version of British council-house sales.

Already the more radical reformers in the Soviet Union, such as Oleg Bogomolov, Pavel Bunich, Gavriil Popov, Vasily Selyunin (an economic journalist) and Boris Kurashvili, are criticising the state enterprise law as inadequate, or pressing for further reforms, or both. So long as debate remains open and the leadership remains actively reformist, incremental 'reforms of the reforms' are possible, and could in the very long run improve performance.

Some extension of the cooperative law's application to the main existing (but hitherto 'state-ised' and nominal) cooperatives – the collective farms – could have dramatic effects. Moves in this direction are already being touted in the Soviet press. Article 34.1 of the final version of the Law on Cooperation seems to establish that collective farms, like the new-style cooperatives, will not be subject to compulsory directives. On paper, at least, the era of compulsory procurements is drawing to a close (*Izvestiya*, 8 June 1988, pp. 1–4; see also the interpretation given in Aleksei Ponomarev's speech to the USSR Supreme Soviet, Moscow 1, 26 May 1988). It has also been made clear that the high rates of personal taxation on earnings in cooperatives are being reconsidered (Ponomarev's speech).

## CONCLUSION

The drive for reform from above is supported, it seems, by a substantial group of the more socially active members of the population, who share an earnest desire that their country should become a country they can be proud of. The most important social and political considerations that will determine the success of *perestroika* are the following: whether that group of active, reform-minded officials and other citizens is in reasonable agreement about what should be changed and how; and whether, if they are in reasonable agreement, there are enough of them to provide a critical mass of support for radical political and economic reforms; and not just for promulgating such reforms but for carrying them through.

## Notes

1. For more detailed description and analysis see Hanson, 'The Enterprise Law and the Reform Process', Radio Liberty *Research*, RL 269/87, 14 July 1987; 'Reforming the Foreign Trade System', Institute for Defense Analyses, May 1987; 'Foreign Trade: the Restructuring of the Restructuring', RL 58/88, 9 February 1988; Gertrude Schroeder, 'Anatomy of Gorbachev's Economic Reform', *Soviet Economy*, 3:3 (July-September 1987), pp. 219–42; Ivan Ivanov, 'Restructuring the Mechanism of Foreign Economic Relations in the USSR', *ibid*, pp. 192–219; Richard E. Ericson, 'The New Enterprise Law', The Harriman Institute Forum, 1:2 (February 1988).
2. Based on Hanson, 'The Draft Law on Cooperatives: An Assessment', RL 111/88, 15 March 1988 and 'Ownership and Economic Reform', RL 154/88, 6 April 1988.
3. The author is indebted to Colin Lawson for this point. He suggests that all of the 'special earnings of foreign trade' may be treated in this way, and that they can be formulated as

$$SEFT = (PmQm - P \times Qx) + R(P^* \times Qx - P^*mQm)$$

where P and Q denote prices and quantities, the former in rubles, $P^*$ denotes prices in foreign currency and R denotes the official exchange rate.

# 4 Agriculture

## KARL-EUGEN WÄDEKIN

Mikhail Gorbachev was obviously aware of the need to reorganise the Soviet food economy and had ideas about how to do it while he was Central Committee (CC) secretary for agriculture and even earlier, when he was first secretary of Stavropol krai, a large and agriculturally important area. Since March 1985 his thinking seems to have been developing and changing over time. The Gorbachev who in his political report to the XXVII Party Congress seemed to believe in the fundamental viability of state and collective farms, with some organisational improvements, is not the same politician who in October 1988 maintained that it was Stalin's agrarian policy, and implicitly, the kolkhoz system which have produced the present distressing state of Soviet agriculture. He has advocated long-term 'leasing' of land to peasant families or small cooperative groups of collective farmers. (For the speeches, see *Pravda* and *Izvestiya*, 26 February 1986; 30 July and 14 October 1988.)

It would take up several pages merely to list all the major legislative and organisational measures affecting agriculture under Gorbachev, not to speak of possible unpublished decrees and instructions. Therefore only an outline of some of the major developments can be given below; others will have to be neglected or only mentioned in passing. Developments up to the XXVII Party Congress will only be touched upon occasionally as they are covered by Wädekin in McCauley 1987, pp. 118–34.

In the early stages of Gorbachev's tenure as General Secretary his agrarian policy did not aim at fundamental change. It tried more vigorously to achieve an integrated food economy, to practise a more tolerant policy towards the private (personal) sector and it emphasised the agricultural renaissance of the Russian Non-Black Earth zone. In so doing he basically continued the policies of his predecessors and of the 1982 Food Programme in particular which were likely to have been influenced by him since 1978. The early changes under his leadership were not deviations of principle from the Programme.

70

Thus when the 1986–90 Five Year Plan was proposed and approved in spring 1986, the scaling-down of the ambitious production goals of the Food Programme was veiled by relating them, not to the 1986–90 average, but to the final year, 1990. However, the grandiose river-diversion plans, which he had conspicuously failed to endorse already at the CC plenum of October 1984, were shelved for the foreseeable future, the growth in agricultural investment was cut and the grain-sown area reduced simultaneously, while fodder crops and summer fallow areas were expanded.

Equally, the organisational format for a comprehensive food complex was already revealed by that programme. The raion agro-industrial associations (RAPOs) were generally introduced by 1983, and the USSR State Committee for the Agro-Industry (Gosagroprom), when formed in November 1985, merely transformed the former Council of the same name into an administratively stronger institution (Wädekin in McCauley 1987, pp. 127–8). So far, no positive effect of these reorganisations on the production performance of agriculture and the food industry has been discernible. More and more criticism is heaped on the RAPOs. The leaders of an Estonian raion, for example, were determined in early summer 1988 to liquidate the local RAPO and replace it by a raion cooperative organisation (*Selskaya Zhizn*, 18 June 1988, p. 3). There is also the attempt to pursue the integration of agriculture with the processing and distribution spheres (its downstream linkages) along lines which are determined by a given local production orientation rather than by the administrative borders of a raion. Again this dates back to the pre-1985 period. A prototype, the Kuban Agro-Industrial Combine was founded in 1984 after the approval by the Politburo of a proposal by the RSFSR government (*Pravda*, 8 June 1984). Its performance has met with much praise but also with some criticism. The mid-1988 statistical report (*Pravda*, 24 July 1988) recorded the existence of some 187 such combines and similar agro-industrial associations as well as 63 'agrofirms'. A few weeks before the XXVII Party Congress, V. S. Murakhovsky, head of USSR Gosagroprom, floated some innovations, and during the Congress, Gorbachev adopted them publicly. They may be put under three headings: *prodnalog* (tax in kind); farm autonomy, and family links. They became important parts of the comprehensive decree of 20 March 1986 'On Further Perfecting the Economic Mechanism in the Agro-Industrial Complex'. (The text is in *Spravochnik partiinogo rabotnika*, XXVII, Moscow, 1987, pp. 369–92, and *Pravda*, and *Izvestiya*, 29 March

1986.) The decree still euphemistically said 'perfecting' while the term 'reform' and even 'radical reform', used by Gorbachev at the XXVII Party Congress, was more and more often encountered in authoritative statements.

Gorbachev has always said, and continues to do so, that the socialist economy and society are to be retained. Yet without abandoning this principle he seems to have come, during 1986, to the conclusion that a more efficient organisation of the economy, combined with more effective incentives for those working in it, would just not do, if real improvements, or 'perfecting', and the resulting 'acceleration' (*uskorenie*) of economic development and growth were to be achieved. He said so at the CC plenum in June 1986 (*Pravda*, 17 June 1986), when he complained about the slow implementation of *perestroika*. He did not only have agriculture in mind.

At the CC plenum in January 1987 Gorbachev was even more outspoken. *Perestroika* would have to extend to the political structure, including the CPSU, so as to safeguard the civil rights of the population and activate workers' self-interest through participation (*Pravda*, 28 January 1987). As regards agriculture he emphasised farm autonomy and the necessity of changing the kolkhoz model charter so as to make them true cooperatives with greater rights for their members. According to Boris Meissner (*Osteuropa*, no. 11/ 1987, p. 827) a 'programmatic definition of the strategy of regeneration' was approved during the session.

## FARM AUTONOMY AND STATE ORDERS

Of the intentions contained in the three headings mentioned above, that of farm autonomy is the most difficult to put into practice by mere lelgislation. In fact, it has long existed in law and is an economic as well as political principle. As long as kolkhoz farm managers and members kept within the law and socialist principles and fulfilled state plans, which already under Khrushchev were explicitly delivery, not production orders, administrative interference was illegal. In practice, however, kolkhozes were under what was called the 'petty tutelage' of the raion authorities. This fact needs little elaboration here; but some recent evidence will be cited. The chairman of Surkhandarya oblast gosagroprom complained in spring 1988 (*Ekonomicheskaya Gazeta (Ekon. Gaz.)*, no. 16/1988, p. 10): 'As before there are the prescriptions – what to sow on which areas, what hectare yields to achieve, what numbers of livestock with what productivity to have'. Two aspects of this need to be considered, in addition, however. The first is that the recent stronger emphasis on farm autonomy may exert a certain influence on present administrative practice. The other is that state farms, put directly under a special administration (whether its own Ministry or a department of the Ministry of Agriculture, or recently Gosagroprom or specialised state farm trusts), are closer to being merely executive production agencies of the state. For the reconversion, after 1985, of a number of Lithuanian sovkhozes into kolkhozes, the possibility of more autonomous management was given as the main reason, in conversation with the present writer. If Soviet public farms (kolkhozes and sovkhozes) are to be managed – relatively! – independently, their actual parameters of activity will have to be changed. The core of these parameters are the obligatory plan tasks, and change was heralded by *prodnalog*, which by 1987 and 1988 has more and more been replaced by state orders (*goszakaz*). The intention is that not only should the number of plan indicators be reduced but also that the centrally-imposed obligatory deliveries be limited to a small number of the most important products. These tasks should not fully exhaust the productive potential of the farms. Regional plan tasks should also leave some room for above-plan output which the farms should be able to sell at their own discretion, including free market sales.

It goes without saying that the whole system of planning and public administration, of the state as well as the party hierarchy, will have to undergo fundamental changes if the managerial autonomy of farms (as well as of other Soviet enterprises) is to become reality. Among other things, the relatively recent arrival of RAPO as an organisation, established by order from above within the territorial boundaries of each administrative raion, is hardly conducive to farm autonomy. It is vested with great powers which, in part, are inherited from, and intertwined with, those of the previous raion administration of agriculture. One suspects that the 'combines' or comparable 'associations' now often possess such directive powers. Gorbachev seems to be aware of all this but less so of the difficulty of overcoming it within the existing Soviet system.

In economic practice, probably the most formidable obstacle to farm autonomy is the pressure of tight procurement goals, which at least in the short-to-medium-term forces planners to continue more or less fully exploiting the production potential of the farms. This was heatedly discussed in connection with the role of state orders in the draft text of the Law on Cooperation in spring 1988. All the same the final version of the law remained equivocal in its assumptions that the farms would find these sales orders 'advantageous' and would voluntarily conclude contracts in compliance with the demands of the state orders. As regards the contents of these, the Preliminary Regulation (*polozhenie*) for state purchases in 1989 and 1990, approved on 25 July 1988 by the USSR Council of Ministers, is very revealing. At least for 1989 the intention is to place all sales of major farm products 100 per cent under *goszakaz* (*Ekon. Gaz.*, no. 30/1988, p. 11. For the text of the regulation see *Ekon. Gaz.*, no. 31/1988, pp. 18–19).

Notwithstanding such systemic problems, the reform ideas and demands were put in concrete terms in three important legislative acts in 1987 and 1988 covering agriculture (and the economy as a whole): The Law on the State Enterprise (Association) of 30 June 1987. As regards agriculture it concerns those farms which are under state ownership – overwhelmingly sovkhozes. It should be noted that sovkhozes now dispose over half of all agricultural land and fixed assets and half the labour force in socialised Soviet agriculture. A draft of the new Kolkhoz Model Charter, was discussed and accepted in general terms by the IV Kolkhoz Congress in late March 1988. In its final form, which has not yet been published in the generally accessible press, it was approved by the Council of Kolhozes on 3 August 1988.

## THE LAW ON COOPERATION OF 8 JUNE 1988

This law assigns an important role to cooperative forms of economic activity, including small cooperatives formed on citizen's private initiative. It contains a special section on kolkhozes which, in part, overlaps with their new Model Charter. The idea of small cooperatives within the larger cooperative of the big farm, as laid down in the law, is in line with the *podryad* system.

### The *Podryad*

Under these conditions, possibly the only operational way to greater efficiency and elasticity in agricultural production is to begin with autonomy within the farms, in other words, their subsections in relation to overall farm management. Therefore the *podryad* (contracted production commitment, not contract in the sense of a freely negotiated agreement) system of organisation and remuneration of work within the farms appears to be the most important element of those changes which are, at present, being implemented. (Among the vast Soviet literature on *podryad*, see Poshkus 1988 pp. 72–204; Shmelev 1987a; as well as Shmelev and Zavyalov 1987, a collection of papers presented at an all-Union conference in Makhachkala in 1986.)

As a system of remunerating labour, the *podryad*, without using the term, was already in 1961–2 part of the wage reform introduced on state farms and recommended to kolkhozes. As such it did not require new legislation. It was merely reemphasised in connection with the 1982 Food Programme and in subsequent publications and official statements. By 1982 already almost a quarter of permanent (not seasonal) farm labour was working under the system and numbers continued to grow afterwards. (See the statistics for 1982 in Narkhoz 1984, p. 327 and in subsequent Narkhoz volumes. The *podryad* was recommended for the construction sector and 'other branches' of the economy by a CC decree on 10 October 1986.) Until 1986 *podryad* referred mainly to rather large units of a few dozen workers, the brigades or livestock sections (*ferma*) and – in theory rather than in actual practice – to the remuneration of their work based on productive performance.

What is new is the change of emphasis within the *podryad* system towards new forms of organisation, small groups, even families. It became official policy only in early 1986 (see Wädekin in McCauley 1987, pp. 131–2), although in semi-legal, not generally publicised practice it had existed locally for several years. The decree of 20 March 1986 (*Spravochnik XXVII*, pp. 369–92, point 16) permitted state farms and recommended kolkhozes, 'starting from concrete local conditions of production, to apply the family and personal *podryad* in field and animal husbandry as one of the forms of collective *podryad*.' However, it added that the payment of work per output unit should be the same as for larger *podryad* groups (brigades and links). Another CC decree of 6 December 1986 (*Spravochnik XXVII*, pp. 508–9) endorsed it again but at the same time was very critical about the implementation of *podryad* in practice and revealed that people were, not infrequently, pressured into concluding stereotyped *podryad* contracts:

Among the various forms of collective *podryad*, those proving more successful are the limited number of small links and brigades of intensive work, to which the land, machinery and other means of production are assigned on a contractual basis for a lengthy term. In all regions of the country the family *podryad* is becoming more and more widespread.

However some formalism and irresponsibility are evident in connection with the installation (*vnedrenie*) of self-accounting (*khozraschet*) and collective *podryad*.... Frequently there is no guaranteed supply of resources and there are only weak incentives for economising on them....

Not infrequently, in working with *podryad* links, brigades and livestock sections, an administrative approach prevails, the democratic principles of management are violated, the role of the labour collectives is held in low esteem and their rights infringed upon....

It is proposed ... to develop in every way the through (*skvoznoi*, i.e. comprising a whole production process or more than one stage of it) and family *podryad* and other progressive forms of organising and stimulating work. Special attention is being paid to the inadmissability of a formalistic approach, to stereotyped ways and of campaigning in this important matter.

The agricultural *podryad* was incorporated into the Law on the State Enterprise. At the same time, in June 1987, Gosagroprom and Goskomtrud (State Committee for Labour), together with the All-Union Council of Trade Unions, recommended the implementation of family and individual *podryad*. (These recommendations are mentioned by Shmelev 1987b, p. 33). It was also incorporated into the new Kolkhoz Model Charter in 1988.

As in the brigades of the reformed wage system of 1961–2, the intention is that the workers in a small *podryad* unit or family are not paid a wage determined by work norms and tariffs. This group as a whole is paid for its output minus the value of the inputs and services supplied by the overall collective or state farm. The quantities of produce to be delivered to that farm are fixed in the contract. They are paid at contracted unit prices of 'evaluation' (*rastsenka*) below the state procurement prices received by the overall farm. Yet the factors of calculation are largely determined by the expected (planned) yields and the 'normatives' of material inputs and of required labour expenditure at fixed tariffs. In this way the old plan goals, work norms and tariffs come in again; the essence is that of a working contract based on them, not a production contract. In exchange, the *podryad* workers do not bear the full production risk, as the contract usually provides for a minimum payment similar to the previous minimum wage on the farm. Yet if the expected yields (indirectly, the plan goals) are set too high, as frequently is the case, only that guaranteed minimum payment will be achieved, whether the *podryad* workers make an effort or not.

What, then, in reality, is the advantage of the *podryad*? It is now normally a small, usually family, kinship or friendship group of workers. The link between each member's skill, effort and careful execution of work and productive results is visible and the reward is distributed internally (though with regard to fulfilled work norms and skill tariffs). The problem of 'freeloaders', is more easily solved than in larger groups. Moreover, the *podryad* unit is – or should be – free to organise or time its work, very often in excess of what labour legislation stipulates. If so, the diseconomies of day-to-day management and organisation in oversized farms are avoided at least for those parts or stages of the production process which are executed under the *podryad* contract. Such a *podryad* corresponds to contracting public production out to private households and their plot-farming, which might as well be considered family cooperatives on *podryad*.

For the contracted production, the plot-owner may receive a piece of land and keep animals over the legal limits. However, at the same time he might produce part of the contracted output on his original plot and with the animal numbers privately owned kept within the legal limits. In animal production, which dominates plot farming, the plot holder usually provides small livestock premises and labour, and often the young animals. The public farm, depending on circumstances, often supplies indoor premises, small machinery (rented or sold), veterinary services, sometimes the young animals, etc. and – most important – some feed.

Thus the boundary between private (or personal) and contracted production for the socialist sector become blurred in this variant of contracted production or *podryad*. To quote current Soviet usage: private and socialist production are integrated. The subject is dealt with in more detail below, in connection with what might be termed individual production, because it is neither completely private nor completely socialist.

## The Tenancy *Podryad*

Since the summer of 1987 a new term has been increasingly used: *arendnyi podryad* or simply *arenda*. This means a production commitment contract on a land rent basis (*arenda* means rent, land lease or tenancy). During the CC plenum in late July 1988, Gorbachev strongly advocated it as a long-term land lease 'for 25–30 and even 50 years' (*Ekon. Gaz.*, no. 31/1988, p. 4). Numerous and rather differing examples have been cited in the press. On 12 October 1988 a conference of specialists on the subject was held in the CC, CPSU under Gorbachev's chairmanship. A number of points emerge from the (fully?) published proceedings and are summarised here on the basis of *Selskaya Zhizn*, 14 October 1988:

(i) Only supporters of *arenda* attended, according to an interjection by Gorbachev. Hence there were no dissenting voices present.

(ii) *Arendnyi podryad* or *arenda*, as distinct from simple *podryad*, so far only exists in a minority of cases and has taken very different forms. E. S. Stroev, First Party Secretary of Orel, announced during the conference that in his oblast more than 4000 'tenancy collectives of differing profiles' had been formed, of which only 390 were on a family basis and 53 on 'tenancy *podryad*'.

(iii) There is great uncertainty about admissible and desirable forms. There are not only adversaries of the initiative but also many people who hesitate since they are not certain of the staying power of the present policy.

(iv) Gorbachev himself is for the new venture. He stated: 'The *podryad* is a big step forward. Renting out of land is also a kind of *podryad*, but one of a higher order, the tenancy *podryad*, when a person takes land and the means of production for a certain time.' He does not want to make this a campaign but wants it to be propagated. At the same time, he is in favour of many farm and regional variants.

(v) The radical logic of dissolving unprofitable public farms and handing their land over to small and family groups of tenants, as advanced by Nikolai Shmelev, one-and-a-half years earlier (*Novyi mir*, no. 4/1988, p. 164), found no support at the conference, or at least not in the published proceedings. It was more or less implied, however, by the demand of Mart Saldre (Estonia) that the land be sold to him, not leased, and the proposal of the writer I. A. Vasilev that deserted land be rented out to *arendatory* by local soviets, not public farms. The envisaged ideal case seemed to be that the large farm retain a number of overhead functions and technical services, for which it is better qualified. Large-scale farming, possibly by bigger tenancy brigades, as a better instrument of performance accounting and wage distribution, should continue where favoured by the product, e.g. in dry-land grain farming – see the indirect plea by V. V. Shvets at the conference.

(vi) A law on the *arenda* is in preparation and should bring some clarity. This is urgently needed because the present Land Law and Civil Code explicitly forbid leasing and renting of land. Landed property remains a state monopoly.

Small-scale tenant farming would be a radical departure, but at least for the time being the term *arenda* has to be interpreted restrictively. It is not even clear whether there is a monetary rent being paid for the use of the land. At the October conference, V. I. Gusenkov, from Moscow oblast, complained that 'no normative of a hectare of land has been fixed'. Only one case of monetary land rent was mentioned during the conference by Mart Saldre, a tenant from Estonia, but Estonia seems to have gone farthest down this road. Possibly, the rent in many or most cases continues to be levied by the difference between the state procurement price (paid to the 'landlord' public farm) and the calculated price paid to the tenant by the same farm, as is the case, in fact, with all kinds of *podryad*. At any rate, machinery services may be paid as such, which, in practice, has a monopoly on all such inputs otherwise unavailable to the tenant.

In only a minority of cases, mainly in the Baltic republics, perhaps also in Belorussia, in some Central Asian mountainous areas and in the agrarian depressed regions of Central, North Western and North Eastern Russia, parts of Siberia and the Soviet Far East does a tenancy exist in the sense of the tenant having some autonomy over how he manages his land and animals, and markets his output. Even though there may be rent contracts on many collective and state farms, they usually account only for a small proportion of the farm's production.

In the great majority of cases the tenant is a share-cropper in a production programme drawn up by the farm and is afforded little room for individual entrepreneurship. This is by far the predominant situation in the fertile agricultural regions. An official West German delegation, in late summer 1988, found that leaseholding contracts play a minor role on successful public farms.

It is also clear that windfall superprofits from either simple or tenant *podryad* farming are not feasible. This is in accord with the ingrained beliefs not only of communists but also of large segments of the Soviet population. On the other hand, labour-earned income, if derived from more and or better work, should not be restricted, although this has happened in many cases. It will, of course, be difficult to draw a clear dividing line, and there seems to be a bias in many places to draw it in a restrictive way. Much depends and will depend on contract conditions. In an interview (*Izvestiya*, 1 October 1988), A. A. Nikonov, President of the Lenin Academy of Agricultural Sciences, stated that recommendations on rent agreements were issued by USSR Gosagroprom in August 1988, and had the following to say on the subject:

> What is often at present called rent, is in reality far from being such ... this form, which is new to us, and the existing economic mechanism, the system of planning, management and accounting, have not been adapted to one another. According to the recommendations, he [the tenant] has the right only to a superprofit, if he has performed superwork...
>
> In the regulations, the advantages of the enterprise (public farm) are taken into account, not those of the other partner. The tenant is still powerless in his relations with the kolkhozes, sovkhozes, authorities, *vis-à-vis* those on whom he depends ... the tenant must be made equal before the law. We know of more than one case where the tenants have been discriminated against, humiliated and aggravated, where deliberately unbearable conditions were written into the contracts. And all this is being done under the guise of defending state interests and social property against some supposed attempts to 'erode' them.
>
> Existing agreements do not guarantee the tenant the full duration of his tenancy. At any time (with two months' notice) the enterprise may terminate the contract with him. Thus, we declare an ownership term of half a century, but in fact we prove that the tenant is a timeserver, whom we do not trust. This puts a heavy brake on the move to tenancies and also eliminates trust in the irreversibility of the present course of agrarian policy.

If the land rent is not too high, it might even make economic sense to pay tenants produce prices below those of the state procurement agencies, which are high by international standards. This is so because the present procurement prices are too high for most of the huge Soviet public farms given their potential for economies of scale. The standard of their labour organisation and capital utilisation are too low, making production too expensive. Efficient and hardworking small-scale producers can make handsome profits, given these prices, although at the expense of long working hours. Yet this also depends on the quality and price of the inputs they receive from the public sector, and here many complaints were raised at the October conference, as well as in the Soviet press. What matters, after all, in a country with excess demand for the better foods, is not the total outlay on agricultural products, but the cost per unit of output, especially for those products which are in real demand. And this is what the small-scale producer achieves with his higher yields per hectare and per animal.

It does not seem difficult to find a minority of Soviet people who, even under the adverse conditions described by Nikonov, are ready to work hard and efficiently, in order to derive an above-average income. Numerous such cases are quoted in the Soviet press. But will there be a majority, or at least a sizeable proportion of the population, sufficient for them to have an impact on Soviet agriculture as a whole? This is very much an open question because there is the additional factor that latent distrust of long-term state and party policy is justified by historical experience.

## SLOW OVERALL IMPROVEMENT WITH MAJOR FLAWS

Soviet indices of gross agricultural output reveal a 1981–5 average only 5 per cent above that of 1976–80 (for the livestock sector, 7 per cent). This rate was not significantly above population growth. Moreover, food demand per head rose due to income growth. In the public sector (excluding kolkhozes and not to speak of the second economy) average nominal wages by 1985 were 30 per cent higher than in 1975 and the labour force was 15 per cent greater. (Gorbachev, in his Krasnoyarsk speech on 16 September 1988 dwelt on the subject (*Selskaya Zhizn*, 18 September 1988). Our data are taken from *Statisticheskiy 1987*, pp. 380, 387.

Some output growth is discernible in 1986, but it cannot unequivocally be ascribed to the new policy, since livestock production growth had already resumed in 1982 after the stagnation of the years 1978–81.

Apart from the slowness of output growth, a major flaw is that during 1985–7 labour inputs in socialised agriculture remained practically unchanged at 10 million agricultural workers (12 million if non-agricultural are included) on sovkhozes, and decreased only slightly on kolhozes from 12.7 million (with 22.39 days worked per

TABLE 4.1    *Official indices of gross output of agriculture, 1981–7*
*(1980 = 100)*

|                        | 1981 | 1982 | 1983 | 1984 | 1985 | 1986 | 1987   |
|------------------------|------|------|------|------|------|------|--------|
| Agriculture<br>of which | 99   | 104  | 111  | 111  | 111  | 117  | 100.2  |
| Crop production        | 97   | 106  | 113  | 111  | 110  | 117  | 98–99  |
| Livestock<br>production | 100  | 103  | 109  | 111  | 112  | 117  | c.102  |

*Sources*:   *Statisticheskiy 1987*, p. 169; *Narkhoz 1986*, p. 213; and, for 1987, estimated on the basis of *SSSR 1987*, p. 111.

month) to 12.5 million (with 22.54 days per month). (Derived from *SSSR 1987*, pp. 136–40.) At the same time, the sum of labour costs increased by more than 8 per cent and thereby exceeded output growth, while investment also increased. In other words the rise in the costs of agricultural production also seriously concerns Soviet leaders by affecting the overall availability of investment capital. Most likely, this is another important reason why forms of farming are being sought which mobilise labour, and economise on inputs, thereby saving capital, as is expected of the *podryad*.

Detailed investment data for 1987 are not yet available but productive fixed capital assets per worker reveal an annual increase of 7 per cent by 1987 over 1985, i.e. at roughly the same annual rate as during 1980–85, though much less than the increases during the years 1970–80 (ibid., p. 107). It seems, however, that under *khozraschet* (economic accounting) and somewhat greater autonomy, public farms in 1987 began to cut back on their machinery purchases. Compared to 1985, the number of tractors decreased (total h.p. increased insignificantly), and the same happened with grain combine numbers (ibid., p. 130). It remains to be seen whether this is a once-and-for-all change, or signals more selective buying in the future. On the other hand, public farms' lorry park continued to grow at an accelerated rate, which seems rational, given the severe transport bottlenecks on Soviet farms.

It is sensible to combine production results for two years, as the Soviets are prone to do. The year 1986 brought a great increase and 1987 again stagnation, the result of very unfavourable weather. The 1986–7 combined growth average of gross agricultural output is quite respectable compared to 1985 (plus 5 per cent) as well as compared to the 1981–5 average (plus 9 per cent). It should be added that the 1987 wet harvest weather reduced the quality of grain and potato output, so that above-average deductions due to be storage losses have to be made to that year (see below). Most important is the fact that the supply of food continued to lag behind demand during the current period, as it has for the last quarter of a century. Gorbachev left no doubt at the XIX Party Conference that this is, together with excess demand for other consumer goods and a shortage of housing, a central concern of his government. Politically, it is clearly more important for him to achieve a marked improvement in food supplies. This may have contributed to his step-by-step acceptance of reform proposals which appear radical in a Soviet context.

## THE CROP SECTOR AND THE PROSPECTS OF GRAIN AVAILABILITY

The overall quantitative improvements in crop production are not spectacular, but reveal a change of trend compared with the early 1980s. More remarkable are the increases in hectare yields of important crops such as grain, sunflower and sugar beet. For grain (see Table 4.3) they almost equalled the 1978 all-time Soviet record,

TABLE 4.2(a)  *Output of main non-grain crops, 1976–87: absolute quantities, millions of tonnes*

|  | *1976–80* | *1981–5* | *1986* | *1987* |
|---|---|---|---|---|
|  | 5 year averages |  |  |  |
| Oilseeds | 6.04 | 5.71 | 6.25 | 7.24 |
| Potatoes | 82.6 | 78.4 | 87.2 | 75.9 |
| Sugar beet | 88.7 | 76.4 | 79.3 | 90.4 |
| Cotton, unginned | 8.55 | 8.31* | 8.23 | 8.09 |

TABLE 4.2(b)  *Main non-grain crops, 1976–87: yields (centners per hectare)*

| Sunflower seed** | 11.8 | 11.9 | 13.7 | 14.6 |
|---|---|---|---|---|
| Sugar beet | 237 | 218 | 233 | 266 |
| Potatoes | 117 | 115 | 113 | 119 |
| Cotton fibre (Soviet recalculation) | 8.6 | 7.6 | 7.7 | 7.0 |

*This is the recently corrected figure and is lower than those published earlier
**Sunflower accounts for 85–90 per cent of oilseeds
*Source*:  *SSSR 1987*, pp. 110–11, 116 and 117

although on a somewhat smaller sown area. Cotton production, however, continues to suffer from worsening soil conditions and salinisation, perhaps also from the aftermath of the 'Uzbek Affair' – padding of cotton production figures. Potatoes, half of which are grown on individual plots, also showed no rise in yields.

Soviet statistics of grain production are in bunker weight and require adjustment to make them comparable to Western data and to reduce them to quantities actually available for human, animal and industrial consumption. (On the definitional aspects see *Prospects 1979*, pp. 58–61; and *Prospects 1983*, pp. 77–81.) In these publications the present writer arrived at an average adjusting deduction of 14–17 per cent, higher than that applied for dockage and wastage by the USDA group, but most recently confirmed in conversation with a prominent Soviet economist. Due to excessive moisture content in 1987 the same economist put the necessary adjustment for that year as high as 20 per cent. The drying and storage facilities could not cope with moisture contents of up to 40 per cent and this meant that much grain was spoiled after delivery. If the necessary statistical adjustments are less for 1988, Gorbachev's announcement on 16 September 1988 that the grain harvest will be below that of 1987, sounds less alarming.

Some official Soviet spokesmen still cling to the goal of producing one metric ton of grain per head of the Soviet population. This seems greatly exaggerated by Western standards. Thus, one metric ton per head enables France to export sizable quantities of grain. However, the Soviet goal refers to bunker weight. If an adjustment of minus 14–17 per cent (see above) is made, this would bring the figure down to 850 kg per head. This looks reasonable in an international context and should be sufficient to achieve adequate domestic supplies of meat and higher living standards all round.

One might also envisage slowly improving grain harvesting and utilisation techniques which could reduce the necessary adjustment by, say, 5 percentage points. More than that, a reduction in the enormous pre-harvest losses (which nobody has dared quantify) by another 5 percentage points would result in a bunker yield 5 per cent higher. Applying such – admittedly highly speculative, though not utopian – improvement factors, the present writer arrives at the 'potential' output of Table 4.3.

The figures reveal how critical the situation was during the early 1980s and again in 1987/88 because of the bad harvest conditions of that year. They also show the great compensating impact of grain imports.

TABLE 4.3   *Soviet grain output, 1976–88*

| | 1978 | 1976–80 | 1981–5 | 1986 | 1987 | 1988 |
|---|---|---|---|---|---|---|
| | | 5-year averages | | | | |
| Official bunker weight, output, mill. tonnes | 237.4 | 205.0 | 180.3 | 210.1 | 211.3 | 195 |
| Bunker weight, yields per ha | 18.5 | 16.0 | 14.9 | 18.0 | 18.3 | |
| Adjusted output, mill. tonnes** | 197–204 | 170–76 | 150–55 | 174–80 | 169* | |
| Adjusted output, kg/head*** | 754–81 | 651–74 | 550–68 | 621–42 | 597* | |
| Net imports, mill. tonnes**** | 21.2 | 19.9 | 38.3 | 23.9 | | |
| Adjusted availability (inc. imports) mill. t. | 218–25 | 190–206 | 188–93 | 198–204 | | |
| kg/head*** | 836–63 | 727–50 | 691–709 | 707–28 | | |
| Potential net output, mill. tonnes***** | 213–27 | 189–96 | 167–72 | 194–201 | 177* | |
| kg/head*** | 815–69 | 724–51 | 612–31 | 675–717 | 625* | |

*Assuming a 20 per cent – instead of 14–17 per cent – downward adjustment of bunker weight in 1987 (see above).
**Adjusted (= net) output: bunker weight minus 14–17 per cent (but 20 per cent for 1987, see above).
***Mid-year and mid-quinquennium population numbers.
****Import minus export grain (excl. legumes) tonnage according to FAO Trade Yearbook, Vol. 30.
*****Potential net output = bunker weight output plus 5 per cent for avoided pre-harvest losses, then minus 9–12 instead of 14–17 per cent for post-harvest loss adjustment (cf. above).

In order to achieve 850 kg per head of domestic grain actually available for an estimated population of 302–3 million by 1995, a net output of about 257 million metric tons would be required instead of the over 300 million metric tons bunker weight implied by the current plans. Even the 257 million metric tons would not all be needed, if during the same timespan the feed-conversion ratio improved or/and the percentage share of concentrates in feed consumption diminished. The relative overconsumption of concentrate feed, and thereby the saving potential, for grain is particularly significant where cattle are concerned. (According to a Soviet source it was possible to reduce this consumption per unit of live weight gain by 25 per cent between 1982 and 1985. See Cook 1988, p. 20. Also compare the feed consumption ratios (in oats units), which are almost double those in Western industrial countries.) With harvesting and utilisation techniques improving by an assumed 5 percentage points each, and the feed conversion ratio by another 5 per cent, the required increase of net output by about 20 per cent over the 1986–7 bunker weight average, during the years to 1995, seems easier to achieve than the official goal of over 40 per cent, expressed in bunker weight figures. However, these are possibilities, not assured prospects. As to the feed conversion ratio it will be shown below that there are indeed signs of a slow but steady improvement.

## THE LIVESTOCK SECTOR

In animal husbandry, qualitative improvements have been more marked than in crop production. (For a competent recent overview, see Cook 1988, passim.) Comparing the published statistics per 1 April and 1 July 1987 and 1988 (*Selskaya Zhizn*, 26 April and 24 July 1988) one finds that with smaller herds on public farms, total (including private herds) output of meat and milk was greater in both the first and the second quarter of 1988 than during the corresponding periods of 1987. At the same time the public sector herds were rebuilt after the winter and spring decline. This conclusion, being based on rough and preliminary data, cannot be totally reliable, but it is probable that either animal productivity increased at an almost incredible rate or the private sector contributed a growing share (see below).

A rise in animal productivity over the mid-term is most visible when milk yields per cow are examined. After near-stagnation during the 1970s at 2100–2200 kg per milch cow, they had risen to 2330 kg by 1985 and by another 7 per cent during only the two years 1986 and 1987 (2501 kg). As a result, milk output increased while cow numbers declined. Similarly, pork output per pig (beginning of year numbers) was dismayingly low. With 70–80 kg and at an average slaughter weight of sold pigs of 100–105 kgs (Narkhoz 1985, p. 250), it implies that, on average, it takes about 15 months to fatten a new-born piglet (including, of course, those which died). Yet from a low of 70 kg in 1980, annual pork output per pig has increased at an accelerating rate: by 7 per cent by 1985 and another 5 per cent during 1986–7. The output of all kinds of meat rose much faster than the numbers of annual average livestock units. It should be added, though, that Soviet meat statistics include fats and edible subproducts, so that at least 10 per cent has to be deducted to render them comparable to Western data.

Due to severe drought throughout most of the Soviet Union, the

TABLE 4.4  *Animal numbers, feed consumption and animal production, 1975–88*

| | 1975 | 1980 | 1985 | 1986 | 1987 | 1988 |
|---|---|---|---|---|---|---|
| **A  Animal numbers, millions at beginning of year** | | | | | | |
| Cows | 41.9 | 43.3 | 43.6 | 42.9 | 42.4 | 42.0 |
| Other cattle | 67.2 | 71.8 | 77.4 | 78.0 | 79.7 | 78.5 |
| Pigs | 72.3 | 73.9 | 77.9 | 77.8 | 79.5 | 77.3 |
| Sheep and goats | 151.2 | 149.4 | 149.2 | 147.3 | 148.7 | 147.0 |
| Poultry | 782 | 981 | 1143 | 1165 | — | — |
| Livestock units, annual average* | 146.8 | 154.9 | 161.5 | 162.7 | — | — |
| **B  Feed consumption** | | | | | | |
| Oats units consumed, mill. t | 368.5 | 398.1 | 436.1 | 444.2 | — | — |
| of which: concentrate feed** | 118.9 | 143.9 | 147.4 | 150.8 | | |
| Oats units per annual average livestock unit, t | 2.51 | 2.57 | 2.70 | 2.73 | | |
| **C  Animal production** | | | | | | |
| Overall: meat units, mill. t*** | 34.7 | 35.3 | 39.1 | 40.9 | 41.6 | |
| Milk equivalents, mill. t | 90.8 | 90.9 | 98.6 | 102.2 | 103.4**** | |
| Eggs, billions | 57.0 | 67.9 | 77.3 | 80.7 | 82.1**** | |
| Wool, greasy, thous. t | 467 | 443 | 447 | 469 | 455 | |
| Meat, slaughter weight, mill. t | 15.0 | 15.1 | 17.1 | 18.1 | 18.6**** | |
| Pork, per pig, kg | 78 | 70 | 75 | 78 | 79 | |

* Annual averages, derived from Soviet data on feed consumption in absolute quantities of oats units and consumption per livestock unit, probably including horses, poultry and some other livestock.

** Roughly 85 per cent consisting of grain, legumes and grain byproducts.

*** 1 kg of meat = 1.0; 1 kg of milk = 0.167; 1 kg of wool = 3.57; 1 egg = 0.05 meat units.

**** According to Gorbachev at Krasnoyarsk, the 1987 figures were: 104 million for milk; 18.9 million for meat and 82.7 billion for eggs.

*Sources: Narkhoz 1975*, pp. 391, 395, 401, 412; *Narkhoz za 60 let*, pp. 337, 349; *Narkhoz 1980*, p. 245; *Narkhoz 1985*, p. 239; *Narkhoz 1986*, p. 206; *Narkhoz za 70 let*, pp. 258, 267; *SSSR 1987*, pp. 120, 122.

data for 1987 understate feed consumption and overstate meat output per animal because of emergency slaughterings, in particular of pigs. Some above-normal slaughterings took place in 1980 in the wake of the part-American embargo of grain. With this in mind, the steady increase of output after 1980 emerges yet more clearly. Production measured in meat units increased faster than feed consumption and average annual numbers of livestock. (For a breakdown of the feed conversion ratios up to 1985, based on various Soviet sources, see Cook 1988, Table 9.)

Both the declining feed consumption (per unit of output!) and the growing share of non-grain feed in it, if it continues, will have important implications for Soviet grain consumption and thereby for import requirements and/or domestic milk and meat supplies. Most likely, the growing imports of protein feedstuffs (instead of grain) has had a positive impact, but when it comes to growth in most recent years, it should be borne in mind that Soviet grain imports (basically for feed) decreased after 1985 so that in essence the protein imports merely made up for this decline.

## THE PRIVATE OR INDIVIDUAL PRODUCTION SECTOR

According to G. I. Shmelev, probably the most competent Soviet specialist on the subject, 47–8 million Soviet families, or 'more than two thirds of families in our country are in one way or another involved in running a family agricultural concern' and they produce approximately 25 per cent of gross Soviet agricultural output (Shmelev 1987a, p. 14, including footnote 6).

Various decrees favouring the individual sector of private animal holdings have been promulgated since 1977 (see Wädekin in McCauley 1987, pp. 119–20). The most recent are those of 15 May 1986 on suburban individual gardening under collective organisation and, more generally for the non-agricultural population, of 25 September 1987. All the same, the area of individually-used land has not expanded fast, except for the so-called collective gardens (allotments). The same is probably true of other individual users, such as those of gardens around urban houses or of holders of 'service plots', who account for a small but not negligible share. (They may amount to for up to 500 000 ha, which is the difference between the 8.02 million ha given in *Narkhoz 1982* and the 'more than' 8.5 million ha of *priusadebnye uchastki* for the same year quoted in Perelygin 1986,

p. 31; on the 'service plots', see ibid., p. 40.) In total, one may estimate the share of individually-used land, excluding contract plots and total pasture, at 3.5 per cent. However, this sector is most important for animal production since very little grain and practically no technical crops are grown.

TABLE 4.5 *Private livestock holdings (million head at beginning of year) and individual land use (thous. ha), 1975–87*

|  | 1975 | 1980 | 1985 | 1986 | 1987 |
|---|---|---|---|---|---|
| Cows | 13.7 | 13.2 | 13.1 | 12.9 | 12.8 |
| Other cattle | 9.7 | 9.8 | 11.0 | 10.8 | 10.6 |
| Pigs | 12.2 | 14.0 | 13.9 | 13.6 | 13.6 |
| Sheep and goats | 29.4 | 30.2 | 33.1 | 33.4 | 33.2 |
| Arable and garden land hay meadows | 8020 | 7950 | 7990 | 8110 | |
| of which: orchards and vineyards | 1140 | 1522 | 1295 | 1257 | |
| In addition: allotments | 516* | 622 | 811 | 854 | |

* In 1970

*Sources: Statisticheskii ezhegodnik 1987*, pp. 199–205; *SSSR 1987*, p. 120. For land use: *Narkhoz 1975, pp. 343, 379: Narkhoz 1980*, pp. 219, 235; *Narkhoz 1985*, pp. 222, 236–7

The discrepancy between the growth of total output and that of total labour cost on public farms, as outlined above, would be even greater if Soviet statistics did not overstate recent growth by 2–3 percentage points (estimate based on *SSSR 1987*, pp. 106, 111–12, 122, 139) by treating as socialist production the output of the individual plots of the population. There is a certain, though limited justification for this misleading practice, as most of the sales of plot output to socialised farms is based on contracts with them. The contracts may refer to livestock in public ownership, which is handed over to households or individuals for tending and fattening, or to privately-owned animals. Some scattered, mostly indirect previous information (e.g. that disclosed by G. I. Shmelev, as quoted in Wädekin in McCauley 1987, p. 120; and more recently in Shmelev 1987a and 1987b) on the intra-farm animal product flows was available and was collected and analysed by the present writer (see *Berkeley-Duke Occasional Papers on the Second economy in the USSR*, no. 10/April 1987, Appendix). For the first time the 1987 Soviet statistical pocketbook published official data on them. The quantities, which increased after 1980, involved 6.4 million tonnes of milk, 1.2 million tonnes of meat and 15 000 tonnes of wool by 1987

(*SSSR* 1987, p. 122, in the table headed *Realizatsiya produktsii zhivotnovodstva lichnymi podsobnymi khozyaistvami kolkhozam i sovkhozam v sootvetstvii s zaklyuchennymi dogovorami* where the footnote states explicitly: '*Proizvodstvo etoi produktsii uchetno v obeme produktsii kolkhozov i sovkhozov*'). There were also some similar but very much smaller transactions before 1980 (see Wädekin 1973, pp. 232–46). In Table 4.6 they are included in the private sector percentages. Apparently they do not refer to those contracted quantities which are produced by animals owned by the public farms, but kept on household plots and premises.

TABLE 4.6   *Percentage shares of private herds at beginning of year and of meat, milk and wool output, 1975–88*

|                                  | 1975 | 1980 | 1985 | 1986 | 1987 | 1988 |
|----------------------------------|------|------|------|------|------|------|
| Cow numbers                      | 34.0 | 30.5 | 30.7 | 30.7 | 30.5 | 30.5 |
| Milk, calculated                 | 29.8 | 28.5 | 27.4 | 26.9 |      |      |
| Milk, Soviet data                | 31.0 | 30.0 | 28.0 | 22.0 |      |      |
| Other cattle nos                 | 15.4 | 13.7 | 13.8 | 14.0 | 13.5 | 13.5 |
| Pig numbers                      | 18.9 | 20.0 | 18.1 | 17.9 | 17.1 | 17.6 |
| Meat, calculated                 | 31.3 | 31.1 | 32.7 | 31.7 | 32.3 |      |
| Meat, Soviet data                | 31.0 | 31.0 | 28.0 | 27.0 |      |      |
| Sheep nos per cent               | 18.8 | 17.4 | 19.3 | 19.9 | 19.9 |      |
| Wool, greasy, calculated         | 20.1 | 21.7 | 26.0 | 25.6 | 26.2 |      |
| Wool, Soviet data                | 20.0 | 22.0 | 26.0 | 27.0 |      |      |
| Eggs, Soviet data                | 39.0 | 32.0 | 28.0 | 27.0 |      |      |
| Potatoes, Soviet data            | 59.0 | 64.0 | 60.0 | 55.0 |      |      |
| Vegetables, Soviet data          | 34.0 | 33.0 | 29.0 | 28.0 |      |      |
| Fruit, berries and grapes, Soviet data | 43.0 | 42.0 | 43.0 | 40.0 |      |      |

*Sources*: *Narkhoz 1975*, p. 381; *Narkhoz 1980*, p. 235; *Narkhoz 1985*, pp. 185, 217, 240–41; *Narkhoz SSSR za 70 let*, p. 236; *SSSR 1987*, pp. 121–2. For Soviet percentage data of animal products in 1986; Shmelev 1987b pp. 14–15.

Significantly, the share of private meat production, as revealed by Soviet statistics, exceeds the private share in cattle and pig holdings. In part this is due to the date of the counts at the end/beginning of the year. This is when private owners hold less animals because of the winter feed shortage.

Then there are the statistically unrecorded sales of milk, meat and wool. For 1985, Shmelev (1987a, p. 17) reports that 'agricultural enterprises' bought from 'the population' 5.73 million head of horned cattle, of which 3.36 million were 'by contract'; for pigs, the corresponding figures were 2.26 milion and 1.88 million; for sheep and goats, 1.98 million and 1.13 million. The total meat purchases in 1985 amounted to 1.31 million tonnes, of which 0.84 million was on contract. So the remaining 0.47 million tonnes of meat is an additional contribution by the private sector, which is likely also to be statistically registered under social production. Compared to 1984, total production declined, but those 'on contract' increased as a percentage of them. Milk seems entirely to be bought 'on contract', probably since this is continuous production and can be accepted only on a current contract basis.

The rural agencies and stores of the practically nationalised – *ogosudarstvlennye*, according to Prime Minister Nikolai Ryzhkov (*Pravda*, 25 May 1988) – consumers' cooperative organisations buy sizable quantitics of eggs. These do not seem to be separately reported in published statistics. The same holds true for greater quantities of potatoes, other vegetables and fruit, some of them produced by urban individual gardeners, organised in 'collective gardeners' associations' (allotment holders). It is not clear to what extent they are accounted for in the overall statistics.

The public farms supply some, though by far not all of, the feed required for the meat, milk and wool output produced individually, on contract or not, and some feed may be bought from state stores. This is an important contribution by the socialist sector, given that feed is in short supply in Soviet agriculture. This fact is invariably pointed out in Soviet publications as being a socialist sector contribution. However, it has to be paid for, as well as almost all other resources and services individual producers receive. And if it is given as labour payment in kind, it is not a gift either, but has to be earned by collective work. Yet why do public farms conclude such contracts instead of utilising all the available feed to increase their own milk, meat and wool output? The point is that in the case of contract production only part of the privately-owned animals' needs is provided by the socialist sector. The other part, usually over half, is provided by the individual producers from their plots, including their haymaking and grazing rights, and by the labour required to produce or use those resources. Most of this labour is such that the public farm is not entitled to or able to mobilise it, and as a rule it is applied with greater care and intensity than in collective work. Thus, not only is additional labour mobilised, but the feed consumption is also lowered per unit of output, though not necessarily per animal.

Given the above, the contribution of the 'personal subsidiary economy' to gross food production, as usually given by Soviet authors, may be an understatement. Even if it is not, the question remains, whether a slowly declining percentage share of meat and milk production is not being compensated by the increasing wool output and growing potato, vegetable and fruit production of non-agricultural individual gardeners. At any rate, in absolute terms the contribution of individual production has been increasing rather than decreasing over the last few years. This is no mean achievement, given the declining rural population. This sector, though, contributes to the overall Soviet food economy, in the main, by not allowing its output to drop.

It is of little relevance to Soviet consumers whether food originates in the public or individual sector, except that, not only in the free markets (legal, semi-legal or illegal) but also in the consumers' cooperatives, they pay higher prices than in state retail trade stores. If Soviet consumers complain about the lack of improvement or too-slow improvement of supplies in the state and cooperative stores, they do not give the public system credit for the additional supplies which originate in the individual sector. In a way, this is justified, but it should also be kept in mind that the Gorbachev regime, by being more tolerant, has permitted the individual sector to play this compensatory role.

## THE PRODUCTION EFFECTS OF GORBACHEV'S AGRARIAN POLICY

Has Gorbachev's agrarian policy had a noticeable effect on the productive performance of Soviet agriculture? Even if this were so, it is almost impossible to establish clearly a causative link between policies and improvements. Above all, the time span is too short to judge whether the observable changes and improvements will continue and reveal a new trend. This is even more valid for their causes.

The point can be made that Gorbachev, in his earlier role as CC Secretary for Agriculture, had already influenced the formulation and initial execution of the 1982 Food Programme and some earlier measures. The degree of that influence cannot be measured. The political aspect, however, is of a different kind. In the eyes of the population and of many party and state cadres he only bears full responsibility for the food economy since 1985. The following conclusions emerge from a review of the main areas of agrarian policy and their effects since 1985.

## Administrative Reorganisation

Present doubts about the effectiveness of the administrative reorganisations have been spelled out above. As regards the possible diminution of the petty tutelage of farms by state and party authorities, only reports over a longer time span and from many areas will reveal whether it is a reality, but some positive signs should not be ignored. Yet it is self-evident that the self-financing and financial responsibility, under which all farms are to operate, beginning in 1989, can have an economically positive impact only after the reform of the price system, scheduled for 1990 and 1991, has been implemented.

## Prices

Large increases in agricultural producer prices were announced as part of the 1982 Food Programme and put into effect by the beginning of 1983. Hence this is not part of agrarian policy under Gorbachev's leadership. A new rise, decreed in May 1987, concerned only oilseeds. Another one of May 1988, for high-quality grain, cannot have had an impact on the stated production results.

## Investment

The published data on investment policy do not demonstrate rising growth rates. The cancellation of the northern rivers' diversion project has either not yet freed resources for other agricultural uses or these resources have not been channelled into agriculture. Much is being said about increased investment in rural infrastructure and the food processing industry. However, under overall declining investment growth they will hardly have grown faster than before in absolute terms, even if within the agro-industrial complex their percentage shares may have done so.

## Fertilisers

The increase of fertiliser deliveries to agriculture must have had a positive influence, but it should not be overestimated. After a slump in the early 1980s, they accelerated only slightly during 1985–7. It should have benefited crop production but the crop sector performed less well than the animal sector. (For protein feed imports, see the section on the livestock sector above.)

## The Russian Non-Black Earth Zone

A massive improvement programme for the region was announced in 1974 (subsequent data are from *Narkhoz RSFSR 1985*, pp. 115, 178–9; *Narkhoz RSFSR 1986*, pp. 228–9). The programme showed no visible success for the first eight years. Suddenly, in 1982–3, it recorded an amazing success. Total gross output of agriculture, on average over these two years, exceeded the 1980–81 average by 18 per cent. In crop production the increase was 34 per cent. Grain yields per hectare even rose by 64 per cent on an almost unchanged sown area. Yet fertiliser deliveries are not likely to have been the main cause. They increased – for the whole of the RSFSR, it is true – by only 15 per cent. Anyway, the upsurge in this zone preceded Gorbachev's election to General Secretary. The years 1984–6 were again characterised by near-stagnation.

## Intensive Technology

The implementation of so-called 'intensive technology' (not dealt with in the present chapter) is often raised as a success story. The statistical 'proof' produced for it is of doubtful validity. In essence, this technology is nothing more than improved farming methods, the only point being whether these should be introduced throughout the Soviet Union or concentrated in certain areas. Pros and cons for both approaches can be adduced. Again it is part of the 1982 Food Programme, hence is not specifically of the Gorbachev era.

## Individual Small-Scale Production

Two policy measures remain: tolerance of the private or individual producer and the *podryad*. Both also predate 1985. However, Gorbachev has identified himself personally with them more than with any other policy, except for the administrative reorganisation. They are not tantamount to the abandonment of large-scale mechanised farming but imply an important supplementary role for smaller production units. It seems significant that progress has been more marked in livestock farming. Here the degree of mechanisation is still relatively low and household plots still play a considerable role. They may be combined with, and enhanced by, the family *podryad*. Such progress is likely to continue, if not held back by shortcomings in transport, storage and processing and also by ideological considerations. Its importance lies not only in increasing supplies of animal products but also in savings of feed grain and investment. This is not to say that under present Soviet conditions such small-scale animal production will solve all problems. Yet it may provide some relief, so urgently needed for economic as well as political reasons.

# 5 Foreign Trade*

## MICHAEL KASER and
## MICHAEL MALTBY

Gorbachev's domestic restructuring, both economic and political, would be much easier if the USSR were earning the huge profits on energy and gold on which Brezhnev drew in the 1970s. He is well aware of the protection from the realities of the command economy which the oil and gas boom afforded his predecessor. He pointed out in a speech to the February 1988 Plenum of the Central Committee that the increase in the increments to Soviet national income over twenty years were attributable to sales of energy and vodka. Merely between 1977 and 1981, the USSR doubled the value of its exports to the industrial West but decreased the volume of those exports by 10 per cent (that is, earning twice as much for quantitatively one-tenth less) and importing over one-third more in real terms. Such windfall gains, if available today, would enable Gorbachev to buy Western consumer goods to offer workers and farmers as incentives under his restructuring, but he has had no such luck. In addition, after a somewhat better showing in the first years of his administration, Soviet agriculture still produces much less than the country needs, making hard-currency imports a heavy drain on earnings. The 1988 harvest of 195 million tonnes of grain was well down on the 211 million tonnes achieved in 1987. Even though agriculture is a priority area, with a Plenum devoted to it in March 1989, these reforms are unlikely to have any effect before the 1990 harvest; and the USSR continues to buy 30 or more million tonnes of grain on Western markets. Gorbachev's first three years in power, far from bringing any improvement in the USSR's external balance, have in fact seen it worsen.

*Acknowledgement is made to the ESRC for the three-year grant for research into the contemporary Soviet reforms at the Institute of Russian, Soviet and East European Studies at the University of Oxford, and to Tom Adshead for research assistance within that project.

As Table 5.1 shows, imports from non-socialist countries (in 1987, 13bn valuta rubles from the industrial West and 4.7bn from the Third World) had to be held constant in real terms when both the world oil price and Soviet production began to decline (1983 to 1985) and in 1986 and 1987 were cut by 17 per cent to the point that they were back to the volume imported in 1979.

TABLE 5.1 *Volume of Soviet foreign trade, 1983–7 (constant prices, 1975 = 100)*

| | | 1983 | 1984 | 1985 | 1986 | 1987 |
|---|---|---|---|---|---|---|
| Socialist countries: | Exports | 124 | 129 | 130 | 137 | 138 |
| | Imports | 163 | 176 | 188 | 188 | 188 |
| – of which CMEA: | Exports | 121 | 125 | 126 | 131 | 132 |
| | Imports | 162 | 172 | 183 | 184 | 187 |
| Other countries | Exports | 164 | 164 | 146 | 169 | 179 |
| | Imports | 162 | 162 | 162 | 139 | 135 |
| Total | Exports | 140 | 143 | 137 | 151 | 156 |
| | Imports | 163 | 170 | 177 | 166 | 163 |

*Source*: *Vneshnyaya torgovlya SSSR*, various years.

Even to permit such imports, the USSR had to borrow heavily in convertible currency (its net debt at the end of 1987 totalling $25bn against $11bn in 1980), and to increase its sales of gold (from 55 tonnes in 1983 to 338 in 1986 and 270 tonnes in 1987). The experience of the USSR in trading with Finland, one of its most important non-socialist trading partners, is an example of the cutbacks. Trade between the two countries is conducted on a bilateral, clearing basis, imports equalling exports, over five-year periods. The original agreement for 1986–90 envisaged Finnish exports of FM 19.3bn annually to the USSR. In its first year the level was FM 16.5bn and this fell a further 14 per cent in 1987 to FM 14.2bn. The shortfall is primarily attributable to the overwhelming share (90 per cent) of oil in USSR exports to Finland: the decline in the price of oil constrains the volume of imports that it can afford.

Table 5.2 shows trade with all partners since Gorbachev's accession, with the USSR earning 6 per cent less for its exports, while exporting quantitatively 12 per cent more; its reaction has been to buy 13 per cent fewer imports at current prices, but 6 per cent less by volume.

Table 5.3, drawn from these returns, reveals how seriously the USSR terms of trade with the socialist bloc and the West have shifted since 1983.

TABLE 5.2    *Soviet foreign trade, 1985–8 (billion rubles)*

|          |          | 1985 | 1986 | 1987 | 1st half 1988 |
|----------|----------|------|------|------|---------------|
| Exports: | Current  | 72.7 | 68.3 | 68.2 | 33.0          |
|          | Constant | 72.7 | 79.4 | 81.5 | —             |
| Imports: | Current  | 69.4 | 62.6 | 60.7 | 33.4          |
|          | Constant | 69.4 | 66.1 | 65.5 | —             |

*Source*: *Ekonomicheskaya gazeta*, No. 15, 1988.

TABLE 5.3    *USSR terms of trade, 1983–7 (1983 = 100)*

|                         | 1984 | 1985 | 1986 | 1987 |
|-------------------------|------|------|------|------|
| Socialist countries     | 102  | 103  | 102  | 97   |
| Non-socialist countries | 102  | 101  | 78   | 84   |

*Source*: *Vneshnyaya torgovlya SSSR* 1984, 1985, 1987.

The postponement and small extent of the fall of trade with socialist partners is overwhelmingly attributable to the application of a five-year moving average of world pieces for intra-CMEA quota transactions. The terms of trade improvement *vis-à-vis* these latter led to a Soviet input by 1985 of about 50 per cent more by volume from Eastern Europe than in 1980 while the USSR counterdelivered about the same as in 1980. Even so the USSR had to extend credits to the East European partners of about the same value ($25bn) as it itself became indebted to the West. Whether it be to import consumer goods and food to provide workers with something worthwhile to buy with the rubles they earn, or to purchase machinery and technology to raise the quality and variety of production in the consumer good industry, the Soviet Union can no longer pay almost solely with oil and gas exports.

Expectations of a radical change in the composition of Soviet trade were announced by the Chairman of the USSR Council of Ministers, Nikolai Ryzhkov, at the XXVII Party Congress in February/March 1986. Exports were to be increasingly of manufactures in order to reduce dependency on energy and raw materials. The danger of that reliance had been demonstrated: in 1983 oil earned 65 per cent of Soviet sales to the industrial West, but only 49 per cent in 1987, even though the volume then sold, 83mn tonnes (on a tonne-for-tonne basis of crude and refined as shown in the official trade returns) was at a record level (e.g. 78mn tonnes in 1983, 67mn tonnes in 1985), both for these partners and for all destinations (a grand total of 196mn tonnes in 1987 compared to, for example, 130mn tonnes as recently as 1975). Sales of gas have likewise increased as output has boomed. With however, only one per cent of imports by the United States, Western Europe and Japan coming from the Soviet Union, the haul to export diversification is sure to be long. Results have so far been poor: a study in *Ekonomicheskaya gazeta*, No. 15, 1988, states; 'Expressed in constant prices, that is, according to physical volume, our exports of machines and equipment fell by, on average, 1 per cent per annum in the first two years of the present 5-year plan' (1986–7). Since exports to industrially developed countries form only 3.9 per cent of the exports of this sector, the hard currency earned will not buy many machines to improve the quality of exports, let alone the output of the entire sector; not that Soviet production will be much affected by the need to make competitive such a tiny proportion of its export output (and, *a fortiori*, of its total output).

It is the need to generate more competitive manufactures for sale on Western markets that calls for the reform of the Soviet foreign-trade system. Six decades of protection behind the monopoly of the Ministry of Foreign Trade and the complete separation of domestic from world-market prices (the so-called *Preisausgleich* system) have blunted export promotion and inhibited competition from imports. A more competitive export sector, stimulated by general economic reform, would permit more imports of equipment and know-how, to improve efficiency further, and of consumer goods to mop up inflationary purchasing power and give concrete backing to incentive earnings. Something of the same can be expected from trade with the other socialist countries, particularly from fellow-members of the CMEA, and in Gorbachev's time measures have been taken for closer integration with the latter. Having subsidised CMEA members in Europe between 1973 and 1980 – Raimund Dietz (in *Comparative Economic Studies*, No. 2, 1986) estimates the aggregate as $74bn – the USSR has, as already indicated, benefited from a rising five-year moving price average for its exports since 1980.

In the interests of development and of consumer satisfaction the recent import-cuts will soon have to be restored; but the shift away from natural-resource exports will take time. Rather than borrow too heavily on the international capital markets, the USSR has launched two new vehicles of capital inflow. The first and most important was the opening in 1987 of its territory to joint ventures, as described in the second section of this chapter. The second, but so far modest type of inflow has been the issue of Soviet bonds. A small issue (SFr 100mn) was launched successfully in the conservative Swiss market in January 1988, followed by a DM 500mn issue in the FRG in July; the success of both of these admittedly minor flotations demonstrates the willingness among Western European investors to accept this new form now that the Soviet Government has paid back nearly all of the country's pre-revolutionary obligations, and is willing to disclose somewhat more statistical information about the economy. The repayment of obligations of Tsarist times and of compensation for Soviet nationalisations to UK residents in 1987 may be an indication that the USSR may soon enter the large London-based Eurobond market. A third new channel for capital inflow, the concessional (or 'soft') loan is now being mooted. One version (written up for the *Financial Times*, 20 June 1988) was advocated at the Potsdam conference of the Institute of East–West Security Studies by the Hungarian-American financier George Soros. Another, advocated by the Italian Premier De Mita after visiting Moscow in October 1988, was concerted Western support for a Soviet programme which would be a new 'Marshall Plan'. It was not well received by Western governments: Sir Georffrey Howe immediately parried in the annual Cyril Foster Lecture at Oxford that Alfred, rather than George, Marshall's ideas were more appropriate to the Soviet Union today. Nor was it certain whether such soft loans were acceptable to them: the Soviet Ambassador to the UK, Leonid Zamyatin, said in a letter to the *Daily Telegraph* on 27 October; 'We will resolve our problems on our own', while, on the other hand, Leonid Abalkin, the Director of the Institute of Economics of the USSR Academy of Sciences, wrote in *Literaturnaya gazeta*, 2 November 1988, that imports of consumer goods may be necessary in order to counter repressed inflation.

Viktor Gerashenko, Vice-president of Vneshekonombank, announced (as reported in the *Financial Times*, 21 January 1988) at the ceremony to sign the Swiss bond issue, that the Soviet Union plans to finance about 2 per cent of its domestic investment needs from hard currency borrowing. This, and the linkage of recent large syndicated loans to certain trade deals (in particular the £1bn trade credit arranged with Britain in October 1988 and the DM3bn with the FRG the following month), are well within the bounds of Soviet creditworthiness. Financing present debt ($27bn) requires, on OECD estimates, only 5 per cent of export revenues.

## THE REFORM OF FOREIGN ECONOMIC RELATIONS

The foreign trade reforms, announced in August 1986 to take effect from 1 January 1987, are an integral part of the reform to which this book is devoted (translations of the law and of its 1987 revision are in *USSR Foreign Trade*, Nos 5 and 12, 1987). Their success is, in turn, dependent on the coherence of the overall reform process. At the heart of the new reform model is the Law on the State Enterprise (Association) which took effect on 1 January 1988.

The broad outlines of the foreign trade reforms emerged in late 1986, although they were subsequently modified to make them consistent with the Law on the State Enterprise. They encompass two broad areas: first, an attempt to rationalise the administrative and planning structure and, secondly, a decentralisation of foreign trade decision-making powers from the centre to the enterprise, including the possibility of engaging in industrial cooperation with foreign companies. The decision of the CPSU Politburo of 2 December and of the USSR Council of Ministers of 9 December 1988 implements the opening of the Soviet economy to limited foreign competition by setting a realistic rate of exchange for the ruble, moving to end currency inconvertibility and allowing majority foreign ownership of capital on Soviet soil.

The first organisational changes were centred on the creation of the State Foreign Economic Commission to regulate foreign economic relations. The aim was to increase the coordination of all those agents involved in activities associated with foreign trade and to improve the planners' ability to formulate and implement policy. Policy was to be implemented using primarily parametric methods, such as incentives and credit terms, and was broadly intended to promote export diversification (quantitatively, a 50 per cent increase in manufactured exports by 1990), in particular to the CMEA, and to foster import substitution. For the duration of the 12th Five year Plan (1986–90), though, a substantial use of state orders was envisaged to ensure that targets would be fulfilled. The organisations which had existed up to 1986 were thrown into turmoil by the administrative changes, and hardly had these new structures been announced than in January 1988 the Ministry of Foreign Trade (MFT) and the State Commission for Foreign Economic Relations (SCFER), which together had gained the responsibility for much of the supervisory work associated with foreign trade, were merged into a new Ministry of Foreign Economic Relations of the USSR (MFER).

The self-financing of enterprises is being extended to foreign currency earnings, albeit within severe import restrictions. Certain enterprises obtained direct access to foreign markets through the creation of their own foreign trade firms (the initial list was published in *USSR Foreign Trade*, No. 3, 1987). The rest were to affect trade through intermediaries – foreign trade organisations either newly-created in selected ministries or remaining under the aegis of the MFER.

During 1987 numerous difficulties became apparent in the new system. Many were associated with the lack of personnel to staff the new foreign trade organisations and firms (as Ivanov describes in *Soviet Economy*, July–September 1987 in a broad review of the reforms). Within the CMEA countries, continued currency inconvertibility raised obstacles to the use of enterprise currency reserves. Another issue (as described by A. Zverev in *Ekonomicheskaya gazeta*, No. 23, 1988) was the allocation of profits and foreign exchange earnings between an exporting enterprise, its subcontractors and, where necessary, the intermediary. However, the greatest problem to emerge was associated with the inability of enterprises to assess the opportunity costs of the trading opportunities confronting them.

The non-comparability of domestic and foreign price structures complicates any comparison of the opportunity costs of production for the domestic and foreign markets. The transitional reform measures attempted to address it by use of differentiated currency coefficients (DCCs), designed to relate foreign to domestic prices; but drawbacks in their application as well as in their conception had become apparent within a year of their authorisation in August 1986. Originally, 1500 were introduced, a figure which has, according to one of the most outspoken reformers, Nikolai Shmelev (*Novy Mir*, No. 3, 1988) since reached an astounding 10 000, being set separately for imports and exports, and according to S. Zakharov in *Ekonomicheskaya gazeta*, No. 29, 1987, ranging in value from 0.3 to 6.0, but later (according to N. Astrakhantseva and V. Kuznetsov in the same journal, No. 35, 1988) from 0.2 to 6.6. This is a virtual return to the *Preisausgleich* structure whereby there were as many implicit exchange rates as there were traded goods.

The issue was intensively debated in the Soviet specialist press, notably in *Ekonomicheskaya gazeta* (articles by S. Zakharov and by A. Burov in No. 20, 1987; by V. Kuznetsov in No. 26, 1988; by S. Zakharov in No. 33, 1988; and by A. Zverev and V. Telegin in No. 35, 1988) and *Voprosi ekonomiki* (A. Shurkalin in No. 5, 1988), with a consensus emerging for abandoning the practice of differentiating coefficients by product, whether it is being imported or exported, and by the currency for which it is being bought or sold. One scheme was that the DCC should be the same for all enterprises in a particular branch of industry, but the most popular proposal was that there should be a single coefficient for each currency in which trade is taking place. This line of argument points out that the more differentiated coefficients are, the more they act as subsidies and the less they measure efficiency. There will still be subsidies, but they would be patent, allowing the financial organs correctly to appraise enterprises' foreign trade activities. In the event, the December 1988 decision called for the abandonment of currency coefficients on 1 January 1991, when the ruble would have been devalued (by 50 per cent on 1 January 1990 and by more as required in 1991) and wholesale prices would have been realigned to absorb the differentials indicated by the present coefficients. By envisaging foreign-currency auctions, the decision builds on an embryonic internal currency market, where enterprises and organisations buy and sell hard currency at free prices in parallel to the State allocation system; exporting enterprises can already retain some of their foreign sales in the earned currency (between 1 and 50 per cent is the range) but may only lend, not sell, to other enterprises. The procedure of the 1988 decree was foreshadowed in an article signed by officials from Gosplan and Gosbank (Zverev and Telegin, op. cit.), who damned with faint praise the corresponding experience in Poland and implied that such a market should be very tightly controlled and not open to foreign participants. The ease and completeness of this transition must be heavily conditional on the realism of the wholesale and retail price reforms, planned for the years 1990 and some two or three years later respectively.

The December decrees also widened the scope of the various forms of industrial cooperation with both socialist and non-socialist partners (the original laws are in *USSR Foreign Trade*, No. 5, 1987). Western firms were initially given the legal opportunity of becoming minority shareholders in joint ventures on Soviet territory in partnership with Soviet enterprises. Such concerns were to be exempted from the planning process, dealing with the domestic economy through the foreign trade system at prices based on those prevailing on the world market. The new regulations raise the limit for the foreign shareholder to 80 per cent.

Certainly, there is some motive for Western participation to take the opportunity of the new laws to obtain Soviet technological know-how, but, as Western technology is significantly more advanced than Soviet, a more realistic motive for direct Western imports is to realise a reduction in production costs using existing technology – based, that is, on a product cycle model of technology transfer (as shown by Philip Hanson in *Trade and Technology in Soviet-Western Relations*, Macmillan, London, 1981). But, in such a model it is the combination of lower labour costs and control of quality of output which ultimately provide the incentive. While production is likely to be marketable within the USSR, difficulties may well be experienced in promoting hard-currency exports. This is also moderated by the new regulations, because the old regulations presented obstacles to the transfer of profits in hard currency abroad – permitted as long as the joint venture has earned sufficient hard currency itself to cover all purchases abroad, the salaries of expatriate staff and the repatriation of profit, itself taxed under two regimes (30 per cent on all profit and 20 per cent on the remaining profit if repatriated, or 44 per cent in all). Consequently, export promotion, including earnings from tourism, has played a dominant and limiting role as far as the establishment of joint ventures is concerned, although other motives, such as import substitution (including for the domestic consumer market) on the Soviet part can be identified. There is a danger that some joint ventures may prove to be only short-term, if Western firms take advantage of the two-year tax holiday, but subsequently withdraw.

A decision attractive to Western investors which is also foreshadowed concerns 'special' zones, within which fully-owned foreign enterprises would be permitted. One of four such zones has been highly successful in China, although it is only recently that Soviet reformers have started to recommend them. Oleg Bogomolov, Director of the Institute of the Economy of the World Socialist System, advocated them in April 1988 for the Baltic republics, the Black Sea coast and the Far East, and has said that the possibility of their creation is being discussed. Recent political changes in Estonia, together with the success of market reforms in that republic, make it a prime candidate, although the central authorities might balk at giving potential separatists such a powerful weapon.

The possibility of creating joint ventures with firms from CMEA member states has also been provided with no restriction on the relative shareholdings of the two partners. Such joint ventures could, if they so chose, trade domestically through the Soviet wholesale trade network. In addition to joint ventures, two other forms of industrial cooperation became acceptable for firms in CMEA partner countries. The first are 'direct links', primarily intended to coordinate research and development, especially in connection with the Scientific-Technological Programme of 1985, and the second is the formation of International Organisations and Associations, operating outside the domestic plan. However, continued commodity and currency inconvertibility has continued (as with intra-CMEA trade generally) to retard progress.

# 6 Employment

## ALASTAIR McAULEY

### INTRODUCTION

Soviet economists attribute their current difficulties to the fact that central planning has failed to stimulate sufficiently rapid technical progress. *Perestroika* aims to substitute autonomous enterprises for the present system of bureaucratic administration. Such a change entails consequences for the Soviet labour market. In particular, if *perestroika* is effective, it is likely to reduce the job-security currently enjoyed by Soviet state employees. In future, workers are more likely to be exposed to the risk of unemployment. Those most likely to experience unemployment are semi-skilled male manual workers – members of the traditional working class. Middle-aged women in low-skilled and routine white-collar jobs may also be vulnerable. *Perestroika* is also likely to lead to an increase in inequality and, perhaps, to the emergence of pockets of deprivation. Such developments will encourage the growth of opposition to Gorbachev's policies; or, at the very least, they may be exploited by those opposed to *perestroika* on other grounds.

### THE ECONOMIC CAUSES OF *PERESTROIKA*

At the June 1987 Plenum, Mikhail Gorbachev stated that the USSR was in a 'pre-crisis' situation; six months earlier, he had referred to 'pre-crisis phenomena'. This was the culmination of a process in which the General Secretary expressed increasing concern at the state of affairs in the Soviet economy and society. At the XIX Party Conference, he claimed that the USSR had 'halted the drift towards social, economic and political crisis'. Many observers feel that the actual position in 1986–7 was even worse than Gorbachev was prepared to admit; there is also scepticism about the improvement achieved since the XXVII Party Congress.

106

In large measure, the causes of this crisis are economic. Secular decline in the rate of growth threatens the legitimacy of the Communist Party in the USSR (Hewett, 1988a, p. 57). The authorities were faced with the problem of defence, the consumer and investment in future growth of the system. In the early 1970s, it appeared that their strategy had failed all three. The economy was stagnating, despite the commitment of substantial resources to investment (Hewett, 1988a, pp. 70, 74). Its failure to come to terms with the new information technology meant that there was a growing risk that it would be incapable of producing the next generation of weapons (Deutch, 1987, p. 424). Finally, in the early 1980s, for the first time in almost forty years, real wages started to decline (Aganbegyan, 1988, p. 231).

The misfortunes of Soviet consumers were aggravated by the particular problems of Soviet agriculture – made worse by an unexpected run of bad weather. And, predictably, the conflict between declining incomes and rising expectations resulted in the build-up of popular frustration. The sense of disillusionment with the system was compounded by feelings that the system was in moral decay. As the official socialist system increasingly failed to satisfy popular economic expectations, consumers turned to private and quasi-illegal sources of supply. This resulted in the growth of corruption, a phenomenon that was reinforced by the tolerant *immobilisme* of the late Brezhnev years (Jowitt, 1983).

Soviet economists do not emphasise this growing gap between expectations and economic capacity in their discussions of the crisis; rather they focus upon the material causes of the decline in the rate of growth. Their analysis of the causes of economic failure also points to the measures that they believe should be adopted to overcome the deep-seated problems in the system of economic administration. (The account given in the next few paragraphs is taken from Aganbegyan, 1988, pp. 49–65.)

The facts of Soviet demography (which are largely outside the short-run control of the authorities) have resulted in sharp falls in the rate of growth of the labour supply. At the same time, accessible deposits of raw materials in European Russia have been exhausted; increasingly, the country has had to turn to the climatically inhospitable regions of the north and east for replacements. These, and other, sources of increasing real cost have not been offset by sufficiently rapid technical progress. As a result, the economy has experienced a secular decline in its rate of growth.

Innovation and the rapid diffusion of new products and processes have been inhibited by the bureaucratic system of economic decision-making in the planned economy. Bureaucratic decision-making has also resulted in the sorts of allocative inefficiency traditionally studied by neo-classical economists.

The identification of bureaucracy as a source of economic inefficiency and an impediment to technical progress is not new. This, in essence, was the analysis that underlay the attempt at economic reform undertaken by Khrushchev after 1953. It also provided the theoretical backing for the so-called Kosygin reform of 1965–7. Previous attempts at systemic reform failed, however, because the reformers were unwilling or unable to bring about appropriate changes in social and political institutions.

On the basis of this analysis, Soviet reformers have set themselves the task of modifying the Stalinist system of economic administration in such a way as to facilitate the adoption and diffusion of new technologies. Second, where possible, they wish to encourage static rationality in decision-taking.

Since the bureaucratic structure of directive central planning has been identified as the major obstacle to technical progress, it has been decided to replace it by an alternative, decentralised system which provides more scope for enterprise autonomy. (For a detailed description of the organisational changes included in the reconstruction programme, see Berliner, 1987 or Hewett, 1988a Chapter 7.) In practical terms, the *perestroika* proposals mean that the system of obligatory output targets that made up the core of the annual plan will be abandoned. It will be replaced by a set of state contracts, the so-called *goszakazy*. (In the long term, it is expected that enterprises will tender for these in a way similar to that in which capitalist firms bid for defence contracts; in the transition period, however, they will be obligatory – and thus indistinguishable from output targets.)

Ultimately, *goszakazy* are intended to account for some twenty to thirty per cent of the capacity of manufacturing industry; managers will be expected to complete their order-books from other sources: consumers, other state enterprises and foreign purchasers. Enterprises will be expected to cover the costs of *all* inputs from sales revenue, without the benefit of subsidies; they will also be expected to finance the bulk of their investment programmes out of net profits. (This is the essence of *samofinansirovanie* and so-called *polnyi khozraschet*.) It is this change in the position of the enterprise that constitutes the core of *perestroika*. But such a radical innovation involves complementary changes elsewhere in the system.

If managers are to make rational decisions, they require information about the relative scarcity of different resources and about the intensity of consumer demands. That is, such a shift in the locus of decision-making authority can be effective only if it is accompanied by a reactivisation of the price-mechanism. The need for this is recognised in theory; but price-reform (and particularly the elimination of subsidies on basic consumer goods) is a politically contentious issue (Aganbegyan, 1988, p. 118). As a result, it is still unclear whether the political authorities in the USSR are prepared to allow state enterprises to determine their own prices. Or whether the intention is to limit price reform to the numerical realignment of individual prices – as has occurred on previous occasions (Hewett, 1988b).

Also, if managers are to have the incentive to search for new ways of satisfying consumer demand they must be allowed to reap the rewards of success. By the same token, however, they must expect to pay the penalty of failure. The central authorities must refrain from their present practice of transferring the bulk of profits to the state budget. They must also abstain from the subsidisation of loss-making enterprises. Inefficient firms must be allowed to go bankrupt.

Third, the new decentralised system calls for increased effort on the part of workers; and it necessitates a greater willingness on the part of labour to exercise initiative. To some extent, increased effort can be generated by a greater emphasis upon labour discipline; and, insofar as it had an economic rather than a moral rationale, the decision to embark upon the anti-alcohol campaign shows that Gorbachev is prepared to adopt this approach (Treml, 1987; Shmelev, 1988, especially pp. 162–3). But effort and initiative are more likely responses to improved incentives. And this explains the third strand to the programme of *perestroika*.

Changes in the financial regime under which the Soviet enterprise will operate are expected to result in a widening of wage and salary differentials (Kostin, 1988, especially pp. 41–3). These will be converted into real income differences if the price reform results in the introduction of market-clearing prices. At the same time, the decision to encourage the growth of private and cooperative enterprises (and the system of *goszakazy*) should make suppliers more responsive to consumer demand; they should also increase the range of choice available. This is intended to reinforce the incentive effects of the growth in wage inequality. Finally, the changes in arrangements that have been described in this paragraph will be magnified by an anti-statist shift in the elite's ideology that appears to have occurred in the last decade or so. (See Hauslohner, 1987b especially pp. 350–52 for a further development of this point.)

Changes in the autonomy of the enterprise and the concomitant modifications to the wider system of economic administration will affect the position of workers and employees in the Soviet economy. These are likely to be of two kinds. The systemic changes to the mechanism for resource allocation will result in modifications to what we may call the labour contract. These are discussed in the next section. If reform is effective, it will result in changes to the pattern of output; these, in turn, will result in changes in the structure of demand for labour. These are the subject of the next but one section.

## PERESTROIKA AND THE SOVIET LABOUR MARKET

The classic (or Stalinist) centrally planned economy is characterised by the following stylised facts. It enjoys full or even overfull employment. In the Soviet Union, full employment has lasted for almost sixty years (Lane, 1986, Ch. 1). On the whole, full employment has not been associated with rapid or accelerating inflation – although the experience of various states (and time-periods) differs somewhat in this respect (McAuley, 1979, Ch. 10; Granick, 1987a, Ch. 2). Despite the ubiquitous labour scarcity, there is evidence of substantial waste: in the USSR, for example, the establishments of imported plants are always much greater than the same plants would have in a market economy (Hanson, 1981, Ch. 11). Similarly, there are frequent anecdotes of labour-hoarding by enterprises (Dyker, 1985, p. 35 and *passim*). Finally, despite official opposition to *uravnilovka*, there has been a progressive narrowing of differentials: wage and salary profiles are relatively flat (McAuley, 1979, Ch. 9; Granick 1987a, pp. 40–49).

Centrally planned economies are characterised by very high rates of labour force participation – for women as well as for men (McAuley, 1981, Ch. 3). This implies that such systems have few reserves and that they are likely to lack flexibility (Winiecki, 1987, pp. 71–2). (Or, to be more precise, their reserves, in the form of hoarded labour, are not readily accessible to other enterprises.) They will therefore not be very effective in responding to the random shocks to which all real-world economies are exposed. In particular, such economies are likely to take a relatively long time to adjust to changes in the structure of demand, and disequilibrium in the labour market may well be perceived as shortage.

Western observers disagree about the most appropriate theoretical explanation of these phenomena. There now appear to be three competing models. First, there is what may be called the conventional analysis. This assumes that the labour market in a centrally planned economy operates in a way that is similar to that of a market economy. That is, we can talk about a well-defined labour demand function; this has the usual arguments and its derivatives have the expected signs. According to this analysis, full employment can be attributed to planners' tension. Labour hoarding is a rational response to the supply-uncertainty generated by bureaucratic decision-making; it is analogous to the accumulation of other types of inventory (Gregory and Stuart, 1986, pp. 226ff; Granick, 1987a, Ch. 2).

Second, there are explanations that derive from Kornai's shortage economy model. This asserts that socialist economies are characterised by non price-guided markets. In such circumstances, the appearance of shortage (e.g. of overfull employment) is a necessary characteristic of equilibrium. It is the disruption caused by the non-availability of key personnel, the difficulty of obtaining additional workers and the psychic costs that managers experience as a result, which put a limit to the tendency for individual enterprises to expand. Again, such a model leads to the prediction of labour-hoarding. (Buck and Cole, 1987, pp. 96ff; Granick, 1987a, Ch. 2).

Finally, David Granick has published an analysis in which the right to a particular type of job security is postulated as the first argument in a lexicographic social preference function. This, too, leads to a prediction that full employment will necessarily characterise positions of economic equilibrium (Granick 1987a).

The changes to the system of economic administration, outlined in the previous section, will have different implications for the position of labour, depending upon which of these three theories corresponds best to underlying relationships that characterise the labour market in a Stalinist economy. For example, the replacement of obligatory output targets by a system of *goszakazy* should result in a reduction in the level of planners' tension in the economy. If such tension is the source of overfull employment and labour hoarding, as the conventional model suggests, there should be an immediate improvement in the labour market. That is, enterprises will 'shake out' unwanted labour and, at the same time, they will find it easier to fill some of their present vacancies. Labour market inflexibility will have been reduced. If, however, the Soviet labour market is better described as non price-guided in the spirit of Kornai's shortage economy, there will be no apparent change: enterprises will still experience difficulties in filling vacancies and they will still have a strong incentive to hoard labour.

This possibility has now been recognised by the Soviet reformers, although it is not clear that the measures they propose will avoid it. The requirement that enterprises should meet the conditions of *polnyi khozraschet* and *samofinansirovanie* appears to be designed to harden the enterprise's budget constraint. That is, the authorities intend to eliminate the preconditions for the emergence of a shortage economy. But the Hungarian experience suggests that imposing strict financial discipline is no easy matter. Further, Gomulka's analysis would imply that the elimination of shortage phenomena may entail a degree of price-flexibility that is politically unacceptable (Gomulka, 1986, Ch. 5).

Of course, if David Granick is correct, there will be no change in the Soviet labour market. The authorities will continue to be prepared to pay a high price in efficiency terms in order to confer particular job rights upon Soviet workers. It has been suggested, however, that even if Granick's analysis provided a correct description of the Soviet system in the 1960s and 1970s, the present Soviet leadership is no longer willing to pay the efficiency price: *perestroika* can be seen as an attempt to renegotiate the implicit social contract between the CPSU and the Soviet working class. (This argument is made most cogently in Hauslohner 1987a; see also Teague 1987.)

There is still significant uncertainty about the content and long-term consequences of *perestroika*, but let us start with the assumption that the reform package outlined above is introduced in full. To recapitulate, this consists of a regime of *polnyi khozraschet* under conditions in which *goszakazy* do not absorb the full capacity of industry and an active price mechanism. (This assumption is probably unrealistic; opposition from different groups – and second thoughts on the part of Gorbachev and his supporters will almost certainly result in modifications to the programme over the next five years or so. But the assumption that *perestroika* will be fully realised, provides a basis against which to judge actual future outcomes.)

If the programme is introduced successfully, job security as it has been understood in the past will no longer operate. If the authorities are successful in hardening enterprise budget constraints, there will be a reduction in labour hoarding; greater attention will be paid to the economical use of labour. This is likely to result in a reduction in the demand for labour. It may even lead to some unemployment.

Second, the economic reform imposes new tasks upon the central authorities. They are required to learn new methods of demand management. Initially at least, it is to be expected that they will find it difficult to maintain a constant level of economic activity. Fluctuations in the pressure of demand may reinforce the likelihood that Soviet workers will experience unemployment in the 1990s.

Third, a reactivisation of the price mechanism implies that greater reliance is to be placed upon wage differentials to allocate and reallocate labour between sectors and regions. The level of inequality in society is likely to increase. If greater inequality is associated with a lower average pressure of demand (and hence with some unemployment) it may entail real poverty for some sections of the population.

It is thus not clear that *perestroika* represents a Pareto improvement for risk-averse households. The successful reform of the Soviet economy will result in far-reaching changes to the implicit contract between workers and the Soviet state. The guarantee of security for all and a modest but relatively equal standard of living irrespective of one's efforts will be withdrawn. In its place, the authorities hold out the prospect of a much less certain future. For the enterprising, the skilled (and, perhaps the lucky) there will be substantially increased rewards. But, instead of being shared out among all households, the costs of adjustment, of making wrong decisions, will be concentrated upon a minority. The chances are that this minority will include the incompetent, the unskilled as well as the unworthy. The new system will create innocent victims as an unintended consequence of its redefinition of social justice. In consequence, one must expect the development of political opposition to the reform programme.

## *PERESTROIKA* AND STRUCTURAL CHANGE

The economic reform outlined above entails changes in the structure of output as well as changes to the system of management. These output changes also have implications for employment over the next decade.

A primary objective of *perestroika* is to eliminate featherbedding in manufacturing. It is hoped that other measures will also contribute to a sharp increase in the growth of labour productivity. It is intended that the so-called productive sphere (industry, agriculture, construction and part of trade and transport) will have shed some 13–19 million employees by the end of the century (Kostakov, 1987a; p. 80). Of these, 3 million are scheduled to go by 1990 (*Izvestiya*, 11 Sept 1987); Leonid Kostin, deputy chairman of Goskomtrud, reported that at least 300 000 had been released by the middle of 1987. At the same time, *perestroika* enivsages an expansion of employment in the services sector in response to the growth of consumer demand as incomes continue to rise (Aganbegyan, 1988, Ch. 10).

At first glance, a change of this magnitude seems feasible. Voluntary labour turnover in manufacturing in the late 1970s amounted to some 15–18 per cent per annum (say 6–7 million employees) (Granick, 1987a, p. 15). There is no reason why it should have fallen dramatically in the last decade. With turnover on this scale it should be possible to eliminate sixteen or twenty million positions in the next twelve years. On further consideration, however, an element of doubt arises: it is not clear that the authorities possess the instruments with which to organise and control a redundancy and retraining programme on this scale.

If Soviet industry follows the priorities suggested by the reformers in its introduction of new technology, the jobs that will be shed will involve disproportionately manual and auxiliary activities. Those at present employed in such positions are, typically, above average age, with less than average education. Many of them are male. Such a group is not *prima facie*, likely to be attracted to the services sector. Nor are they likely to prove attractive to potential employers.

A second group that might emerge as a target for labour shedding are women employed in routine clerical positions. There are large numbers of such *planoviki, schetovody* and *ekonomisty* employed in Soviet industry. They enjoy very little esteem within the official ideology; most of them are married with families; such groups have traditionally been targets for shake-out and they are vulnerable under *perestroika*. But they may well find it easier to adapt to the psychological and physical demands of a job in the newly expanding services sector than the men described above.

It is not clear how effective the existing network of job placement agencies will be in securing the redeployment of this labour (Granick, 1987a, pp. 20–2). After all, they were not designed with such a task in mind. And, since there is as yet no extensive infrastructure capable of retraining redundant workers with skills relevant to the services sector, the mismatch between the skills needed and those available in the labour force is likely to persist for some time. Thus, the USSR may well experience structural unemployment similar to that which accompanied the decline of shipbuilding and heavy engineering in Scotland in the late 1950s and 1960s.

It is possible that the Soviet authorities expect the recently revived cooperative sector to absorb a significant proportion of redundant workers (Aganbegyan, 1988, pp. 128–9; Hewett, 1988a, pp. 340–42; *Zakon*, 1988). But such expectations may be over-optimistic. Scotland and the north of England have had much more extensive and more recent experience of an enterprise culture than most of the USSR, but the local economy proved very sluggish in creating alternative employment opportunities for the structurally unemployed, both after the rundown in staple industries in the 1960s and also after 1979.

Finally, the Soviet authorities have taken only the first tentative steps towards providing a system of financial support for those declared redundant. (See *Izvestiya* 20 January, 1988). In January 1988 a decree was adopted which provides those who lose their jobs, with redundancy pay – equal to one month's wages! In certain circumstances, workers are to receive payments equal to their previous wages for a period of up to three months after being declared redundant. After that, nothing. There is some evidence to suggest that such payments have been made to Soviet workers on previous occasions, for example during a rundown of the coal industry in the 1960s; but they have certainly not been widely available in the past (Granick, 1987a, p. 97). Again, if British experience of structural unemployment is anything to go by, such a system is an inadequate response to the problems of long-term unemployment faced by redundant workers.

It may be inferred then, that the structural changes which follow a successful *perestroika* will entail significant adjustment costs for Soviet employees. It seems likely that these costs will not be evenly distributed among the labour force as a whole. They will be borne disproportionately by older, less educated workers (and by their dependents). Thus, Mr Gorbachev is likely to encounter political opposition from the traditional working class. As in Hungary in the early 1970s, this may make it easier for opponents of reform to mount an effective resistance campaign by appealing to ideologically potent symbols.

# 7 The Socialist Legal State*

## NICK LAMPERT

### INTRODUCTION

The 'socialist legal state' has emerged as a central theme of the Gorbachev reforms. It is not the first time that there has been a strong emphasis on legality in Soviet political discourse, but current developments suggest an unprecedented amount of self-searching. In the history of the Soviet state the stress on legality has had a double aspect. On the one hand it has signalled the search for greater predictability and central control over unruly political officials and wayward citizens. On the other hand it appears as a necessary condition of a democratic political order and of the protection of the citizen in the face of arbitrary power. The language of legality is therefore open to a statist ('law and order') and a democratic ('rule of law') interpretation. Both are present in recent Soviet comment, but it is the rhetoric of rule of law that now prevails. The term 'legal state' was mooted in academic circles in the 1970s, but was not allowed to appear in print because it sounded too close to bourgeois notions of rule of law (in the Anglo-American variant) or of *Rechtsstaat* (in the German variant) (V. Savitsky, Institute of State and Law, Moscow, in private discussion). Now the idea has been officially adopted, enshrined within the resolutions of the XIX Party Conference (*Izvestiya*, 5 July 1988), and assigned an important part within the wider project of political and economic reform. The stated intention is to ensure the 'dominance of law in all spheres of life', to establish 'mutual responsibility of the state and its citizens', to 'protect society from abuses of power' and to 'generate citizens and organisations their rights and freedoms' (*Pravda*, 12 July 1988, editorial; Gorbachev 1987, pp. 105–10).

*I would like to thank the Nuffield Foundation for a grant which made possible research on this chapter.

116

The ramifications are numerous. The main connotations of the newly adopted slogan – not attempting an exhaustive account – seem to be the following. First, it is part of a discourse on democracy, raising questions about the role of the electorate, the legislature and the Party itself, and about the scope for political–civil freedoms. Second, there is an attack on the proliferation of administrative as against legal norms within the system, under a banner that reads 'everything is permitted that is not forbidden by law'. This is central to economic reform, to the extent that such a principle is a necessary condition for greater enterprise autonomy. Finally, there is a call for a reform of the criminal justice system, to take the law-enforcement machinery out of the control of local political fiefdoms and to provide basic guarantees of fair investigation and trial.

## I  LAW AND DEMOCRACY

The main political idea behind the talk of a socialist legal state is the search for some form of constitutionalism and thus a change in the basis of political authority. In one sense the conditions of a 'legal state' might be met by any system that was able to devise laws and abide by them – a requirement that could as well be satisfied by an authoritarian regime.* However, in the current Soviet discussion the intimate link between legality and democracy is constantly reiterated. 'In adding the concept "legal" to the characterisation of our state,' says one of the theses for the XIX Party Conference, 'it should be emphasised that it is not only citizens who bear responsibility before the state but also the state which bears responsibility before citizens. The state is obliged to show constant concern for strengthening the guarantees of Soviet people's rights and freedoms' (*Pravda*, 27 May 1988).

The rhetoric of legality seems to reflect the need for a new form of legitimation. In Weber's terminology one could see the process as a projected shift towards a 'legal–rational' mode of domination in its modern democratic variant: that is, one which is seen to be legitimate because its rules are the outcome of generally accepted democratic procedures (Weber 1947, Part III). The rulers of the Soviet state have

---

* It has been remarked that the codification of Roman law under Justinian occurred under a regime whose constitutional maxim was that the Emperor's will was law (Lloyd 1981, p. 32). The term *Rechtsstaat* was coined by a conservative monarchist and was concerned with setting limits to the operation of the state, not with the sources of state authority (Neumann 1957, Ch. 6).

always stressed the superiority of Soviet over bourgeois forms of democracy. But the language of political legitimation in the USSR has other sources, since the leading role of the party is linked to its position as keeper of a sacrosanct (if changing) body of ideas about society and its needs, as guardian of a secular theocratic state. The type of authority that has emerged on this foundation, which one writer christened 'partynomial' to indicate its 'non-rational' characteristics – a play on Weber's 'patrimonial' form of 'traditional' domination (Z. Bauman, 'Officialdom and Class' in Parkin 1974, pp. 136–40) – now looks increasingly fragile. The 'rule of law' suggests an alternative, but it does not sit well with the party's leading role. The critical question is therefore how far this fundamental pillar of the Soviet system is indeed open to change.

Making links between legality and democracy has two sets of implications. First, it points to a change in the law-making process in the broadest sense, in turn raising questions about the role of the Party. Second, it raises a number of issues concerning the relationship between law and political–civil freedoms.

**The Separation of Powers**

The search for a new form of legitimacy is leading to a reappraisal of the role of the soviets and of the electoral system. That theme in its wider implications is dealt with elsewhere in the present volume. Within this broader context, writers on the legal state have highlighted the position of the legislature itself, adopting in one or another form the concept of a separation of powers.

The highest elected state body, the USSR Supreme Soviet, has played only a ritual part in the law-making process. It is pointed out that even in a strictly formal sense very little *legislation* proper has been passed by the USSR Supreme Soviet. Between 1938 and 1980, if one excludes legislative acts relating to the plan and the budget, 144 laws were passed, of which 87 (63 per cent) were ratifications of previously adopted decrees of the Presidium of the Supreme Soviet. Between 1980 and 1985, 48 laws were passed, of which 33 were ratifications of decrees. Furthermore these decrees in a number of cases significantly altered existing legislation. For example, between 1961 and 1988 about 3000 alterations and additions were made in this way to the criminal law (V. Kudryavtsev, *Izvestiya*, 1 June 1988).

Constitutional principles have been 'systematically violated' over several decades. With rare exceptions, draft legislation has been presented to deputies just before the sessions of the Supreme Soviet, after approval from the 'directing organs' (ibid). The legislative 'kitchen', says one specialist with experience of the Supreme Soviet commissions whose job is to prepare draft legislation, remains a closed sphere. A more or less ready draft appears 'from nowhere'. Who drafted it first, which departments were involved, what their views were, is 'not to be made public' ('*ne dlya oglasheniya*'). Instead of providing political guidance, the party apparatus often takes a hand in the detail. Commission members may spend ages poring over every word, to find that the final result bears little relation to these deliberations (V. Savitsky, *Literaturnaya Gazeta* (*Lit. Gaz.*), 11 May 1988, p. 12).

It is agreed that a 'separation of powers' is a necessary condition for the emergence of a law-making body with any life in it. This will involve some form of sitting parliament, and is taken to mean that members of the executive would not normally sit as deputies. (Resolutions of XIX Party Conference, *Izvestiya* 5 July 1988; V. Savitsky, *Lit. Gaz.*, 11 May 1988, p. 12). However, different glosses are put on the notion of separation. Some formulations say that under socialism the division of powers between executive, legislature and judiciary need be thought of only as a division of labour or competences, since 'power belongs to the ruling class and cannot be divided' (O. Temushkin, *Lit. Gaz.*, 8 June 1988, p. 11), and since a 'strict division of functions' is coordinated by the party (V. Terebilov, *Lit. Gaz.*, 27 April 1988, p. 11). Others emphasise the need to prevent monopolistic political control (A. Levikov, *Lit. Gaz.*, 30 March 1988, p. 11).

To speak of strengthening the position of elected state bodies is to raise basic issues about the role of the Party. 'In our conditions', suggests one legal scholar, 'the democratisation of the Party is itself the very first and the most essential condition for the creation of a legal state.' The trouble is that at present one cannot give an adequate legal definition of the idea of the Party as the 'nucleus' of the political system. Reference to its role in the *nomenklatura* system of appointment is no longer adequate since that system is itself under challenge (A. M. Yakovlev, *Lit. Gaz.*, 8 June 1988, p. 11). The Constitution, says another observer, stipulates a leading and guiding role, but 'in what laws, articles and instructions are "leadership" and "guidance" embodied and how should they be implemented?' (L. Ionin, *Moscow News*, 19/1988, p. 10).

The question is what it would mean for the party itself to be subject to constitutional control. In theory the party acts within the law and is 'not a subject of state power' (M. Vyshinsky, USSR Deputy Minister of Justice, *Lit. Gaz.*, 8 June 1988, p. 11). In practice it is immune from any challenge based on appeal to law, since there is no agency that would take up such a challenge. Also the Party is 'above the law' in the sense that decisions which on the face of it are internal Party matters may have serious civil-legal consequences. Suppose, suggests one writer, that the chief engineer of a large plant is expelled from the Party for some moral offence connected with family life. Such a person would be highly unlikely to remain in his or her post, although there is no legal act that sanctions a dismissal in these circumstances, and no law that would defend one's rights as an employee. (Yu. Feofanov, *Izvestiya*, 21 June 1988). Similarly, it is argued that the Party Regulations in effect establish a presumption of guilt for Party members subject to criminal charges. The regulations say that members who have committed criminal acts (*nakazuemye v uglovnom poryadke*) are expelled from the Party. That formulation does not in fact give the authority for expulsion before conviction by a court, but it is perhaps vague enough to allow of such an interpretation. (A. Vaksberg, *Lit. Gaz.*, 8 June 1988, p. 11; for the Party Regulations see *Pravda*, 2 November 1985).

The demand, then, is that the Party must be brought within the orbit of the law and that the notion of 'guidance' should be clarified. In some of the contributions there is an implicit challenge to the one-party state, although nobody says so openly. Since the political edifice rests on the claims of the Party to a special guiding role, the notion that a body standing outside it might independently define the permitted character of Party activity is not credible. Hence the calls for constitutional control over the Party are tantamount to a rejection of the one-party state itself. It is not therefore surprising to find that this particular line of thought fails to appear in the resolutions of the XIX Party Conference or in the *Pravda* editorial explaining the significance of the socialist legal state (*Pravda*, 12 July 1988).

## Political Freedoms and the Law

In the language of Soviet reformers, the legal state is one whose authority is circumscribed and in which the political–civil freedoms proclaimed in the Soviet Constitution are backed up by legal guarantees. In the past law was seen only as an instrument of state repression, as a means of struggle against crime (*Lit. Gaz.*, 8 June

1988, p. 11). When administrative will was 'raised to a norm of law ... there remained one "law" – the right of power to publish any norms ensuring, in its view, "the state interest"'. That situation reflected the special and uncontested role of the apparatus in society, leading to a 'serious restriction of the defensive (*garantiinyi*) side of law'. (V. O. Mushinsky, *Sovetskoe Gosudarstvo i Pravo* (SGiP) no. 2/ 1988, p. 7).

A number of legislative enactments have been drawn up or are in various stages of preparation, with the stated purpose of strengthening this 'defensive' side. Important among them are the laws on *glasnost* and on the media. The law on *glasnost* is to deal with access to information and the obligations of ministries, law enforcement agencies and other bodies in that connection. The law on the media is likely to lay down a framework for the activities of the press, TV and radio, the rules for publication of critical materials, and forms of control over the media (V. Yasmann, 'Soviet jurists discuss draft press law', *Radio Liberty Research*, 1 June 1987; 'Law on glasnost in preparation', *Radio Liberty Research*, 13 April 1988).

These are highly contentious areas, which no doubt explains why the publication of the draft documents has taken such a long time coming – considerably longer than originally predicted, since it was at first intended to publish a draft press law in 1986 (ibid., 1 June 1987). It is reported that during the preparation of the draft law on *glasnost*, alternative recommendations included a 'positive' formulation specifying the scope of *glasnost* and a 'negative' one favouring a new law on secrecy: closed matters would be listed, but everything else would be allowed. A scholar involved in the drafting explained that the commission adopted the former (more conservative) variant because 'we bore in mind the lack of legal awareness (*pravosoznanie*) of our people, and because of the need to overcome resistance to *glasnost* mounted by those who dislike it and see it as a threat to their positions' (ibid., 13 April 1988).

A law on *voluntary societies* is being drawn up to determine 'the status of unofficial associations and the principles of their relationship to state institutions and public organisations' (N. Izymova, *Moscow News* 19/1988, p. 10). A copy of an early draft of the law was obtained by some of the new informal political clubs, and subjected to intense criticism, because it gave local soviets the authority to decide if a club was worthy of registration and if, therefore, it would be a legal organisation. A meeting was organised at which club members confronted representatives of the drafting commission.

Among other things it was urged that any group should be permitted to register as a voluntary society, and that all groups should have access to printing facilities and accommodation (reported by G. Pelman, who attended the meeting, in private discussion, Moscow, May 1988).

It will be interesting to see if this law, and the laws on *glasnost* and the media, are given a public airing in the way that occurred with the legislation on cooperatives. There seems to have been relative unanimity at the top in support of the cooperative movement and perhaps no great danger that a public discussion would get out of hand. This is not the case with legal definitions of freedom of the press and of association, which are ultra-sensitive. In general it seems that *glasnost* has been weakest in just those areas where the proper extent of *glasnost* and democracy is itself under dispute, and one could therefore expect a more abrupt procedure for the more politically sensitive legislation. It is noteworthy that the rules on 'meetings, rallies, street marches and demonstrations', issued in July 1988, took the form of a decree of the Presidium of the USSR Supreme Soviet rather than a full-blooded law (Decree of 28 July 1988, *Summary of World Broadcasts*, SU/0219 B/1, 2 August 1988). Meanwhile a law of July 1987, 'On the nationwide discussion of important questions of state life' was itself not subject to any national discussion! (*Pravda*, 3 July 1987).

There is a strong commitment among reformers to law as a lever of political change, and as an instrument with which to create a political space for 'civil society'. This was vividly symbolised at a political demonstration in Moscow in May 1988, organised by several political clubs, where prominent banners read: 'We demand a law on demonstrations'; 'We demand a law on the press'; 'We demand a law on social organisations' (Demonstration in Pushkin Square, 28 May 1988). Abstracted from political realities this might look naive. The historic political developments of the Gorbachev period – the greater tolerance of diversity, the change in the definition of dissidence, the encouragement within certain bounds of informal associations and clubs – have occurred without benefit of law. Conversely, in the absence of the necessary political conditions, plenty of good legal provisions have remained on paper. Furthermore, the new rules that will define the scope for political and civil freedoms are designed not only to give legal backing for more political openness, but also to establish state controls that were previously absent. The July 1988 decree on demonstrations is a case in point. While it details the rights to march and demonstrate that were only vaguely stated in the Constitution, it also allows the local soviets to prohibit meetings whose purpose is deemed to be 'contrary to the USSR Constitution' or is a threat to public order (Decree of 28 July 1988). This gave the Moscow city soviet the legal authority to prohibit, for example, a demonstration by the Democratic Union to commemorate the 20th anniversary of the Soviet invasion of Czechoslovakia – a meeting that went ahead and was broken up by the police. The refusal was given not only on public order grounds but also on the grounds that the initiators 'attempt to present the policy of the Soviet government in a clearly distorted form' (G. Ovcharenko, *Pravda*, 24 August 1988). Meanwhile an editorial note in *Pravda* commented that the leaders of the Democratic Union 'deliberately go beyond the bounds of a socialist pluralism of views, provoking violation of legal order (*pravoporyadka*)', and noted that law enforcement agents, 'fearing accusations of excess', had recently weakened their struggle against such violations. Such a policy was 'diametrically opposed to the principles of a legal state' (*Pravda*, 26 August 1988).

Like 'socialist legality', the rhetoric of the legal state can then be put to different uses depending on the vantage point of the observer and the political needs of the moment. However, it would be rash to conclude that because the problem is primarily political, the law is of no great consequence. If this were so, it would be hard to explain the way in which law and legislation become so highly contested, and the secrecy that still prevails in relation to key parts of the rule-making process. Soviet historical experience and political culture have established no informal rules that could sustain the political freedoms which the reformers hope to achieve. Under those conditions formally and 'positively' stated legal freedoms are of great symbolic importance, and provide the necessary mechanism of protection when political conditions *are* favourable. This is illustrated, for example, by some recent libel cases in which newspapers were instructed to retract hostile statements against named individuals. See, for instance, *Pravda*, 6 April 1988; 26 October 1987; 6 January 1988; *Guardian*, 20 July 1988, the latter a report on a successful libel case by a political club member attacked in *Komsomolskaya Pravda*, 31 January 1988. Admittedly libel law is a double-edged weapon, since it can be used by opponents of reform to limit the damage from *glasnost*. But it is also an important potential instrument for *perestroika* enthusiasts maligned in the press.

## II  LEGALITY AND ADMINISTRATIVE POWER

In the legal state the production of *extra-legal* norms are to be limited
and controlled. The proliferation of administrative rules is therefore
a central target of the discourse on legality. It is a major theme in the
context of economic reform, and more generally in the search for
limits to administrative power over citizens.

### Law and Economic Reform

A change in the legal framework of economic activity is a necessary
condition for a change in the powers of disposition over property, in
particular for a change in the status of enterprises and farms in
relation to ministries and other state agencies. Here the key slogan is:
'everything that is not forbidden is permitted', which is to replace the
governing principle that 'anything that is not permitted is forbidden'
(XIX Party Conference Resolutions, *Izvestiya*, 5 July 1988). Establishing the former principle would mean radically reducing the weight
of non-legal norms in the system, which constantly inhibit enterprise
autonomy. Reformers complain that under the present arrangements, the USSR Council of Ministers is in effect an extra-legal
institution; that laws on economic activity are of little significance
until translated into ministerial directives; that managers have
precious little interest in law – it is what your superior says that
counts; that laws are eroded and rendered useless by ministerial
directives; that numerous administrative rules contradict the law or
the Constitution. (See round table discussions in *EKO* 1/1988,
pp. 24–46; *Pravda*, 2 August 1988; *Pravda*, 12 July 1988, editorial).

A major re-examination of administrative regulations that limit
managerial initiative is said now to be in progress (*Pravda*, 12 May
1988, editorial), in an attempt to stem the 'bacchanalia of prohibi-
tions which today characterises departmental and local norm-making'
(*Pravda*, 12 July 1988, editorial), and there are proposals to set up a
mechanism of review of administrative norms to assess their legality
(V. Prozorov, *EKO* no. 1/1988, p. 40). However, the more fundamental complaint is the lack of a clear definition in law of what it
means to be in charge (to be *khozyain*) of an enterprise. The powers
of ministries and other higher organs are at present described in a
way that establishes no precise boundaries of competence. Injunc-
tions on economic matters constantly talk about 'increasing' this or
that agent's 'responsibility' for ensuring this or that, but these

directives have no juridical consequences (ibid., pp. 25–6). Enterprise directors have no effective avenues of redress, whether 'horizontally' or 'vertically', in the pursuit of compensation. The state arbitration service, which deals with 'horizontal' legal suits and is supposed to be strengthened in the forthcoming legal reform (XIX Party Conference resolutions, *Izvestiya*, 5 July 1988), has at present no second line of defence to make its decisions stick. A recent change in the law gives arbitrators the right to 'instruct' rather than 'recommend' management to ensure the payment of compensation, but no further measures of enforcement are stipulated (*Vedomosti Verkhovnogo Soveta SSSR*, no. 7/1987, p. 92, cited by V. Prozorov, *EKO* no. 1/1988, p. 30).

The changes in the legal framework of agricultural activity, in particular the provision for self-financing, has recently encouraged some farms to seek support from the courts for their proclaimed autonomous status, but the results have not been encouraging for them. In January 1988 ten collective farms in Bashkiriya refused to sign contracts with grain purchasers on the grounds that the latter were making unreasonable demands for compulsory purchases. If the new rules on self-financing were for real, then the farms must have some say in the volume and assortment of grain written into the contract. The farms were taken to court, and nine of them lost. In the case of the tenth, the suit was withdrawn after one hearing, but it was not clear from the press report if the farm had been able to get the sort of contract it wanted. There was some sympathy from officials with the farm's point of view, but the purchasers protested that 'chaos will start if the collective farms themselves establish plans for grain deliveries', and that they themselves would be in trouble because the republic inspection people would not accept an 'incomplete contract'. The Bashkir *obkom* secretary explained that 'Today a free market approach in this matter is impossible. Imagine if we declared: trade as much as you want and how you want. Chaos would begin. One cannot manage without state orders. The appropriate organs must know beforehand how to plan the activity of the grain processing industry. . .' (*Izvestiya*, 7 July 1988; 19 July 1988).

This example illustrates the ambiguity that surrounds the idea of autonomy – an ambiguity that has been especially criticised in the case of the 1987 Law on the State Enterprise – and which leads to demands for clearer definitions of competence. In a sense this is to put the cart before the horse, because the 'lawlessness' of the much-criticised economic bureaucracy is part and parcel of the directive planning system. Ministries and other higher agencies could not perform the tasks assigned to them without wide powers. As a Deputy Minister of the Automobile Industry explained: 'on the one hand we are told to ensure the stable work of enterprises, on the other hand not to touch their independence'. If the ministries were not needed, then they should be abolished and an alternative system established. But if they were needed – and this was not at present in question – then they must have the appropriate powers, including the power to interfere, to transfer resources from more-successful to less-successful enterprises (interview with V. Novikov, *Izvestiya*, 5 August 1988). Hence one could expect a radical legal change only as part of a fundamental reform of the economic mechanism as a whole. However, economic law is sure to remain an important arena of political argument and in that sense to contribute to the total fortunes of reform.

### Administrative Power and the Citizen

Administrative power is under criticism not only in the context of economic management, but also in the context of the relationship between individual citizens and officials. The less naive reformers accept that non-legal rules are bound to play an important part in the life or organisations, since legislative enactments cannot provide the necessary detail and flexibility. However, safeguards must be established. In particular it is vital that administrative rules are open, that they are subject to some form of systematic review, and that individual citizens have the right to appeal against official decisions that they deem to be illegal.

The openness of rules appears as a basic condition of a law-governed social order. The heavy weight of unpublished directives has therefore come under strong attack, and it is suggested that only published rules should be regarded as legally binding (Yu.Feofanov, *Izvestiya*, 1 August 1988). There are also moves to strengthen legality by establishing a mechanism of review of administrative acts. At present this job is assigned to the procuracy, which can bring 'protests' against local rules and administrative directives judged to be illegal. But it is generally agreed that this is not an adequate mechanism. Over the years, said the then newly-appointed USSR Procurator, the procuracy had lost independence and had 'gradually become an adjunct of the command-bureaucratic system of management' (*Lit. Gaz.*, 31 August 1988, p. 12). Also, if a ministry rejects a protest 'the law is not clear about what to do next' (O. Temushkin, ibid., 8 June 1988, p. 11). Some have suggested the establishment of a system of judicial review, allowing the procuracy and other agencies to take appeals about the legality of administrative rules to the courts (V. Terebilov, ibid., 27 April 1988, p. 11). The XIX Party Conference did not go down this road. Instead it proposed, along with a strengthening of the supervisory role of the procuracy, to establish a committee of constitutional supervision, to be elected by the Supreme Soviet (*Pravda*, 12 July 1988). Just how this might work remains to be seen.

In addition to controls over the rule-making process, reformers have put a lot of emphasis on widening the scope for redress by individual citizens against official decisions. This matter has been on the agenda for many years, in connection with article 58 of the 1977 Constitution, which says that 'actions by officials which conflict with the law or exceed their authority and infringe upon the rights of citizens, may be appealed in court' and that 'citizens of the USSR have the right to compensation for damages resulting from unlawful actions by state organisations'. These provisions are backed up by reference to a statement of Engels that 'the first condition of any freedom is the responsibility of all officials for their official actions in relation to any citizen before the ordinary courts and in accordance with general law', and by reference to the first programme of the Bolshevik Party which stipulated 'the right of each person to take any official to court in the normal way' (Hecht 1983, p. 37; Engels is cited by V. Savitsky, *Izvestiya*, 8 April 1988, the Bolshevik programme by V. Romm, *EKO* no. 1/1988, p. 43).

In July 1987 a law was finally brought in, extending the possibilities of appeal to the courts against official decisions. Until then such a right existed for labour disputes (with some important exceptions) and in relation to a number of other matters (such as electoral registers, decisions on deprivation of driving licences, confiscation of property in connection with tax claims and eviction orders. V. Savitsky, *Izvestiya*, 8 April 1987), but it was narrowly defined. The new measure was announced with some fanfare but was quickly criticised as very ineffectual because it contained no right of appeal against *collegial* decisions, only against the decisions of individual officials. Hence the most pressing matters that concern the greatest number of people (for example, decisions about allocation of housing or pensions), are excluded. As before, complaints on these matters will be dealt with only through administrative channels. The law therefore remains at odds with the constitution (V. Savitsky, ibid.). It is also noteworthy that no additional protection was given to employees who come within the so-called Lists 1 and 2 (mainly people with administrative-managerial responsibilities), who are still barred from recourse to the courts in the event of dismissal. These lists, appended to the Regulations on Work Disputes of May 1974, were long ago described as unconstitutional (see, for instance, S. Ivanov and R. Lifshits, *SGiP*, no. 4/1978, pp. 14–24). The restrictions have helped to ensure a minimal response. For example, during the first three months after the introduction of the law, 200 complaints were taken to Moscow city courts, 40 to Moscow oblast courts, 60 to Leningrad courts and less in other territories (V. Savitsky, *Lit. Gaz.*, 11 May 1988, p. 12). A. M. Yakovlev has remarked that the law was stillborn (*Lit. Gaz.*, 8 June 1988, p. 11).

The law on appeal to the courts against official decisions was not subject to public discussion. It has been suggested that had it been published in draft form 'people's reaction would surely have been so sharp and furious that one would hardly have been able to limit oneself to half-measures' (V. Savitsky, ibid., 11 May, 1988, p. 12). It is possible that if the law had been framed with broader terms of reference the ordinary courts would have been inundated, especially with housing disputes, and physically unable to cope. However, this was no doubt a secondary consideration in deciding the shape of the law. More likely there was the sense that large areas of administrative discretion needed to be preserved and that it was inappropriate for the courts to meddle in them, whatever the constitution might say.

This outcome will help to ensure that Soviet citizens remain *petitioners* in relation to the state, soliciting help, asking for favours, using what pull they have, rather than asserting their 'rights'. This state of affairs is absolutely customary for Soviet people – it is a way of life – yet is also the source of intense frustrations, as was well-expressed in a letter to *Literaturnaya Gazeta*:

Why, throughout my life, must I be an eternal supplicant, begging and imploring things to which I am entitled according to all the rules? Why, from the school bench to ripe old age . . . should I live as if with an outstretched hand, always, everywhere, every day – in the shop, the housing department, the dressmakers, the ispolkom? What am I after all, a citizen of my country or a supplicant in my country, and how long can this go on? (31 August 1988, p. 12)

To judge from regular brief encounters with Soviet life and from a reading of many, many letters to the Soviet press, this *cri de coeur* would find an echo with millions of Soviet people. The response of legal reformers is to urge the creation of a legal framework in which people might be transformed from *supplicants* into *claimants* (Yu. Feofanov, *Izvestiya*, 21 June 1988). That too is part of the meaning of a legal state. It may be that the idea of everyone becoming a potential litigant would not find a lot of popular sympathy among the Soviet population – the adjective 'litigious' seems to carry a greater pejorative weight in Russian than in English. However, this would be the drift of things if the legal reformers got their way. Since that has not yet happened, the problems with the present law are likely to stay on the agenda.

## III  CRIMINAL JUSTICE

Very soon after Gorbachev took over the leadership in 1985, an urgent discussion began on legality in the system of criminal justice, raising a number of issues that were familiar from the Khrushchev years. In the Khrushchev period there had been major reforms in the area of criminal law, but they left intact a number of the features of the Stalin inheritance. The main effect of the post-Stalin reforms was to diminish the powers of the security police, and to reduce the level and scope of repressive sanctions (N. P. Mironov, 'Vosstanovlene i razvitiye leninskikh printsipov sotsialisticheskoi zakonnosti (1953–1963)', *Voprosy Istorii KPSS*, no. 2/1964, pp. 17–29). But these changes left law enforcement agencies (in particular the procuracy, police and courts), within the control of territorial political fiefdoms, creating the conditions for what was to become an entrenched system of 'dual legality'. In the sphere of economic crime (bribery, theft of socialist property and other forms of economic or official crime), which has occupied a great deal of the attention of the investigative organs and criminal courts, the powerful were generally well-protected, while the small-fry and the less favoured were much more likely to find themselves under scrutiny. As a result, as Gorbachev put it, 'serious crimes against the interests of our society and citizens' were left undisturbed while, as in the Russian saying, 'they shot at sparrows with cannon' (*Pravda*, 28 January 1987).

This pattern became particularly striking in the later years of the Brezhnev era, when increasing economic difficulties, together with political protectionism, fuelled a growing corruption into which law enforcement agents and party officials were increasingly drawn. On the one hand local elites who were up to their necks in corrupt networks were left alone. Accounts of some of the more notorious cases are in *Lit. Gaz.*, 26 October 1987 (the role of top officials of the Ministry of Internal Affairs); *Pravda*, 18 January 1988 (on Armenia); *Pravda*, 23 January 1988 (on Uzbekistan). On the other hand, investigators and judges were under pressure to show that something was being done in the struggle against crime, and they were not encouraged to be fussy in the methods used to secure confessions and convictions. It is the sense that people who get caught up in this system are very weakly protected, as well as the sense that the level and scope of repressive sanctions remain much too great, that has provided the main moral impulse for reform. All this has been assisted by a flood of reports in the central press detailing miscarriages of justice ('legal errors' in Soviet parlance) arising from these pressures within the system. (For a few cases relating to managers convicted in connection with their necessarily illegal activities, see *Pravda*, 17 June 1986; 24 August 1986; 18 April 1987; 6 June 1987).

A legal state is one which gives people protection from unwarranted detention, investigation and prosecution, and in which the judiciary is not subject to outside pressures, whether to protect big-shots from legal responsibility or to ensure the conviction of others. Obviously, no legal system is without fault according to these criteria, but recent comment in the Soviet Union has been very damning.

In the USSR, the main agencies responsible for investigation are the procuracy (more serious offences), the Ministry of Internal Affairs (preliminary inquiry in a wide range of cases and investigation of less serious offences) and the KGB (political and some economic – e.g. currency speculation – offences). The attention of reformers in this context has focused on the role of the procuracy. At present its function as 'supervisor' of legality throughout the system is joined by two other roles as investigative and prosecuting arms of the law. As a result the procuracy has a strong vested interest in continuing with a case once criminal proceedings have begun (*Lit. Gaz.*, 15 April 1987, p. 11), offering a very weak barrier against unjustified detention (the rate of detention is said to be much too high and the length of detention inordinately long, I. Petrukhin, *SGiP*, no. 6/1987, p. 79), against reliance on confessions (V. Kudryavtsev, *Pravda*, 14 March 1988), and hence against flimsy and ill-founded indictments.

The courts, which in principle should act as a filter, have had very little room for manoeuvre. Failure to secure a conviction has come to be seen as a major upset for the investigation and prosecution (in effect a big black mark for the procuracy), and thus indirectly as a failure on the part of local party apparatus, which is held responsible for the state of law enforcement in its territory. These criteria of performance led, among other things, to the almost complete disappearance of acquittals (P. H. Solomon, 'The case of the vanishing acquittal: informal norms and the practice of Soviet criminal justice', *Soviet Studies*, Vol. XXXIX, no. 4/1987, pp. 531–55).

Under the present system, judges are formally elected for a five-year term; in practice they are selected by the local party apparatus. Judges who refused to adopt a prosecution point of view and to take into account 'local interests' could not expect to hold on to their jobs for long; they would be blackballed the next time round. One judge put it like this:

Yes, the People's Judge is independent. In theory. In life everything is more difficult. The material well-being of the court and its workers depends on local party and soviet organs. This concerns the repair of court buildings, the allocation of flats, installation of telephones and much else. One way or another in such conditions judges begin to feel their dependence on local powers. And let us be frank: if in the course of five years ... a judge does not establish good relations with the local power, you can be sure that he will not be elected for a new term. (I. Tivodar, *Pravda*, 14 March 1988)

This state of affairs, along with more direct forms of political pressure on the judiciary from political officials (for example, meetings with local party secretaries in connection with particular law-enforcement campaigns), has led one reformer to speak of the 'humiliating, degrading position of the court in our society and state' (V. Savitsky, *Lit. Gaz.*, 30 March 1988, p. 11).

A 'prosecution bias' has thus become entrenched within the system, and it is this that reform of criminal justice is above all designed to confront. A number of changes, hastened by Central Committee resolutions in summer 1988, are in the pipeline. They are likely to take the following form.

First, the procuracy is, with some exceptions, to be freed from responsibility for investigation. Most investigations will pass to a separate department within the Ministry of Internal Affairs, not subordinated to the local offices of Internal Affairs. Also, defence lawyers (*advokaty*) will be given more rights of access to their clients in the pre-trial period (*Izvestiya*, 5 July 1988). (Previously, defence lawyers usually had access to a case only on completion of the preliminary investigation.) In these ways it is hoped to reduce the number of ill-founded detentions and forced confessions, and to make prosecutions more secure.

Second, there will be changes designed to increase the independence of the judiciary in relation to investigators, prosecutors and local political officials. Reform proposals in this connection have included the following: (1) Moving to a system of selection of judges, preferably with life tenure, and removing them from the *nomenklatura* of lower-level party organisations (V. Savitsky, *SGiP*, no. 9/ 1987, pp. 29–35). (2) Increasing the number of People's Assessors (lay judges). At present there are two assessors in the lower courts, who are easily manipulated by the judge. More of them would, it is argued, make them less readily influenced (G. Anushkin, *Lit. Gaz.*, 15 April 1987, p. 11). Some commentators would like to see a jury system for certain types of trials, though such a radical change is unlikely. (Z. M. Chernilovsky, *SGiP*, no. 9/1987, pp. 79–86). (3) Improving salaries, and moving financial responsibility for the courts from local authorities to the central budget (Yu. Feofanov, *Izvestiya*, 21 June 1988). (4) Making officials legally liable for interference in the course of justice (*Lit. Gaz.*, 27 April 1988, p. 11).

It is also stressed that there is a big job ahead to train more and better lawyers. The training of judges, especially, needs to be greatly improved, with more careful selection of applicants and less reliance on part-time education. In 1987, 73 per cent of judges in the RSFSR had had extramural training, leading to 'mass production of very mediocre lawyers'. It is pointed out that the Soviet Union has three times fewer judges in relation to population size than the USA, and four times fewer than England. The number of defence lawyers has remained almost the same in relation to population as during the immediate pre-revolutionary period. There should be 'at least twice as many' lawyers overall as at present (M. Vyshinsky, USSR Deputy Minister of Justice, *Pravda*, 6 June 1988).

The brief indications that came out of the XIX Party Conference – in particular, election of judges by higher-level soviets for longer terms than at present, and more assessors for some trials – suggest that the final shape of the reform will be a partial shift in the direction proposed by the more radical legal reformers.

The main thrust of the proposed changes in criminal justice is to provide legal agencies with weapons with which to resist outside influence on the law-enforcement process. Tighter procedures will assist. However, a remaining difficulty is that the reforms do not directly confront the problem of criteria of performance of the agencies involved. So long as investigators and judges are held responsible for the state of crime in a territory, which has been the case up to now, they will be tempted to ignore legal niceties. Similarly, so long as the party is held responsible for law enforcement and the criteria of success include, for example, the clear-up rate and the rate of 'bad' prosecutions, it will tend to support the efforts of investigators even at the expense of legality, and will put pressure on judges, directly or indirectly, to secure convictions. A more radical change could occur if the party were to withdraw from state administration in the way that is now being suggested in some quarters. But this is not yet happening, and with the introduction of a joint first party secretary-soviet chairman, is not likely to in the near future.

## CONCLUSION

This chapter has been concerned primarily with a discourse of reform. The discussion on the legal state is only in its first stages and, with the exception of criminal law, it is hard to tell what significant concrete changes, if any, it may bring. One can, however, see in broad terms why the rule of law has come to occupy an important place in he reform debate. It has a vital function in the context of a shift towards greater use of the market, since legal guarantees are a necessary condition of predictable contractual relationships. More broadly, the popularity of rule of law is a manifestation of the current strength of westernising influences within the Soviet intelligentsia and within the reformist wing of the Party apparat. Western-orientated intellectuals have been borrowing more and more uninhibitedly from a liberal-democratic tradition, which may be compatible with but is certainly distinct from the socialist one with which it is in tension as well as dialogue. It could indeed be argued that the legal state slogan corresponds above all to the interests of the intelligentsia broadly defined, who would be most likely to make use of a more independent legal system and for whom guarantees of professional autonomy are particularly important. Yet there is more than that at stake. The talk of the legal state arises from a sense of crisis of political authority and is part of a wider effort to strengthen the legitimacy of the Soviet state. Whether that is possible given the preservation of a monopoly of political power is a question that remains to be answered.

# 8 Nationalities*

## BOHDAN NAHAYLO

In no other area has the impact of *glasnost* and democratisation been as dramatic as in the nationality sphere. The push by the Baltic republics for the restoration of the sovereignty of the non-Russian republics; the conflict between Armenia and Azerbaidzhan over Nagorno-Karabakh; riots in Kazakhstan and Yakutia, mass meetings in the Ukraine, Belorussia and Moldavia; the vigorous national assertiveness being shown on a broad front by the non-Russian cultural elites; as well as the numerous demonstrations by Crimean Tatars and the sinister activities of the Russian ultra-nationalist *Pamyat* group, have brought home to the Kremlin and to the outside world the scale and seriousness of a nationalities problem which for years Moscow had denied even existed.

If, at the time Mikhail Gorbachev took over as Party leader, the Soviet Union's nationalities problem seemed to be well under control, by the fourth year of his period in office it had forced its way into the open and established itself high on his political agenda. Indeed, in January 1989, the Soviet leader himself acknowledged that the success or failure of *perestroika* would 'depend to a decisive extent' on how this complex and acute question is dealt with (*Pravda*, 7 January 1989). On the two previous occasions, before Gorbachev, when Stalin's successors (Beria and Khrushchev) attempted to distance themselves from Stalinism, the need for a fundamental review of the Party's policy towards the non-Russians was recognised. There is no evidence, though, to suggest that the present Soviet leader realised the necessity for this, nor, indeed, that he was particularly interested in the nationalities question when he came to power.

For Gorbachev, like Andropov and Chernenko before him, the significance of the nationality question lay not so much in its potential

*This chapter draws on an earlier article by the author written for Radio Liberty. See Bohdan Nahaylo, 'Putting Current Nationality Problems in Historical Perspective', in *Glasnost and Empire: National Aspirations in the USSR*, RFE/RL Studies, Munich, 1989, pp. 17–27.

threat to the stability of the system, as in the bearing which it had on the Kremlin's ability to deal with key problems in the socio-political, economic and military spheres. During the first half of the 1980s, both the Party and the specialists had begun acknowledging some of the difficulties in the nationality sphere but had offered little in the way of solutions.

By the early 1980s, economic stagnation had become a major headache for the Kremlin. Even during Brezhnev's final months it was made apparent that Moscow intended to reassert its central control and that the republics would have to pull their weight. After his death, a major crackdown on corruption and economic inefficiency was launched by Andropov and continued under Chernenko. Its main target was the Central Asian republics, particularly the USSR's main cotton producer, Uzbekistan.

Moscow was also becoming anxious about the long-term implications of the population explosion among the USSR's traditionally Muslim peoples and their growing assertiveness and resistance to Sovietisation and assimilation. Not only did a high proportion of them still have little or no knowledge of Russian, but also they were reluctant to migrate from their homelands, even though these were 'labour surplus areas', to regions in Siberia and elsewhere where there was a shortage of manpower. At the same time, Russian and other settlers had begun moving out of the Central Asian republics. Furthermore, by the beginning of the decade, 28 per cent of draftees were being drawn from Central Asia and the Transcaucasus, and they, together with other non-Russians had to be integrated into multinational units in which Russian was the sole language of command. By 1988 this proportion was to rise to 37 per cent (*Argumenty i fakty*, no. 35, 1988, pp. 1–2).

Consequently, Moscow toughened its policy towards the Central Asian republics: apart from the drive against corruption, affirmative action policies were abandoned and emphasis was placed on the 'inter-republic exchange of cadres'. Moreover, more effort was put into expanding the teaching of Russian and combating the influence of Islam. What this amounted to was a unilateral abrogation of the implicit *modus vivendi* that had existed during the 1970s between Moscow and the Central Asian elites.

The first half of the 1980s was also a time when, apart from growing social and economic difficulties at home, the USSR was embroiled in Afghanistan, when Iran was in the grip of Islamic fundamentalism and when events in Poland were causing the Kremlin considerable discomfort. Moreover, the era of detente was over and in the Soviet Union anti-Western attitudes and a siege-mentality were being fostered. In nationalities policy this frosty climate was reflected in an even greater emphasis on integration, 'internationalisation' and ideological vigilance, in the intensification of the promotion of the study and use of the Russian language, as well as in the harsher treatment of non-Russian activitists.

On coming to power, Gorbachev made no attempt to change course in nationalities policy. He made it quite clear that he was primarily interested in the economic aspects of the national question. In fact, his initial attitude seems to have been to avoid tinkering with the thorny nationalities question unless economic exigencies demanded it.

For all the early talk of reform, there was no hint of any economic decentralisation that would restore prerogatives to the Union republics, nor for that matter, that Russification would be eased. During his first year at the helm Gorbachev made no major pronouncements on the nationalities question, though the general impression – and here the Kremlin's number-two man Egor Ligachev played more of a role – was, if anything, that Moscow was intent on pursuing an even firmer policy towards the republics.

When the draft of the new Party programme was published in October 1985 it was clear from the section dealing with nationalities policy, and from the very restricted discussion of it in the press, that it would be a case of more of the same in nationalities policy. Hardly surprisingly, therefore, there were no new departures in nationalities policy at the XXVIII Party Congress held in February–March 1986 (Nahaylo 1988a). Later, in January 1989, however, Gorbachev was to reveal that behind the scenes there had apparently been strong pressure from some quarters to renew the emphasis on 'merging' the nations of the USSR. As he put it,

> There was even a proposal to embark on the practical merging of the nations. At the time, I managed with great difficulty to oppose the pressure of certain learned gentlemen who were seeking to thrust this formulation into the current Party programme (*Pravda*, 7 January 1989).

The Soviet leader now embarked on getting his economic restructuring drive under way. He soon realised, however, that in order to mobilise the Soviet population behind his reform campaign he needed the support of the creative and scientific intelligentsia, especially the opinion-makers, namely writers and media workers. To win them over, Gorbachev began loosening controls in the cultural sphere, reduced censorship and urged the press to be more critical and candid. At first the main beneficiary of *glasnost*, as this more liberal policy came to be called, was the Russian creative intelligentsia and hence the new thaw was largely restricted to Moscow and Leningrad.

The situation began to change in the spring of 1986 as *glasnost*, given impetus by the Chernobyl nuclear disaster in the Ukraine in April, began to spread from the centre to the non-Russian republics. A bolder spirit was discernible at some of the congresses of the Writers' Unions held at this time in the Union republics, and it became more pronounced at the VIII Congress of Soviet Writers which was held in Moscow at the end of June.

Even at this early stage, the different concerns of Russian and non-Russian writers were apparent. Whereas Russian representatives pressed for the easing of censorship and for the publication of the proscribed works of Boris Pasternak and Anna Akhmatova, one non-Russian writer after another expressed concern about the displacement of their national languages from educational and public life by Russian, and about Moscow's control over the national–cultural life of their nations generally. Outspoken terms like 'great-power chauvinists' and 'denationalisation' were used (*Literaturnaya Gazeta*, 2 July 1986).

Even though the Kremlin soon signalled that a return to the liberal nationalities policy of the 1920s – in which deRussification of the non-Russian republics had been a major element – was out of the question (Eduard Bagramov on *Radio Moscow*, 13 August 1986; *Pravda*, 14 August 1986), during the next few months the language issue became a major battleground. Non-Russian dissidents had frequently pointed out at their peril that the promotion of Russian has gone well beyond the practical and cogent need to create a lingua franca and that Moscow's policy amounted to nothing less than Russification concealed behind internationalist rhetoric. Now the cry was taken up by representatives of the cultural elites from the Baltic to the Black Sea.

Even in Belorussia, the most Russified of the non-Russian republics, a remarkable campaign began in the local press in defence of the native language. Belorussian patriots pointed out that in the entire republic, where according to the 1979 census, 80 per cent of its 7.6

million Belorussian inhabitants had given Belorussian as their native language, there was only one urban school providing some instruction in the mother tongue (Solchanyk 1987a). In the neighbouring Ukraine, where in 1979 the Ukrainians accounted for 73.6 per cent of the 50 million inhabitants, it emerged that the percentage of Ukrainian-language schools in the major cities had been reduced to about 16 per cent and that approximately half of the republic's children were being taught in Russian schools (Solchanyk 1987b and c).

Linked to this was the problem of the almost 25 million Russians living in non-Russian republics, only a minimal number of whom had bothered to learn the local language. In Kazakhstan, for example, only 0.7 per cent of the six million Russians living in the republic claimed to know the Kazakh language. This problem was felt particularly acutely in the small republics of Latvia and Estonia where there was growing concern that the indigenous nations would be 'swamped' in a Russian sea. There was also a reverse problem. Many millions of non-Russians living outside their own republics were deprived of basic cultural facilties. For example, six million Ukrainians living in Russia, Moldavia and elsewhere did not have a single school or newspaper in their native language and were effectively condemned to gradual denationalisation (Nahaylo 1988a).

Complaints about the situaton in the language sphere and the way that Russian was squeezing the native languages out of higher education, science and public life generally, soon turned into concrete demands. Ukrainians, Belorussians, Latvians, Estonians and others began calling for the status of their languages to be given legal and constitutional protection. In turn, these developed into proposals that the native languages be given the status of official languages in non-Russian republics, as was already the case in Georgia, Armenia and Azerbaidzhan. Simultaneously, the Estonians and Latvians began to press for some control over the inflow of Russians into their republics.

It soon became increasingly evident that the language issue was only the tip of the iceberg. Intellectuals in the Ukraine and Belorussia, for instance, began expressing their anxiety about the erasure of national memory through the distortion of history. In the Baltic republics calls were made for a truthful depiction of the circumstances in which the independent Baltic states had been incorporated into the USSR. With new editions of the Russian Imperial historians Karamzin, Klyuchevsky and Solovev being promised, and anti-Soviet

Russian literary figures like Gumilev and Nabokov being rehabilitated, the non-Russians started pressing for a more honest account of
their past and for the rehabilitation of their own historians and
political and cultural figures that had been placed off limits.

In one notable case, Russians were given preference over non-
Russians. The Russian Orthodox Church was given a monopoly by
the state over the organisation of the celebrations of the millennium
in 1988 of the Christianisation of Kievan Rus, thereby highlighting
one of the religious aspects of the nationalities question. Although,
according to Soviet historiography, the Russians, Ukrainians and
Belorussians are all said to trace their historical and cultural heritage
from this medieval polity whose centre, Kiev, is the capital of the
present-day Ukraine, the jubilee was approached by both the
Moscow Patriarchate and the Soviet media from an exclusively
Russocentric perspective. Furthermore, in 1988 Gorbachev was to
hail the jubilee as a major milestone in the history of 'Russia's'
culture and statehood, while the then Soviet president, Andrei
Gromyko, was to laud the role played by the Russian Orthodox
Church in the creation and preservation of the Russian Empire
(Nahaylo 1988b).

With Ukrainian and Belorussian national churches still banned in
the USSR, and the appeals from Ukrainian Catholic believers for the
legalisation of their 'catacomb' church falling on deaf ears, Moscow's
attitude towards the millennial celebrations only reinforced existing
resentment among the USSR's two large non-Russian Slav nations.
Interestingly, it was not only Ukrainians who complained about this
double standard. In some of the traditionally Muslim areas the state's
new benign attitude to Russian Orthodoxy was contrasted with its
treatment of domestic Islam (Soper 1988).

In regard to Central Asia, the Gorbachev leadership seemed to
dispense with all tact. Placing a premium on improving economic
performance and strengthening central control, it intensified the
three-pronged campaign against corruption, native power cliques and
Islam (Antic 1987). For instance, the Tadzik KGB chief, V. Petkel,
revealed that in 1986–7 there were 'dozens of trials' in Tadzhikistan
of unofficial Muslim clerics (*Kommunist Tadzhikistan*, 30 December
1987). Moreover, as the local political elites were purged, numerous
Russians were brought in to take over important positions (Sheehy
1985 and 1986). Ideological controls were also tightened. Failing to
heed a warning sounded at the Uzbek Party Congress in January
1986 that this ostensibly economically-motivated crackdown was

being interpreted locally as an 'anti-national' action (*Pravda Vostoka*, 31 January 1986), Gorbachev may have exacerbated matters when in November 1986, during a brief stopover in Tashkent, the capital of the most populous of the traditionally Muslim republics, he tactlessly called for 'resolute and uncompromising struggle against religious phenomena' (*Pravda Vostoka*, 25 November 1986). The following month, when the national sensibilities of the Kazakhs were ridden over roughshod by the replacement of their veteran Party leader Dinmukhamed Kunaev by a Russian, Genadii Kolbin, the famous 'Alma-Ata riots' broke out.

The Soviet news media promptly acknowledged that there had been disorders in the Kazakh capital (Tass, 18 December 1986, and *Novosti*, 23 December 1986) and this, and the subsequent attention given to the protests, were hailed as a victory for *glasnost*. In fact, there was a good deal of distortion and one-sidedness in the Soviet coverage. The demonstrators were depicted as students who had been plied with alcohol and drugs by Kunaev's supporters and the scale of the demonstrations was minimised. Only in the summer of 1988 was it revealed that the protest had affected twelve of Kazakhstan's centres (*Izvestia*, 7 June 1988). As part of the attacks against Kazakh nationalism, *Pravda* accused Kazakh patriots of 'national egoism' for having called for the opening of more Kazakh schools and kindergartens (11 February 1987). Later, however, it was to emerge in the Kazakh press that at the time only 6 per cent of the one million or so children in pre-school facilities in the republic were attending Kazakh schools (Soper, 1987).

At the Central Comittee plenum held in January 1987 Gorbachev changed his tone to the extent that he acknowledged that 'There is not a single fundamental issue that we could resolve, now or in the past without taking into account that we live in a multinational country.' All the same, although he also hinted that 'misunderstandings' and disputes did arise from time to time in the sphere of national relations and called for more tact, the only remedy he offered was the improvement of 'internationalist education'. 'Let those who would like to play on nationalist or chauvinistic prejudices', he warned 'entertain no illusions and expect no loosening up' (Tass, 27 January 1987).

There was, however, a brighter side to the plenum, for Gorbachev did affirm his commitment to *glasnost* and, moreover, signalled that restructuring would be extended to the social sphere. During the next few months, the public discussion of nationality issue became broader and more candid. Within a few months of the protest in Kazakhstan, it was admitted that there were problems with 'nationalism' in other republics, namely Tadzhikistan, Kirgizia and Moldavia. It was to take another two years, however, before the Soviet press revealed that shortly before the protests in Kazakhstan, inter-ethnic riots involving up to 3000 people had broken out in the Tadzhik capital of Dushanbe (*Sotsialisticheskaya industriya*, 18 January 1989).

In April 1987, the Soviet media acknowledged for the first time that Afghan guerrillas had made raids into Soviet Central Asia (*Pravda*, 2 April 1987), while the following month *Literaturnaya Gazeta* carried an article discussing the 'Muslim opposition' and the clandestine activity of the Sufi brotherhoods (*Lit. Gaz.*, 13 and 20 May 1987). That same month, *Pravda* published a forthright article on the nationalities question by the celebrated Armenian poet Silva Kaputikyan in which she argued that it was time to 'harmonise' proclamations about nationalities policy meant for 'the peoples of Africa and Asia' with 'actions in our own house' (*Pravda*, 7 May 1987).

Kaputikyan and others focused on the burning issue of Russification. In May 1987 the Estonian linguist Mati Hint openly condemned Soviet language policy for the one-sidedness of the 'bilingualism' that was being promoted, charging that it reflected an inherently 'chauvinistic' attitude towards the smaller nations (*Edasi*, 29 May 1987; Ilves 1987a). In July, the Kirgiz writer of all-Union fame, Chingiz Aitmatov, also spoke out on the nationalities question. Deploring the old tendency to label expressions of patriotism as nationalism, he attacked 'national nihilists' and 'super internationalists' for their indifferent or disdainful attitude towards national languages and cultures and urged that in the Union republics the non-Russian languages be guaranteed 'equal worth and importance' with Russian (*Ogonek*, no. 26, 1987, pp. 4–9).

By this time, national problems were also being mirrored in the environmental sphere. The non-Russians had begun protesting about the centre's bureaucratic indifference to local interests and started questioning Moscow's right to 'dictate' on where, say, nuclear reactors and chemical plants should be located and how natural resources should be exploited. A leading Estonian economist even compared the central ministries in Moscow to 'trans-national corporations'. (Mikhail Bronshtein, *Radio Moscow*, 3 July 1988). In the Ukraine, writers and scientists headed public opposition to the expansion of nuclear energy in the republic. In the Baltic republics, concern about damage to the environment was linked with resentment at the continuing inflow of Russian workers. In the Central Asian republics, too, where there was considerable disappointment about the shelving of the Siberian Rivers Diversion Scheme, the dessication of the Aral Sea and the problems connected with the cotton monoculture imposed on the region gave an anti-Russian tinge to ecological concerns.

Despite the shock of what had happened in Kazakhstan and the growing pressure from the non-Russians, the Kremlin began to respond by offering palliatives rather than remedies. As in Kazakhstan, in a number of republics modest concessions were made in the language sphere and special republican commissions on international relations were established. A number of small nationalities, such as the Gagauz and the Buryats also benefited and emigration restrictions on Jews and Germans were eased. But in Latvia, Belorussia and the Ukraine, where the language question was most acute, the republican authorities warned that the writers were going too far. In the summer of 1987 editorials and articles in *Pravda* categorically rejected 'demands to restrict administratively the use of the Russian language' and reiterated that the 'equality' of the languages of the nations of the USSR 'does not mean that their social functions are the same' (*Pravda*, 21 July and 14 August 1987).

Although *glasnost* was being extended there was still no sign of restructuring in the area of nationalities policy. The non-Russians were being allowed to get things off their chests, but their complaints and proposals were not producing changes in official policy. What had changed, though, was that fear had receded and that the non-Russians were no longer prepared to take no for an answer. As their frustration grew, so did their radicalisation. In the summer of 1987 there were demonstrations by Crimean Tatars in Moscow and in the Baltic republics, Latvians, Lithuanians and Estonians held large demonstrations on 23 August, the anniversary of the Molotov–Ribbentrop Pact.

For the three Baltic nations, the events of the summer of 1987 were a turning-point. The crude press attacks on Baltic activists who were demanding the truth about the early years of Soviet rule in their republics, shocked and galvanised the native cultural elites. Earlier in the year in Estonia there had already been signs that some Estonian Party officials had begun to back the demands being made by the native intelligentsia. Now, the leading officials of Estonia's cultural unions issued a joint letter of protest and demanded the publication

of the full text of the Molotov–Ribbentrop Pact (Ilves, 1988a).
Furthermore, the poet and head of the Writers' Union of Latvia,
Janis Peters, indicated on 16 September in the pages of *Pravda* that
the issue was no longer one of greater cultural freedom. Not enough
was being done, he stressed, 'to emphasize in our civic consciousness
the idea that each republic is a sovereign state'.

The Gorbachev leadership had so far evaded discussing the
question of whether economic reform would lead to a broadening of
republican powers. It was becoming evident, though, that the new
process of decentralisation would be working to the advantage of
individual enterprises and not of the republican governments. In fact,
republican ministries were being eliminated and enterprises made
accountable directly to Moscow. In September 1987, four Estonian
communists came out with a radical proposal to turn their republic
into a 'self-managing economic zone'. This was a case of non-
Russians taking a general principle espoused by the Gorbachev
leadership – *khozraschet*, or cost-accounting – and applying it to suit
local, or rather national, needs (Ilves 1987b).

The last quarter of 1987 saw Armenian unrest over the issues of
industrial pollution and the disputed autonomous region of Nagorno-
Karabakh, more protests in Estonia and Latvia, and new demonstrations by Crimean Tatars. In Belorussia, the Ukraine, Armenia and
Georgia, new informal patriotic groups sprang up and tested the
limits of *glasnost*. Some of the Ukrainian, Armenian and Georgian
activists even sought to coordinate their activities by forming a united
front (Nahaylo 1988c).

Although there was more talk of the need for greater tact,
Gorbachev was still showing no signs of altering course in nationalities policy. In this respect, his eagerly-awaited speech on the 70th
anniversary of the Bolshevik Revolution (*Pravda*, 3 November 1987)
proved a disappointment. The year ended with *Pravda* referring to
'nationalist epidemics' but issuing the standard warnings that national
narrow-mindedness would not be tolerated (*Pravda*, 30 December
1987). In February 1988 at a Central Committee plenum on education Gorbachev acknowledged the national problem as 'a most
fundamental and most vital issue' facing Soviet society and indicated
that a forthcoming Central Committee plenum would be devoted to
it, though he did not say when (*Pravda*, 18 February 1988). Nevertheless, despite the pressure from the non-Russians, the essentially
discriminatory manner in which different social functions have been
assigned to the Russian and the non-Russian languages was not

questioned and pleas for the learning of the native language in the non-Russian republics to be made compulsory were dismissed.

Only a few days after the plenum ended the country was shaken by events in the Transcaucasus. On 20 February the Armenian-dominated soviet of the Nagorno-Karabakh Autonomous Oblast voted to call for the transfer of the disputed enclave with its Armenian majority from Azerbaidzhan to Armenia. The Kremlin rejected this defiant act but was confronted by protests on an unprecedented scale by Armenians in Erevan and Nagorno-Karabakh. On 26 February, with the Armenian capital paralysed by strikes and 700 000 demonstrators massed in the city's squares and streets, Gorbachev appeared on television and appealed for calm. Just as the Armenian protesters decided to suspend their demonstrations for a month in order to give the Kremlin a chance to come up with a satisfactory solution, ethnic violence erupted in the Azerbaidzhani city of Sumgait which, according to official figures, left 26 Armenians and six Azerbaidzhanis dead.

Gorbachev proceeded cautiously and stressed in mid-March, during a visit to Yugoslavia, that is was 'essential' to 'ensure [the] democratic solution' of nationality problems (Tass, 16 March 1988). He also stressed that the Armenian protests were not 'anti-Soviet' and had resulted from 'cultural and ethnic problems' that had been overlooked and left to accumulate (*Pravda*, 16 March 1988). Curiously though, within a fortnight there was a *volte-face*. First, a press campaign was launched against the Armenian activists and then on 24 March troops were sent into Erevan. At the same time the Armenian demands about the transfer of Nagorno-Karabakh were rejected by the USSR Supreme Soviet, though an attempt was made to soften the blow through the announcement of a conciliatory package of economic and cultural measures designed to improve conditions in the rebellious region. While it is unclear why Moscow suddenly risked alienating the Armenians by resorting to strong-arm tactics, the fact that during this critical period Gorbachev's position seems to have been momentarily shaken by the publication of Nina Andreeva's notorious reactionary letter (*Sovetskaya Rossiya*, 13 March 1988) might have had something to do with it. Whatever the explanation, the unrest in the Transcaucasus continued and at the end of May Moscow replaced the Party leaders of both Armenia and Azerbaidzhan.

In the meantime attention switched to the Baltic republics. Here, the cultural elites came out with bold proposals that challenged the existing relationship between Moscow and the republics. Moreover, mass-based patriotic movements that supported these positions also emerged. The Estonians led the way. At the beginning of April, the leaderships of Estonia's cultural unions issued a radical programmatic appeal addressed to the forthcoming XIX Party Conference in which they expressed their lack of confidence in the Estonian Party and state leaders and asked for broad economic and cultural autonomy, including for Estonian to be made the state language and for the recognition of an Estonian SSR citizenship (Ilves, 1988b). A fortnight later, a grassroots movement – the Estonian Popular Front in Support of Restructuring – was formed to promote these goals and it had tens of thousands of supporters. A quasi-political party, it remained outside the Estonian Communist Party and assumed the role of a loyal opposition committed to securing fundamental changes in Soviet nationalities policy. By mid-June, a commission of the Estonian Supreme Soviet had recommended that the long-banned flag of independent Estonia be restored and that Estonian be made an official language of the Estonian SSR.

In Latvia and Lithuania, where political conditions were more difficult, ferment also continued to grow. In early June, the Latvian Cultural Unions came out with their own bold demands in the form of a resolution to be submitted at the Party conference. Among other things, they demanded membership of the United Nations, a separate Latvian team for the Olympics, and the creation of national military units (Bungs 1988). Meanwhile in Lithuania, also at the beginning of June, a Lithuanian Restructuring Movement ('Sajudis') with similar objectives to its Estonian counterpart was founded (Girnius 1988). Within weeks it, too, showed that it was able to mobilise tens of thousands of supporters.

Faced with this impressive groundswell of patriotic opinion, the authorities in the Baltic republics were forced to retreat. On 16 June the conservative Estonian Party leader Karl Vaino was replaced by Vaino Vajlas, who promptly endorsed some of the goals of the Estonian Popular Front. On the eve of the Party Conference the Latvian and Lithuanian Party leaders also modified their tone and began expressing support for some of the demands being put forward by the unofficial patriotic forces.

In this way the Balts elevated the discussion about the nationalities question to another plane: they pressed for the enhancement of the political and economic rights of their nations and for meaning to be restored to the proclaimed sovereignty of the non-Russian republics. Other economic aspects of the national problem were also being raised elsewhere. In March 1988, the head of the Uzbek Writers' Union publicly criticised Moscow's continuing insistence on excessively high levels of cotton production, and blamed this pressure for the corruption and environmental problems in his republic (*Lit. Gaz.*, 9 March 1988).

While these extraordinary developments were taking place, the Gorbachev leadership stuck to the same line as before in nationalities policy. Despite the salience of the nationalities question, the theses adopted in May by the Central Committee as a platform for discussion in preparation for the XIX Party conference had a familiar ring to them. Apart from a vague reference to the need for the decentralisation of administrative functions 'in full measure to all forms of national statehood and autonomy', they offered nothing new (*Pravda*, 27 May 1988).

But the stance adopted by the Balts pushed matters forward. The far-reaching proposals for economic, cultural and political autonomy that were submitted to the Party conference by the Baltic delegates emboldened representatives from other Union republics to come out with their own demands. The result was the most candid discussion of the nationalities question at a major Party meeting since the 1920s. This time the non-Russians did not limit themselves to the issues of language and national culture. They insisted on a return to the form of federalism and equality between the nations that Lenin had championed in his last writings and on changes to this effect in the Soviet Constitution. As the Armenian Party leader Suren Arutyunyan put it: 'It is now urgently necessary to elaborate new thinking on the nationalities question' (*Pravda*, 1 July 1988). What was significant is that these positions were put forward by republican Party leaders, and not simply representatives of the non-Russian cultural elites.

The attitude of the non-Russian representatives at the Party Conference seems to have taken the Gorbachev leadership by surprise. The difference between what Gorbachev had to say on nationalities policy in his address to the gathering (*Pravda*, 29 June 1988) and what ended up in the conference's resolution on the national question (*Pravda*, 5 July 1988) was quite striking. Undoubtedly, the discussion of the nationalities question at the conference and the resolution on this issue marked a watershed. The non-Russians went away buoyed by the belief that their united stand had altered official attitudes and secured recognition of the necessity for a fundamental review of Soviet nationalities policy, and especially of the relationship between Moscow and the republics.

At a Central Committee plenum held at the end of July 1988 Gorbachev seemed to confirm this impression. Moreover, he also acknowledged for the first time the 'special acuteness of language problems', adding that 'it would clearly be worth preparing and submitting for broad discussion a draft Union law on the free development and equal utilisation of the languages of the peoples of the USSR' (*Pravda*, 30 July 1988).

The Balts, at any rate, sought to act in accordance with what they considered to be the spirit of the Party Conference's resolutions. Certainly, they seem to have interpreted the results of Politburo member Aleksandr Yakovlev's visit to Latvia and Lithuania in August as evidence that Moscow was prepared to tolerate what they were doing. In all three republics (a Latvian Popular Front was formed in early October), the popular fronts established themselves as mass organisations promoting national renewal and spearheading the quest for greater autonomy. In October all three held their inaugural congresses, which turned into remarkable demonstrations of free assembly, free speech and national assertiveness.

There were attempts in other republics to follow the Baltic example. At the end of May 1988, the Writers' Union of Moldavia issued an outspoken appeal to the Soviet leader which in many ways resembled the platform adopted by the Estonian cultural unions. During the summer of 1988 two new Moldavian informal organisations, the Democratic Movement in Support of Restructuring and the A. Mateevich Literary–Musical Union, organised a number of mass public meetings in Kishinev that were attended by hundreds of thousands of Moldavians. During June and July, similar meetings, though on a smaller scale, took place in the Western Ukrainian city of Lvov, and in Lvov and Kiev attempts were made to found Ukrainian popular fronts. In both republics the local authorities attempted to suppress the new independent patriotic movements.

The problem of Nagorno-Karabakh continued to simmer away. Armenian disappointment that the XIX Party Conference had not produced any new approach to this issue was expressed in new protests. On 5 July troops stormed Erevan airport to clear it of demonstrators and there were casualties among both the protesters and the security forces. On 18 July the Presidium of the USSR Supreme Soviet ruled that Nagorno-Karabakh should not be transferred to Armenia. Soviet television aired the proceedings and showed Gorbachev forcefully laying down the law and frequently interrupting Armenian and Azerbaidzhani representatives. In mid

September there was a new wave of strikes and demonstrations by Armenians in Nagorno-Karabakh and Erevan and further clashes between Armenians and Azerbaidzhanis broke out.

In October, the Gorbachev leadership unexpectedly came out with a draft law on amendments and additions to the Soviet constitution that contained provisions which, contrary to what had been stipulated in the resolutions of the XIX Party Conference, would have limited still further, rather than extended, the rights of the non-Russian republics (*Pravda*, 22 and 23 October 1988). The revamped USSR Supreme Soviet was in effect to be accorded the power not only to overrule the formal right of the Union republics to secede from the USSR, but also to annul decisions of republican governments if these were deemed not to correspond with the interests of the Union as a whole. Moreover, in such a case, it was to be empowered to proclaim a state of emergency 'in specific localities ... with the introduction where necessary of special forms of administration'. On top of this, the influence of the Russian republic in the new Council of Nationalities was to be increased.

Not surprisingly, the proposed changes to the Constitution provoked strong opposition in the Baltic republics and precipitated a major constitutional crisis. On 16 November the Estonian Supreme Soviet went as far as to adopt a 'Declaration of Sovereignty' and grant itself the right to veto laws issued from Moscow. This action was immediately condemned by the central media and declared unconstitutional by a commission of the USSR Supreme Soviet. During the tense fortnight that followed, the Supreme Soviets in Lithuania and Latvia also voiced their objections, though they did not go as far as their Estonian counterpart in asserting their 'sovereignty'. In Lithuania, however, the Supreme Soviet did use the occasion to proclaim Lithuanian the state language of the republic and to designate the flag and hymn of independent Lithuania as the official flag and anthem of the Lithuanian SSR.

Opposition to the constitutional changes was not, however, limited to the Baltic republics. There were mass protests in Georgia and on 24 November the Georgian SSR Supreme Soviet also voiced its reservations about the proposed amendments. Demonstrations against the constitutional changes also took place in the Moldavian capital Kishinev.

While the constitutional crisis was unfolding, the Armenian-Azerbaidzhani conflict flared up again, and this time three soldiers were among the victims of the ethnic violence. There were new mass protests in Erevan and Baku (where the protesters are reported to have carried portraits of Iranian leader Ayatollah Khomeini and Islamic flags) and curfews were imposed on the two capitals as well as on three other Azerbaidzhani cities. On 24 November, Armenia's Supreme Soviet also expressed its opposition to the proposed constitutional changes and called on the USSR Supreme Soviet to make provisions for Nagorno-Karabakh to decide its own future.

On 26 November Gorbachev delivered a tough speech at a session of the Presidium of the USSR Supreme Soviet in which he sought to bring the recalcitrant republics into line. In his address, which was later shown on Soviet television, he described the recent Estonian actions as 'political adventurism nudging Estonia onto a fatal path of economic isolationism and destroying the country's unitary economy'. 'Our future is not in weakening ties among the republics', he stressed, 'but on the contrary, in strengthening them and expanding cooperation.' Alluding also to the conflict in the Transcaucasus, he warned that national discord could be 'disastrous' and 'put in jeopardy our *perestroika*'. It was necessary, he added, to 'stop demagogues, those who embark on political speculation by taking advantage of the processes of democratisation and *glasnost*.

Moscow had, however, begun indicating that it was prepared to make some concessions in order to defuse what even Gorbachev described as a crisis. For all his bluster, the Soviet leader did inject a conciliatory element into his speech. He emphasised that Moscow had modified some of the proposed amendments to the Constitution and acknowledged 'the legitimacy of the many real questions which Estonia has come to face and which demand solution' (Soviet television, 27 November 1988). Three days later, at a plenary meeting of the USSR Supreme Soviet, his tone was more placatory and he even admitted that some of the problems could have been avoided if the centre had acted more thoughtfully and tactfully (*Pravda*, 30 November 1988; Sheehy 1988). The crisis, however, was not really resolved but ended in a temporary uneasy compromise. The position adopted by Estonia's Supreme Soviet was declared null and void, yet the Estonians continued to uphold its validity. Moscow did make certain concessions by watering down some of the proposed constitutional changes but this could not alter the impression that the Gorbachev leadership had acted hastily, insensitively and not in particularly good faith.

Gorbachev deferred tackling the crucial issues until the summer of 1989 when, as *Pravda* announced on 12 November, a special Central

Committee plenum was to be devoted to charting the future course of Soviet nationalities policy. The only exception was the Kremlin's decision in December 1988 to round up the leaders of the Armenian 'Karabakh Committee' and the main instigators of the Azerbaidzhani protests.

1989 began with trouble of one sort or another brewing in Moldavia in the southwest of the USSR to Tadzhikistan in the eastern part of Soviet Central Asia. In the Baltic republics, the Russian communities had organised their own popular fronts as a counter-balance to those of the indigenous nations and were voicing their concern about the 'nationalism' of the Balts. In the Ukraine, Belo-russia and Moldavia a gaping rift had opened up between the nationally-minded cultural intelligentsia and the conservative repub-lican authorities, who were still trying to stifle popular forces for national renewal. The situation was particularly acute in Moldavia, where many thousands of demonstrators were taking to the streets to call for an end to Russification and curbs on the inflow of Russians.

In February in the key Ukrainian republic, leading Ukrainian writers defied their republican Party authorities and published a draft programme for a Baltic-type Ukrainian popular movement in support of restructuring (*Literaturna Ukraina*, 15 February 1989). During a visit to the Ukraine later that month, Gorbachev warned that a flare-up of national tensions in this crucial republic would mean the end of restructuring and would put the cohesion of the Soviet multinational state to a severe test (Soviet television, 22 February 1989).

The situation in Armenia and Azerbaidzhan remained tense, and in Georgia, national feeling continued to run high. In the Central Asian republics there were signs of a more assertive attitude on the part of the national elites. It was being reflected in indignation about the scale and duration of the crackdown against corruption, resent-ment of Moscow's economic policies in the region and the serious environmental damage it has caused, as well as in concern about improving the status of the local languages and protecting the Islamic heritage. On 3 February, hundreds of Soviet Muslims demonstrated in Tashkent against the head of official Islam in Central Asia, Mufti Babakhan, and succeeded in having him replaced. Later that month there were ethnic riots in the Tadzhik capital, Dushanbe (*Komso-molskaya pravda*, 22 February 1989). On 19 March, there was a large demonstration in Tashkent by Uzbeks pressing demands that Uzbek be made Uzbekistan's state language. A new national movement also began to develop among another traditionally Muslim people, the six-million-strong Tatars. There were also numerous other national problems that were pressing for attention; among others: the un-resolved Crimean Tatar question, the issue of restoring an auton-omous region for the USSR's ethnic Germans; the plight of some of the small Siberian peoples, and a territorial dispute between Uzbekis-tan and Tadzhikistan. In one crucial area, however, there were signs that Moscow was being forced to yield. In the Baltic republics the local languages had already been made official languages and at the beginning of 1989 it appeared that in both the Ukraine and Moldavia the republican authorities might also give way to popular pressure on this issue.

The debate about the future direction of Soviet nationalities policy was also intensifying. During 1988 certain hitherto sacrosanct princi-ples, such as the notion of 'the Soviet people' and 'Russian-native language bilingualism' came under attack (e.g. Mati Hint, *Druzhba narodov*, no. 5, 1988, pp. 237–42). Moreover, various non-Russians had denounced what they described as 'the Brezhnev–Suslov' assimi-lationist approach to the nationalities policy (e.g. Dmytro Pavlychko, *Literaturna Ukraina*, 21 July 1988). What emerged from all the various discussions of the nationalities question in journals, news-papers, or at conferences or meetings of writers, was the extent of the division over what constitutes the essence of this problem and what solutions should be advocated.

Against this troubled background, Moscow seemed to moderate its tone on the national question and offer reassurances to the non-Russians. On 6 January, speaking before a gathering of representa-tives of the USSR's intellectual elite, Gorbachev explicitly disavowed the concept of the 'merging' (*sliyanie*) of the nations of the USSR and stated that the Party 'cannot permit even the smallest nation to disappear' or 'the language of even the smallest nation to be lost' (*Pravda*, 7 January 1989). Four days later, the Party Central Commit-tee issued an appeal to the Party and to the Soviet people in which, among other things, it pledged that at the forthcoming plenum on nationalities policy it would 'adopt a broad programme' that would result in 'a considerable expansion of the rights of the republics' and their sovereignty. It also put forward the slogan 'a strong centre and strong republics', which, despite the apparent inherent contradiction, is to be the new underlying principle for reform in the nationality sphere (*Pravda*, 13 January 1989).

When, however, on 14 March, *Pravda* published details of draft plans to increase the economic autonomy of the republics, it turned out that the extent of decentralisation that the Kremlin is prepared to tolerate is rather limited. The scheme envisages that Moscow will retain control over most heavy industry and leave the republics with only limited control over their own budgets. Baltic representatives promptly expressed their disappointment, charging that the reforms would not go far enough. Soon afterwards, there was a further blow to the hopes of the non-Russians. On 8 April, Radio Moscow reported that a special working commission of the USSR Supreme Soviet had rejected calls for a new Union treaty that would provide a new basis for relations between the republics and Moscow.

While preparations for the plenum on national relations continued, the Soviet Union was shaken by another major crisis in this sphere, this time in Georgia. On 9 April troops were sent in against Georgian demonstrators in Tbilisi who were calling for broader national rights and protesting against the campaign by the 90 000-strong Abkhaz minority to have its autonomous republic separated from Georgia and upgraded to the status of a Union republic. At least 20 people were killed and many injured. A curfew was imposed on the Georgian capital and leading activists were rounded up. Soviet Foreign Minister, Eduard Shevardnadze, himself a Georgian, was sent to the republic to help restore calm. On 14 April both the Georgian Party leader and prime minister were replaced.

Much of what Gorbachev and the Party have said about changes in nationality policy has remained vague or ambiguous. What is important, though, is that Gorbachev has come to realise that the success of *perestroika* hinges on how the Party handles the nationalities question. Reluctant to budge in this area of its own accord, the Gorbachev leadership has in fact been pushed along by released pent-up forces from below and made to address this intractable issue. Having promised that nationality policy will be reviewed and modified at the Central Committee plenum on the national question, the question is whether, after showing so little initiative and new thinking in this sphere up till now, Gorbachev will somehow find the room for manoeuvre to offer the non-Russians a new deal, for that is ultimately what is called for.

# 9 *Perestroika* and the Soviet Armed Forces

## STEPHEN DALZIEL

### INTRODUCTION

According to official pronouncements, the Soviet armed forces, along with the whole of Soviet society, have been actively engaged in *perestroika* since March 1985. Nevertheless, those pronouncements also admit that the pace of reform is not proceeding as quickly as it should. *Perestroika* in the armed forces seems to have reached a state which can euphemistically be described as 'stability'. It would be more accurate, however, to use the term which now describes the Brezhnev era: stagnation. Official confirmation of the poor state of affairs came about the slow response of the armed forces to the Party's demand for tighter discipline (*Pravda*, 14 October 1988).

### THE XIX PARTY CONFERENCE

The conference was the focal point of Soviet political life in 1988 and thus an obvious starting point for an examination of the state of *perestroika* in the Soviet armed forces. Mention of the army in the conference proceedings was conspicuous by its absence. This was not a slight on the army's prestige but a recognition that, for the time being at least, the military leadership has accepted earlier demands that have been placed upon it by *perestroika* – economically and politically. Furthermore, as far as day-to-day life goes, what is relevant for society is relevant in large part for the armed forces, too. Although the conference was attended by a reasonably large contingent of military officers, only one spoke. This was Lieutenant-General Boris Gromov, designated as an army commander, who is in charge of the Limited Contingent of Soviet Troops in Afghanistan. More than anything else it was a plea to society to have more sympathy for soldiers returning from Afghanistan. It was also an attempt to separate the army from the political questions that are now being asked over the involvement there. One speaker at the conference, G. Ya. Baklanov, criticised the political decision to go into Afghanistan, and the way it was handled. Some candidate members of the Politburo, he claimed, learnt about the decision to send in troops only from the newspapers (Gorbachev was a candidate member of the Politburo at the time). Both speeches are in *Pravda*, 2 July 1988. General Gromov's message was that the political decision had nothing to do with the army. They had reacted to orders in true military fashion, had carried out their duties honourably, and those who had served there should be given due credit for doing their duty before the Motherland, and not be caught up in the political whys and wherefores. Aside from this, the conference had little direct significance for the military, although an analysis of developments since the XXVII Party Congress shows that this was hardly surprising, because the major effects of *perestroika* on the Soviet military establishment had already been achieved.

## THE ARMY IS SUBJECTED TO *PERESTROIKA*

It is now possible to point to a definite period when the Party put the armed forces firmly in the grip of *perestroika*, both economically and politically. The subjection of the Gorbachev military establishment to *perestroika* is arguably one of the greatest successes of Gorbachev's policy so far. This period begins with the XXVII Party Congress, in February–March 1986, and was completed by the appointment of Army General Yazov as USSR Minister of Defence in May 1987. The latter date was certainly not part of any preconceived plan. Herr Rust's arrival on Red Square in his Cessna merely gave Gorbachev the reason to replace the ageing Sokolov with the Minister of Defence he wanted.

Before the XXVII Party Congress there was a heated debate going on in the USSR over the place of the military in the Soviet economy. Military leaders were stressing that the current strategic situation was akin to that of 1941 when the Soviet Union fell victim to a surprise attack by a capitalist power. If this were the case, the armed forces must be provided with all the necessary weaponry to defend the country, even if this were at the expense of other parts of society. A particularly blatant example of this was an article by Colonel-General

Makhmut Gareev, a Deputy Chief of the General Staff, in the important *Voenno–Istoricheskii Zhurnal* (Military–Historical Journal), in November 1985. The article was entitled: 'Konstantin Simonov as a Military Writer'. Using quotations from characters in Simonov's novels, General Gareev clearly argued for greater expenditure on the military to be forthcoming. One character defending the Brest Fortress against the advancing Nazis in 1941 declared almost with his final breath that if he had only known that the Red Army was so short of supplies he would have given up his comfortable life and lived in one room on bread and water.

Gorbachev, it would appear, also added historical perspective to his view of the situation, but went one decade further back. The lesson to be learnt from this was that the USSR must have the right weapons for the right time, and that this could come about only if a sound economic base were established first for the whole of society. This was what Stalin had done during the first Five Year Plan and, as a result, when war came in 1941, although the Soviet Union was initially surprised, it had the right weapons eventually to win the war. An example from the same period of the reverse being true, was provided by Italy. Having chosen to modernise her armed forces at the beginning of the 1930s Italy found by the outbreak of war that it had outdated equipment. If ten years could make such a difference in the 1930s, what technological developments would there be between now and the end of the century? Giving the armed forces all the tanks, aeroplanes and ships they wanted now could leave the Soviet Union with the greatest collection of museum pieces by the year 2000, especially if the West goes ahead with its development of weapons based on new physical principles.

It is quite clear from the Soviet press that after the Congress it was Gorbachev's view that had prevailed. The principle had been established that the country's future military development was inextricably linked to the overall development of the national economy. As was stated in a commentary in *Voenno–Istorcheskii Zhurnal* on the role of the Congress in strengthening the defensive capacity of the Soviet Union: 'Only a strong, modern economic base is capable of providing the opportunity for the maintenance and improvement of the armed forces, and for providing them with the necessary quantities of modern weapons and military technology (April 1986, p. 6). As if to illustrate the historical nature of this link between the military and civilian economies, the then Minister of Defence, Marshal Sergei Sokolov, chose to single out for praise in his order celebrating

Victory Day on 9 May 1987, not the soldiers who had been in the front line fighting the Germans, but the civilian workers in the rear who had kept up the supplies of metal, bread, fuel, raw materials and armaments. One of the clearest admissions of the military's acceptance of the new situation came in October 1988 from General Gareev. When questioned about his article on Konstantin Simonov he stated that times had changed since then, and that both he and the Soviet military now accepted the new economic reality (interview with the author for the BBC World Service, 18 October 1988).

Just as the Soviet military leadership have been forced to accept their place in the economic development of the USSR, so they have been able to say very little against the increase of Party authority over the armed forces. It has always been accepted that the CPSU is the leader in all spheres of Soviet life, including military matters. Nevertheless, the age of *perestroika* ushered in by the XXVII Party Congress has been accompanied by greater and greater emphasis on the party's leading role. As Lieutenant-General Zhilin, then head of the Institute of Military History, said when commenting on the significance of the Congress for the Soviet armed forces: 'The statute on the leading role of the CPSU in all matters concerning the defence of the socialist Fatherland occupies an important place in Leninist teachings' (*Voenno–Istoricheskii Zhurnal*, July 1986, p. 7). The clearest display of the extent to which the armed forces had been placed under Party control came on 7 November 1986. At the parade to celebrate the anniversary of the October Revolution it had become traditional for the line-up on top of the Lenin mausoleum to be headed by the Party General Secretary and the Minister of Defence, flanked on one side by the military leadership and on the other by members of the Politburo and other political dignitaries. For the first time, military representation was reduced to a total of four officers, the four First Deputy Ministers of Defence. (Marshal Sokolov, then Minister of Defence, was prevented by illness from attending the parade). After General Lushev had delivered this address, he retired to the end of the row to join his military colleagues. On this occasion Gorbachev did not replace the absent military commanders with anyone, thus allowing more elbow room for the Politburo. In 1987, to mark the Soviet Union's 70th anniversary, foreign communist dignitaries were invited on to the mausoleum, where they took precedence over the military in the line-up. 1988 saw a similar situation to that of two years previously, with the address being given by Minister of Defence Yazov.

Party influence was seen again in the replacement of Marshal Sokolov as Minister of Defence by Army General Yazov. In the wake of Mathias Rust's flight to Moscow, Gorbachev and the political leadership were quick to retire Sokolov and replace him with the man who was clearly their choice. Yazov's appointment has the mark of *perestroika*. He came to the post of Minister of Defence from that of Chief of the Main Directorate of Cadres of the Ministry of Defence. Although he had held the position only since February 1987, he was appointed to it following the January CC plenum, which brought to prominence the question of *perestroika* and cadres. In the Soviet armed forces this meant that the question of training, of officers in particular, and the 'activisation of the human factor' throughout the Soviet military were of greater importance than ever. Yazov had been put in charge of the training of personnel because, firstly, he already had had some experience working in the Directorate (1974–6) and also because he had long been stressing the values now considered the 'right' ones, such as the importance of the officer in decision-making and caring for his troops. When he was still commanding the Far East Military District he stressed this in an article in the Soviet solider's magazine *Sovetskii Voin*, no. 18, September 1986. General Yazov's meeting with Gorbachev in the Far East in July 1986 no doubt also greatly helped his candidature. However, if he was Gorbachev's man in May 1987, General Yazov has subsequently not turned into Gorbachev's puppet. Whilst he and the other Soviet military leaders have undoubtedly accepted the principle that, if the Soviet armed forces are going to modernise properly in order to keep up with the West, they must accept their place as a part of the Soviet economy, Yazov has not proved to be the slave of *perestroika* or *glasnost*. In discussions on *glasnost* in particular, Yazov has fervently fought the army's corner. At a meeting with editors of military journals in June 1987 Yazov made it quite clear that, whilst the editors should address problems that occur in the armed forces, the treatment of these problems should be positive. Don't just say that a problem exists, show also encouraging ways by which it is being eradicated (*Krasnaya Zvezda*, 20 June 1987). In December 1987, the Minister of Defence tried to do this to civilian editors, too, but received a nasty shock. Civilians do not have the same respect for a military uniform, and cannot be ordered around in the same way as professionals in or connected to the military. Whether for effect, or out of genuine frustration, when criticising the journal *Ogenek* for an article which depicted a general as an alcoholic, he even wiped away a tear (Soviet TV, 16 January 1988; see SWB/SU/0053/B/1). Yazov may be an old sentimentalist who also believes in the Party but the reverse is not true.

Despite Yazov's defence of the military from what he perceives as any attacks from outside, another indication that the Party has the armed forces where they want them has been shown by the maintenance of Yazov's political and military position. He has remained a candidate member of the Politburo; he is still an Army General (yet some officers occupying junior positions to him are marshals); and he has not been made Hero of the Soviet Union, something which Brezhnev was fond of distributing (four of them to himself), but which today must be earned (notably in Afghanistan). All of these points suggest the stabilisation of the military position mentioned earlier.

## MILITARY DEVELOPMENTS SINCE YAZOV'S APPOINTMENT

Much of what has occurred in the Soviet military establishment since May 1987 has coincided with the period of *perestroika*, rather than happened because of it. But *perestroika* is not only about making the Soviet economy work properly. It is also – as the title of Gorbachev's book makes clear – about new political thinking. Certainly, military pronouncements of 1987 and 1988 do reflect this. Some believe that the Warsaw Pact statement on military doctrine of May 1987 marked a new defensive stage in the development of the Pact's military thinking, although a close examination of the document does not support this (*Pravda*, 30 May 1987). The statement did not say a great deal that was new, and appears now to have been a stopgap, put out whilst genuine thoughts on the development of doctrine were being discussed. It was not enough for the statement to say that Warsaw Pact (i.e. Soviet) military doctrine was defensive in nature. The Soviets have always maintained that their doctrine is defensive. Futhermore, the declaration did not remove the rider that has always been put on this idea – that whilst the doctrine is defensive, it also guarantees that the Pact should be strong enough to deal a 'crushing rebuff' to any would-be aggressor. The declaration did not move the Warsaw Pact away from the idea that attack is the best form of defence.

The new political thinking was certainly reflected in General

Yazov's article in *Pravda* on 8 February 1988: 'On the Military Balance of Forces and Nuclear Missile Parity'. For the first time, Yazov put forward the idea that conventional arms control, so vital because of the destructive power of modern conventional weapons, could be achieved by a 'trade-off' of different weapons systems. He admitted that the Warsaw Pact had more tanks in Europe than NATO, but stated that NATO had more aircraft. Instead, therefore, of simply counting numbers of analogous pieces of equipment, he suggested that the Pact could give up some of its tanks in return for NATO removing some of its aircraft. Whilst the military argument put forward by the West shows that, nice though the idea may sound to the layman, it is not such a practical proposition as it appears. It is, nevertheless, an example of new thinking.

More significant for the future may be the proposals put forward by Marshal Sergei Akhromeev, then Chief of the General Staff, during his visit to the USA in July 1988. At the press conference which marked the end of the Marshal's visit, the atmosphere was one of friendship and a great deal more mutual understanding than had been evident before. Akhromeev recognised that in the past the Soviet Union had given military signals which had been interpreted in the West as aggressive. This was particularly true, he said, in the conduct of military exercises. The USSR would now make a conscious effort to change this, in order to foster greater understanding and better relations between East and West. The cynical may still dismiss this as mere Soviet rhetoric, amounting to little more than giving exercises less aggressive-sounding names than *Zapad-81* (the West-81). But the atmosphere in which it was said suggests a genuine hope – and indeed belief – by Akhromeev that the new political thinking could lead to real restructuring – *perestroika* – in East–West relations (CNN TV, 11 July 1988, 1400GMT). Marshal Akhromeev's visit to the USA was reciprocated by a visit to the USSR by US Defence Secretary Frank Carlucci. This highlighted a curious reversal of roles that occurred in the Soviet military high command. Carlucci's visit followed a similar pattern to that of Akhromeev. The Marshal was shown over the B-1 bomber; Carlucci examined the Blackjack. Akhromeev went to sensitive US military bases; Carlucci was the first American ever to be allowed a close-up look at the Black Sea Fleet. But one interesting fact about this military goodwill exchange seemed to be ignored. Carlucci's opposite number in Moscow was Army General Dmitry Yazov, not Akhromeev. Marshal Sergei Akhromeev was Chief of the General Staff and corresponds to Admiral Crowe, his host in the US.

This highlighted the greater political role that Akhromeev began to play in 1988. This was a move away from the traditional roles of the posts of Minister of Defence and Chief of the General Staff. In most countries, including the USSR, the Minister of Defence is a political appointment. He is a member of the government and liaises between that body and the armed forces. He is often (though not currently in the Soviet Union) a civilian. The Chief of the General Staff is usually the most senior military officer, and is concerned with major military decisions which affect the internal workings of the armed forces.

Akhromeev took on tasks that would normally be fulfilled by the Minister of Defence. The trip to the USA was a good example of this. Akhromeev proved himself a skilful diplomat and established a genuine rapport with American military leaders. His approach showed a much greater understanding of Western sensibilities than that of General Yazov, who maintained far more the stance of the military man than the politician. Marshal Akhromeev also played a much more prominent role in the arms-control field than would be expected from the Chief of the General Staff.

It came as a surprise, therefore, when Marshal Akhromeev announced his retirement on the day that Mikhail Gorbachev declared to the United Nations that the Soviet Army was to be reduced by half a million men (*Pravda*, 8 December 1988). Inevitably there was speculation that this was a gesture of protest by the Marshal. He had in the past declared himself to be against unilateral cuts and thus many felt that Gorbachev's action was more than he could stand. But it seems that there was more to Akhromeev's retirement than simply the reasons of ill-health which were cited. It may be that he was sacrificed to appease more conservative elements within the military. Before the announcement there was no sign that Akhromeev's political star was on the wane. Just one week earlier he was one of only two military men appointed to the new CC commissions. He was made a member of the Commission for Foreign Affairs whilst General Lizichev, Head of the Military–Political Directorate, was appointed to the Commission for Party Organisation and Personnel Policy. General Yazov failed to be nominated to any commission. Furthermore when Akhromeev's retirement was announced, it was said that he was to become a personal adviser to Gorbachev on military affairs. When Gorbachev made his next statement on arms reductions, at a meeting with members of the Trilateral Commission in Moscow on 18 January 1989, the only military person present was Marshal Akhromeev (*Vremya*, Soviet TV, 18 January 1989, 1800GMT).

Given the climate of the times, it was not a great surprise that Marshal Akhromeev was replaced by a young, little-known general, Colonel-General Mikhail Moiseev. In some ways this was a return to the early days of the General Staff. After its establishment shortly before the Second World War the Chief of the General Staff tended to be a general in his mid- to late-forties. As more officers gained experience, so the age rose. The appointment of the 49-year-old Moiseev would seem to indicate a desire to revitalise the General Staff.

In terms of age, more surprising was the promotion in February 1989 of General Petr Lushev to the post of Commander-in-Chief of the Warsaw Pact Forces, to replace Marshal Kulikov. At the age of 65 Lushev is one of 'the 1923 generation', as was Akhromeev. Unlike Akhromeev, however, General Lushev seems to enjoy good health. There also seems to be little doubt about his genuine commitment to *perestroika*.

## WITHDRAWAL FROM AFGHANISTAN

The start of the withdrawal of Soviet troops from Afghanistan is another development which cannot be credited to *perestroika*, yet which is a definite example of the new political thinking. The proposal for the withdrawal was described as such by Marshal Viktor Kulikov, writing in *Krasnaya Zvezda* on 21 February 1988 in honour of the seventieth anniversary of the Soviet armed forces. There are undoubtedly sound domestic reasons for the Soviet Army to get out of Afghanistan. The mood in Soviet society is now very much against the continuation of the war, and, even if it is accepted that the decision to go in was a political and not a military one, the army's continued presence is not improving its image in the eyes of the people. Nevertheless, there are strong foreign policy reasons for the withdrawal too. It was difficult for the Soviet leadership to convince the rest of the world that the Soviet Union was adopting a more defensive stance with over 100 000 troops fighting on foreign soil.

Domestically, the Afghan War has raised a number of problems in Soviet society which must be addressed by the new political thinking. For too long there was far too little reporting of events in Afghanistan, which led to ignorance and indifference on the part of many

Soviet citizens. On 9 September 1987 *Pravda* admitted that this had been official policy, when it stated that it was good to see reports now being published on the problems faced by Afghan veterans returning to the USSR. For too long, it was admitted, this had not been reported in the press, but then 'those were the regulations'. The uncaring attitude with which many of those returning from Afghanistan were met led to deep resentment, as ex-soldiers felt that they deserved credit for fulfilling their duty before the Motherland. In 1987 this developed into a coherent movement, dubbed the *Afghantsy* by the Soviet media. In October the first conference of the new movement was held in Tashkent, and was given wide and sympathetic treatment by the Soviet press. Official recognition afforded the *Afghantsy* greater impetus, and in *Literaturnaya Rossiya* on 6 May 1988 the writer Aleksandr Prokhanov described them as 'an ideological force'. Pressure from the movement in autumn 1988 led to the establishment of a memorial in Moscow to the victims of the Afghan War. Hopes for an Afghanistan campaign medal, however, were dashed in December 1988 when it was announced that Afghan veterans would receive a non-specific medal and a diploma for their services. Whilst this was some recognition, it fell a long way short of the expectations of many.

## *PERESTROIKA* AT THE GRASSROOTS LEVEL

When *perestroika* was first applied to the everyday running of the Soviet armed forces, it appeared to be little more than a new tag attached to the old cries of improving combat-readiness and discipline, and encouraging officers to be closer to their men. Some officers, therefore, saw *perestroika* as irrelevant to the armed forces. But the messages from senior Soviet commanders on Soviet Armed Forces' Day on 23 February 1987 made it quite clear that this attitude would not be tolerated. Whereas in the past mere lip-service to these ideas might have been accepted, under *perestroika* something concrete would have to be done. '*Perestroika* signifies decisively overcoming stagnant phenomena in combat readiness and in the training of troops and naval forces', wrote Major-General Danilenko in *Krasnaya Zvezda* on 19 August 1987. By January 1988 there could be no question that this was the accepted case, even though there was still a long way to go before everyone adapted to *perestroika*. It was no exaggeration when Army General Sukhorukov (Yazov's successor at the Cadres Directorate) stated that by the end of 1987 *perestroika* had touched every facet of life in the armed forces (*Krasnaya Zvezda*, 23 January 1988). But there is a great difference between *perestroika* touching life and changing it, and Sukhorukov himself was quick to admit that this had yet to happen.

Since *perestroika* is a political process, it follows that the lead must be given by the CPSU members. The Soviet officer corps represents the largest percentage concentration of communists of any group in the USSR. Over 76 per cent of Soviet officers are Party members, and a further 15 per cent are in the Komsomol (*Sovetskaya Rossiya*, 21 February 1987). The basis for building *perestroika* in the armed forces is the regiment or ship, and it is the responsibility of the primary Party organisations at this level. Of great importance, too, is the Komsomol, since, because of their age, very few conscript soldiers are members of the Party, but the majority are in the Komsomol. In his speech to the XX Komsomol Congress, in April 1987, Mikhail Gorbachev noted that in some places the organisation seemed to be out of touch with Soviet youth:

> At times, when we observe the work of Komsomol activists we are under the impression that young people walk along one side of the street and Komsomol activists along the other, sometimes even in the opposite direction (*Pravda*, 17 April 1987).

This is a tendency which has been noted in the armed forces, too. Komsomol activists have been criticised for displaying a low level of initiative, and for not doing enough to improve discipline. But however much primary Party organisations and Komsomol cells may be criticised, it is up to individuals to ensure that they are putting their best efforts into *perestroika*. Clearly this is still not happening. As with managers in industry, the Soviet officer is used to passing the buck to a higher commander. Colonel Kozlov summed it up in an article in *Krasnaya Zvezda* on 16 January 1988:

> Many have got used to the idea that they are 'cogs'. And if one thinks for everyone then the rest will stop thinking. When one decides for all, then the rest will happily await instructions.

One reason why many officers are clearly content to remain as 'cogs' is because of the confusion which *perestroika* has brought over the question of the relationship between *demokratizatsiya* (democratisation) and *edinonachalie* (one-man command). The accepted principle of command is that the officer in charge at any level is responsible for decision-making. But under the idea of democratisation, everyone is supposed to be able to have their say. Many officers see an inherent contradiction here, claiming that either democratisation applies, and they should have the right to affect decision-making, or *edinonachalie* is the accepted way, and they bow to the commander in everything, as well as passing the buck to him for everything. Despite efforts by senior officers to explain that these two concepts are not mutually exclusive, a great deal of suspicion still exists amongst officers. The continuing debate was highlighted in late 1988 by the publication of an interview with Army General Yazov which took up nearly half of *Krasnaya Zvezda*. The banner headline summed it up: *Demokratizatsiya i edinonachalie* (20 November 1988).

One way in which attempts are being made to overcome the problem of officers refusing to take decisions, is to reform the training system in military colleges and academies. This also fits in with the decisions of the January 1987 CC plenum and the stress it laid upon training in all areas of society. But there are still problems. One cadet wrote to *Krasnaya Zvezda* complaining that although he had heard the word *perestroika* used forty times in one day he could still see no changes (23 June 1987). Although colleges are trying to modify training methods, they are still beset by difficulties in procuring equipment. This is a problem familiar to other areas of the armed forces, and there are regular complaints in the military press about it.

As for the soldiers themselves, the biggest difficulty the officers find is in persuading them that they have a real role to play in *perestroika* whilst they are in the army. One soldier wrote to *Krasnaya Zvezda*:

> In the army *perestroika* affects only the officers and the commanders. Our duty is a soldier's one; whatever they order us to do, we'll do (21 January 1988).

This attitude is, of course, strongly criticised. A soldier is expected to participate actively in *perestroika*. The first stage in this is proper preparation for service, both physically and mentally, before he is called up. On the former point there is grave cause for concern, particularly in some areas of the country. Figures released at the end of 1987 showed that over 50 per cent of conscripts who came into the armed forces with the 'Ready for Labour and Defence' (GTO) certificate from school did not deserve it. In one oblast in Uzbekistan this fell to as low as 3.2 per cent (*Sovetskii Voin*, no. 18, September 1987).

Mentally many soldiers dread the call-up because of the menace of bullying. Although it was long recognised that this went on (a problem not unique to the Soviet Army) it was rarely discussed. *Glasnost* has meant that the problem cannot any longer be ignored. After references appeared in the military press during 1987 to 'non-regulation relations among the troops', the whole question of the organised system of bullying known as *dedovshchina* was revealed in a story by Yury Polyakov which appeared in the journal *Yunost* in November 1987. Although the military is trying now to prove that the problem is in hand – in October 1988 the Minister of Defence, General Yazov, even intervened personally on behalf of one soldier who had been the victim of *dedovshchina* (*Izvestiya*, 21 October 1988) – the publicity that the question has received has made many more young men even more reluctant to serve. Obviously a soldier who is not keen to serve is unlikely to put his best efforts into making *perestroika* a success.

The situation regarding *perestroika* at the grassroots level of the armed forces in 1988 was summed up by General Yazov in February and May. In February, on Soviet Armed Forces' Day, Yazov defined how *perestroika* should be progressing:

We see the main task of this stage [of *perestroika*] in raising the armed forces to a qualitatively new level, especially in terms of an overall improvement in the activity of military cadres, decisively raising the effectiveness of military and political training, and ensuring strict observation of the regulations everywhere' (*Pravda*, 23 February 1988).

In practice, however, Yazov made it clear that there are still serious shortcomings when he addressed the Group of Soviet Forces in Germany Party Conference in May:

among GSFG troops a radical *perestroika* has still not come about in the organisation of combat training.... The influence of ... communists ... upon ... combat training remains rather ineffective. Formalism is being overcome extremely slowly in socialist competition (*Krasnaya Zvezda*, 25 May 1988).

At what was meant to be a celebration to choose the GSFG delegates for the XIX Party Conference, Yazov's words sounded very tough indeed. What makes this even more significant, is that GSFG is supposed to have a higher level of training and discipline than other parts of the Soviet Army. All its units are at Category 1 state of readiness. (This means that they have 80–100 per cent of their troop complement and could be expected to go into action at short notice, if necessary.) It is not overstretching the conclusion to ask if this is the state of affairs there, then how bad are things in Category 3 units, where there may be as little as 20 per cent of combat strength?

## CONCLUSION

Just as society cannot sit back and ignore the demands of *perestroika*, so the military are obliged to put greater effort into achieving genuine successes. However, they face many problems. The military's present standing in society is not high. The image of the Soviet officer is no longer a proud one. Many citizens were shocked that Mathias Rust was able to fly all the way to Red Square unchallenged. There was a feeling that, if the military cannot even defend us from one small plane, what could they do against a real threat? Furthermore, greater publicity of bullying and poor treatment of conscripts has made many young men reluctant to do their military sevice, and many parents reluctant to send them. This is not to say that Soviet society has turned against military service overnight. There are still many – probably the majority – who still agree in principle with the idea of military service, but they feel that conditions must be improved. Some youngsters, on the other hand, have been accused of displaying 'pacifist tendencies', whilst others have declared that they are not against doing their military service, but would rather do it by correspondence course! The Soviet General Staff will also be worried by reports from Eastern Europe where certain countries, notably Poland, are introducing a form of community service for conscientious objectors and others opposed to military service. This will take the place of service in the armed forces.

The biggest problem facing the Soviet military in the long run is, ironically, tied in with the 'new political thinking'. Soviet citizens (and therefore the conscripts of today and tomorrow) are being told that the international situation is improving. As well as the political significance of arms-control agreements, the Soviet people have witnessed genuine human contacts between East and West which show them that chances of living peacefully with the capitalists are genuinely possible. When he was in Washington in December 1987, Gorbachev stopped his cavalcade, got out of the car and met real Americans whose genuine wish was for peace. In May 1988, those same Soviet citizens turned on their television sets to see General Secretary Gorbachev and President Reagan standing on Red Square with their arms round each other in a gesture of friendship. Their own leaders are telling them that not only the need, but also the possibility for these contacts is improving, and that both the governments and the peoples of East and West should have greater contact. From the military's point of view, Yazov explained in his Victory Day article that this must be so:

> Nowadays it is not only possible, but it is essential to unite the efforts of all states behind the common goal of liquidating the threat [of a nuclear catastrophe] and thus behind the goal of the preservation of life (*Pravda*, 9 May 1988).

But surely the rationale of the Soviet armed forces rests upon defending the Soviet Union from a possible attack by the capitalists? Indeed, Marshal Kulikov complained in his article on the occasion of the seventieth anniversary of the Soviet armed forces that:

> A certain section of conscripts display political naiveté, especially as regards the imperialist threat (*Krasnaya Zvezda*, 21 February 1988).

There is an explicit contradiction here which the Soviet military is not going to find easy to deal with in the long term. If the 'new political thinking' really does achieve its international aim, of bringing East and West closer together and genuinely reducing the threat of war in the consciousness of the Soviet people, then the military is going to find that exhortations to defend the Motherland from the capitalist threat fall on deaf ears. Given that many people already hold the military in low esteem because of the bad image it has gained in recent years, this could have very serious consequences. Ironically, it would seem that the military's only hope of regaining its place as a respected part of Soviet society is to carry out a thorough *perestroika* of every aspect of its activity – not in order to develop better discipline for greater combat-readiness, but to develop a more disciplined approach to its own people.

# 10 Foreign Policy

## MARGOT LIGHT

### INTRODUCTION

The warm international atmosphere at the end of the 1980s bears little resemblance to the second cold war that characterised the beginning of the decade. To a considerable extent this is the result of changes in Soviet foreign policy. Soviet diplomacy has changed dramatically in the last four years. Indeed, the foreign policy reforms have been as profound as in the domestic economy and politics. The most obvious consequence has been a resumption of East–West detente. But there have been other surprising developments in Soviet foreign policy, as well as in the theory underlying policy and in the structure of foreign policy decision-making.

This chapter begins by considering why it was necessary to change Soviet foreign policy. In the second section structural reforms are examined: changes in personnel, in the foreign policy apparatus of the Party and state and in the way business is conducted. It then offers a brief synopsis of the conceptual changes which are an essential aspect of the new foreign policy, of the 'new political thinking', as Gorbachev and his colleagues call it. But conceptual and structural changes are not in themselves sufficient to explain the vastly improved climate of international relations. The fourth section looks at some of the substantive policy changes which have contributed to the present spirit of cooperation. The chapter concludes with a brief assessment of the future prospects of the new foreign policy.

### MOTIVES FOR CHANGE

The pressure to reform Soviet foreign policy derived in part from the same source as the drive for domestic change: the poor state of the economy. But in the case of foreign policy, there were also external pressures which encouraged the leadership to reconsider its policies. Soviet foreign policy had suffered a series of setbacks since the beginning of the decade. More importantly, high-priority goals had been sacrificed for less important ones which, despite the sacrifices, had not been attained. In other words, Soviet foreign policy had ceased to be cost-effective, in both the literal and figurative meaning of that term.

As far as the direct effect of foreign policy on the domestic economy was concerned, Soviet foreign policy was, according to the new leadership, simply too expensive (Shevardnadze, *Vestnik MIDa*, no. 2/1987, p. 31). The overmanning, duplication of responsibilities and waste that were criticised in other government and Party bodies, was prevalent in the Ministry of Foreign Affairs (MFA) too. But it was also expensive in the sense that the political or economic returns on Soviet diplomatic investment, and on economic and military aid, were too small.

It was not just a question of making existing policies more cost-effective, however. There were other ways in which domestic economic reform depended upon foreign policy. If investment in the civilian economy was to be increased, for example, defence spending had to be reduced. Moreover if, as Western experts have always maintained, the defence industries were far more efficient and advanced than civilian enterprises, the economy would benefit from the transfer of expertise from the former to the latter. But cutting the defence budget required a decrease in international tension and, in particular, better Soviet–American relations. It also required that America should be dissuaded from research into and deployment of new weapons systems like the Strategic Defense Initiative (SDI) which would require matching efforts on the Soviet side.

Once domestic economic reform had been launched, another connection between it and foreign policy became apparent. The reform required the import of technology. It also needed the encouragement of foreign investment (via joint enterprises) and an increase in foreign trade. The aim was that the socialist economies should be integrated into the world economy. None of these aims could be realised unless Soviet foreign relations improved.

With regard to the external pressures for change, the invasion of Afghanistan had caused intractable and unforeseen problems. Detente was already shaky in 1979 (the causes of the 'second cold war' are analysed in Halliday 1983). The intervention damaged it even further. Any improvement in Soviet-American relations was unlikely as long as Soviet troops remained in Afghanistan. The withdrawal of Soviet troops had also become one of the three conditions set by the Chinese for a normalisation of Sino-Soviet relations (the other two conditions were Vietnamese withdrawal from Kampuchea and a reduction in the number of Soviet troops on the Sino-Soviet border). Moreover, Soviet standing in the Third World had been diminished by the invasion. Despite strenuous diplomatic efforts, Third World countries continued to voice objections to the action. Had the intervention achieved its aims, the cost to other foreign policy goals and to Soviet prestige may perhaps have been worthwhile. In fact, however, it had exacerbated the resistance it had been designed to quell. The civil war in Afghanistan was no closer to being won in 1985 than it had been in 1979 when the Soviet troops intervened.

Like so much else in East–West relations, arms-control negotiations seemed to be at a stalemate in 1985. NATO had responded to the upgrading of Soviet SS-4 and 5 missiles to SS-20s by adopting a dual-track decision to modernise European nuclear weapons while negotiating reductions. An energetic campaign to reverse the decision to deploy Cruise and Pershing II missiles in Europe had failed. When the deployment began in 1983, the Soviet delegation had walked out of the Geneva negotiations. Although new talks were due to begin in March 1985, the prevailing atmosphere made early progress unlikely. Moreover, President Reagan seemed as committed to the idea of SDI as the Soviet leadership was implacably opposed to it. If any serious hopes had been entertained that Western Europe and the United States would become uncoupled over the issues of intermediate-range nuclear forces (INF) and SDI, there was little evidence to suggest that they were justified. By 1985 most of the European NATO countries had agreed to the stationing of INF and many were prepared to cooperate in SDI research.

The Solidarity crisis in Poland at the beginning of the 1980s had contributed to the deterioration in East–West relations. By 1985 the crisis was under control but none of the problems had been resolved. Fears that Polish popular protest would spread to the rest of the bloc had proved groundless (Teague 1988). Nonetheless, the economic situation that had provoked the crisis had not improved. Many other East European countries were also experiencing severe economic problems. In other words, the economies of Eastern Europe were as much in need of reform as the Soviet economy.

Afghanistan was the most acute problem in Soviet Third World policy, but a number of other situations alarmed the new leadership.

The socialist-orientated governments of both Ethiopia and Angola were still fighting civil wars with Soviet and Cuban aid. Moreover, like other socialist-orientated Third World states, they were abysmally poor. Soviet theorists had begun to question whether their transition from socialist orientation to socialism would ever be feasible. Soviet economists had long known that the basis of the transition could not be Soviet economic aid (Valkenier 1983). Soviet activism in the Third World had initiated the deterioration in East–West relations. By 1985 it was clear that it had produced few compensatory rewards. The economic, military and political burdens of client states outweighed the strategic and prestige advantages of the increased size of the world socialist system.

In short, by the time Gorbachev became General Secretary of the CPSU, it must have been abundantly and immediately clear that Soviet foreign policy was in urgent need of an overhaul. He began almost immediately to restructure the foreign policy apparatus and appoint new personnel to redesign Soviet foreign policy.

## STRUCTURAL CHANGES

The restructuring of the MFA and the CPSU Central Committee apparatus took place in two stages. The initial changes were intended, on the one hand, to reflect new realities in the international system and, on the other, to ensure that the people charged with providing information and working out alternative policy options for the Politburo and implementing whatever policy was chosen were sympathetic to the new political thinking. Inevitably, it took some time to effect the necessary personnel changes. The turnover in personnel has continued, in part for 'natural' reasons (in other words, retirement for reasons of age or promotion) but probably also because some people were unable to adapt to the new political thinking. A second set of changes was associated with the decisions taken in 1988 to decrease the size of the Party apparatus, reduce its role and increase the role played by government organs in day-to-day policy, and to 'democratise' decision-making by widening the range of participants.

In the first round of reforms, departments were reshuffled (to reflect geographic changes resulting from the long-past breakup of past empires) and new ones were established to deal with new foreign policy concerns. The MFA, for example, acquired units to deal with humanitarian and cultural ties, with the peaceful use of nuclear energy and space and with the Pacific Ocean area. It also acquired a new information department (under Gennady Gerasimov) which began to deal with Soviet foreign public relations in an extremely professional and successful way. In both the MFA and the International Department (ID) of the Central Committee, arms control units were set up (headed, in the case of the MFA, by the veteran arms negotiator, Viktor Karpov, and in the case of the ID, by Major General Starodubov). A new academic department was also established in the Institute of World Economy and International Affairs to study strategic and security issues. These departments demonstrated both the new urgency with which arms control was regarded and the firm intention to create civilian strategists to provide alternative views to those of the armed forces, which had always monopolised arms control issues. By 1987 sub-departments had also been created or reorganised within the MFA to deal with the socialist countries of Europe and Asia, with the Middle East, North Africa, South-East Asia and South Asia and with the Non-aligned movement. Others were set up for issues such as international law, international economic relations and policy planning and evaluation (Shevardnadze, *Vestnik MIDa*, no. 15/1988, pp. 43–4).

Sweeping personnel changes took place in the MFA during the first stage of restructuring. Eduard Shevardnadze replaced Andrei Gromyko as Foreign Minister (Gromyko became Chairman of the Presidium of the USSR Supreme Soviet until the second round of reforms). Two new first deputy foreign ministers (Yu. Vorontsov and A. Kovalev) and four new deputy foreign ministers (A. Bessmertnykh, V. Petrovsky, B. Chaplin and A. Adamashin) were appointed. By October 1986 more than a third of all Soviet ambassadors had been replaced. A year later the majority of ambassadors and consuls were said to be new (Shevardnadze, *Vestnik MIDa*, no. 15/1988, pp. 45).

The personnel changes within the CPSU Central Committee apparatus were also substantial. A. Yakovlev, V. Medvedev and A. Dobrynin were appointed Central Committee secretaries in charge of the propaganda, liaison with ruling communist and workers' parties and the international departments respectively. G. Shakhnazarov, a known new thinker, was promoted to first deputy head of the department for liaison with ruling communist and workers' parties (Teague, *Radio Liberty Research Bulletin*, RL 111/86). The academic staff of the Diplomatic Academy and the State Institute for International Relations were urged to make their syllabuses and teaching reflect the new political thinking, so that new cadres would be adept at responding to its demands (Light, *Millennium*, 16/2 1987, pp. 293–4).

The XIX Party Conference was the prelude to the second stage of reform. Gorbachev called for more scientific and public discussion of foreign policy, better information and more *glasnost* on international issues, the involvement of legislative organs in discussing foreign policy and the establishment of Central Committee commissions to discuss various aspects of policy, including foreign policy (Gorbachev, June 1988, pp. 35, 79). Shevardnadze raised similar themes at a conference at the MFA in July. He pointed to the establishment a year before of a Scientific Coordinating Centre within the MFA to maintain contacts with scholars in the Soviet Union and abroad. He also mentioned an MFA Centre to study (and shape) public opinion that had recently begun to function. He demonstrated the new 'democratisation' by basing much of his speech on opinions voiced in a survey that had been conducted within his ministry (Shevardnadze, *Vestnik MIDa*, no. 15/1988, pp. 24–46). He emphasised the importance of a closer association between academics and foreign policymakers and of involving the public more in foreign policy.

It was not until the adoption of the amendments to the constitution, however, and the surprise Central Committee Plenum at the end of September 1988 (for which Shevardnadze had to abandon an important visit to the United States) that the shape of the second stage of restructuring became clearer. The constitutional amendments established, amongst other things, a USSR Supreme Soviet in permanent session with proper legislative powers and a voice in foreign policy. The Central Committee Plenum consolidated Gorbachev's power. It also reduced the influence of the Central Committee Secretariat by distinguishing clearly between the sphere of responsibility of individual secretaries and it widened the participation of Central Committee members (as opposed to *apparatchiki*) in making foreign policy.

As far as foreign policy was concerned, the most significant personnel change was Gromyko's retirement and Gorbachev's appointment as Chairman of the USSR Supreme Soviet Presidium (and *de facto* President of the Soviet Union). For the first time Gorbachev acquired a constitutional right to the foreign policy authority he had been exercising since 1985. Anatoly Dobrynin also retired (to become one of Gorbachev's personal foreign policy advisers). The ID and the Department for liaison with ruling communist and workers' parties' departments were fused under the chairmanship of Valentin Falin. Aleksandr Kapto, first deputy head of the now defunct Liaison Department, was promoted to head the iedology department while Aleksandr Yakovlev, its previous head (and reputedly one of the chief creators of *glasnost*), became chairman of a newly-established Central Committee Foreign Policy Commission (Rahr, *Radio Liberty Research Bulletin*, RL 423/88). Vadim Medvedev, previously head of the Liaison Department, was made chairman of a similar commission for Ideology. It was announced that the size of the Central Committee apparatus was to be halved and that all departments that duplicated government ministries would be abolished.

The new Foreign Policy Commission, one of six announced by the plenum, is to meet 'when required, but not less often than once every three months'. Shevardnadze and Yakovlev are both members and so, of course, is Falin, the new head of the ID. The other 21 members are members of the Central Committee and the Central Auditing Commission, but they include eight provincial Party and government officials, four members of the MFA and other ministries, one each from the military and the KGB, one each from the media and the 'creative intelligentsia', three academics, and one ordinary worker (Rahr, *Radio Liberty Research Bulletin*, RL 519/88). The commission is charged with supervising the work of the ID. It will presumaby also supervise further development of the new political thinking which establishes the ideas and principles on which Soviet foreign policy is based.

## THE NEW POLITICAL THINKING

The 'old' political thinking in the Soviet Union was based on the idea that the world was divided into antagonistic capitalist and socialist systems. The correlation of forces was ineluctably changing in favour of socialism as more countries adopted a socialist or socialist-orientated path of development, the economies of existing socialist states became more developed, and as Soviet military power became equal to that of the West. National liberation movements were part of this development. Their struggle for independence should, therefore, be aided by socialist states. Their relations with socialist states, like the relations between the Soviet Union and other socialist states, were based on the principle of proletarian internationalism. Soviet theorists and policymakers maintained that conflict could not occur in this new type of international relations.

Soviet theorists and policymakers believed that conflict between the two systems was endemic and inevitable. Since capitalism was in a state of perpetual crisis and socialism represented a higher stage of development, the conflict would end with the final victory of socialism throughout the world. To avert this outcome, capitalist states would be tempted to attack socialist states. War was, therefore, an ever-present danger, deterred only by the military power of the Soviet Union and the good sense of capitalist leaders who recognised the devastating consequences of nuclear war. This made them accept relations with socialist states based on the principle of peaceful coexistence. This principle did not exclude class and ideological struggle or economic competition. In fact, despite peaceful coexistence, the characteristic feature of the present stage of history was the struggle between socialism and capitalism.

The new political thinking is pessimistic about the present state of international relations, but optimistic that new forms of cooperation can produce a just and peaceful international order. It is based on the recognition that security can neither be achieved unilaterally nor be assured by military means alone. Security is a political problem and it therefore requires political solutions. It is international, indivisible, and interdependent: it either applies equally to all states or it cannot apply to any. Achieving it demands understanding the interests of other states, promoting mutual trust, being prepared to compromise and adopting flexible policies. It also requires understanding that conflict can spread from one geographic area to others, and from one issue to others. Political, economic and humanitarian problems must, therefore, be resolved and local conflicts must be settled, to prevent them spreading and escalating to military confrontation (Petrovsky, *MEMO*, 1987, pp. 15–26; Trofimenko, *International Affairs (Moscow)*, no. 12/1988, pp. 13–25).

Soviet theorists and policymakers maintain that the sheer number of weapons in existence, particularly nuclear arms and more particularly those in the possession of the two main adversaries in international relations, makes military confrontation more likely. They advocate progressive reductions in the military balance (and in military budgets), aiming at the complete elimination of all nuclear weapons by the year 2000. Other weapons of mass destruction should be banned and conventional arms should be reduced to the level of 'reasonable sufficiency' (Zhurkin, Karaganov and Kortunov, *Kommunist*, no. 1/1988, pp. 42–50).

There is an inherent danger that local conflicts will spread, according to Soviet foreign policy specialists, drawing the superpowers into direct confrontation with one another. Far from it being the particular responsibility of the Soviet Union to aid the struggle for national liberation, both superpowers have a responsibility to cooperate in seeking political solutions to regional conflicts. This entails patient negotiation to reconcile the conflicting parties and form viable representative coalition governments, while providing international guarantees to prevent external intervention (Kovalev, *Vestnik MIDa*, 3/10 October 1988, p. 11). The new political thinking about regional conflict stems from the reassessment of political and economic developments in less-developed countries (LDCs) which had begun a number of years before Gorbachev became General Secretary. By the end of the 1970s it had become clear that the economic predicament of socialist-orientated LDCs was no better (and in some cases it was a great deal worse) than that of capitalist Third World states. Previous assumptions that economic aid and political support could enable socialist-orientated states to progress to socialism without an intervening capitalist stage have had to be jettisoned. Soviet prognoses of economic development in all LDCs have become more realistic and less optimistic (Mirsky, *Rabochii klass i sovremenny mir*, no. 4/1988, pp. 118–29).

The new political thinkers have also begun to reconsider the concepts of proletarian internationalism and socialist internationalism (the name given to the principle underlying relations between socialist states). To begin with there seemed to be more disagreement about this aspect of Soviet theory than about any other (except perhaps whether class struggle belonged to the realm of international relations). The argument concerned the precedence of international (in other words, socialist bloc or Soviet) interests over national interests (Dawisha and Valdez, *Problems of Communism*, no. 2/ March–April 1988, pp. 1–14). In effect it was a disagreement about whether or not the Brezhnev doctrine still applied to relations within the socialist system. Many prominent theorists and policymakers now believe that national interests must take precedence and that noninterference and respect for national sovereignty are essential principles in the relations between socialist states to which insufficient attention has been paid in the past (Bovin, *MEMO*, no. 7/1988, pp. 5–15). Every socialist state, according to Gorbachev, 'has the sovereign right to resolve its own problems, to seek its own answers...' (*Pravda*, 24 February 1989).

The concept of interdependence is prominent in the new political thinking. It is used to refer to the indivisibility of security, and the way in which conflicts spread geographically and from one issue to others. It also describes the way in which many domestic problems (for example, pollution) extend beyond national borders to become national, international or even global. The links between the two economic systems and between the individual economies of separate countries also demonstrate how interdependent the world has become. Indeed, Soviet theorists now talk of two types of economy within one single world economic system. Recognition of the need to cultivate and manage the involuntary, interdependent links between European countries that arise from geographic proximity as well as from a shared history and culture has led Gorbachev to coin the term 'common European house' (Gorbachev 1987, pp. 190–95). Interdependence is also the basis for the new cooperative and creative international order that he proposed at the United Nations in December 1988 (*Pravda*, 8 December 1988).

As we have seen in Chapter 1, domestic *perestroika* could not be accomplished without *glasnost*. It was some time, however, before *glasnost* extended to foreign policy. But it gradually became clear that the new concepts could not easily be applied to policy unless old concepts and policies were reappraised. Foreign policymakers could not learn from past mistakes and successes, in other words, unless the history of Soviet foreign policy was open to scrutiny. The political leadership began to encourage historians, theorists and political commentators to fill in the blank pages of foreign policy (Shevardnadze, *Vestnik MIDa*, no. 2/1987, p. 33). Although the result has been far less dramatic than the re-evaluation of domestic history, a number of issues and events have been discussed in the press (see, for example, Dashichev, *Lit. Gaz.*, 18 May 1988, p. 4) and in specialist journals (see, for example, Trofimenko, *International Affairs (Moscow)*, no. 12/1988, pp. 13–25).

A comparison of these ideas and concepts with the brief summary given at the beginning of the section of 'old' thinking makes it clear that the 'new' thinking is indeed new. Some of the individual ideas had been expressed by Soviet theorists before Gorbachev came to power (Glickham, *Radio Liberty Research*, Supplement 2/86). Many of them originate in Western theory (Kubalkova 1989). But the diversity of ideas and the criticism of past theories and policies are new. Whether they are new or old, however, is less important than whether they are designed to mask old foreign policy goals, or whether they indicate substantive change in Soviet foreign policy. We turn now to the effects of the new political thinking on concrete policy.

## CHANGES IN POLICY

One of the earliest effects of the new political thinking and the appointment of new foreign-policy personnel was a change in the style of Soviet diplomacy. Two things, in particular, illustrated the contrast with old ways. First, Soviet officials began to admit quite openly that the Soviet Union had domestic and external problems and that some of these were the fault of past and present practices. As *glasnost* was launched, their revelations of the past became quite dramatic. With very few exceptions, it had been the rule since the 1920s that problems were never acknowledged and that the system was never to blame for anything.

Second, the way in which Soviet diplomats conducted business changed radically. They became more affable and flexible, showed more individual initiative and soon proved that they were adept at using the media to communicate and to project a positive image of *perestroika*. In short, they understood how important public relations could be in winning support and sympathy for the Soviet Union. Their rapid mastery of a more informal style and their rejection of past intransigence caused many Western observers to complain that the Soviet leadership was winning the propaganda war. There were, of course, elements of propaganda in the new thinking and the way it was projected. But there were also substantive shifts in policy. This was particularly evident as a new thaw began in Soviet–American relations.

### Soviet–American Relations

Although the new Soviet leadership began by declaring that the Soviet Union would diversify its foreign policy and would no longer interpret the world through the prism of its relations with the United States, the main thrust of Soviet foreign policy in Gorbachev's first three years as General Secretary was the attempt to resuscitate detente and revive the arms control process. Given the high rhetoric and implacability of President Reagan's first term of office, Gorbachev's success in this endeavour signified that the United States, too, was ready to change. But because of the prolonged electoral process in the United States, there are three distinct phases in Soviet–American relations under Gorbachev: an initial period of mutual suspicion, which lasted until November 1985, a period of heightened activity in bilateral relations which ended when Regan finally retired at the end of 1988, and an hiatus while the foreign policy of the Bush administration was under discussion.

The active period in Soviet–American relations was characterised by summitry and arms control negotiations. Gorbachev and Reagan met four times – in Geneva in November 1985, unexpectedly in Reykjavik in October 1986, in Washington in December 1987 and in Moscow in May 1988. Each meeting produced evidence of a good personal relationship between the two leaders. This in itself helped to reduce tensions in bilateral superpower relations. The summits were interspersed with meetings at Foreign Minister level and below, to make arrangements, fix agendas and agree details. Throughout the period, arms-control negotiators were in session. There was, therefore, constant contact between the superpowers throughout the period. The most tangible product of the contact was the treaty to abolish intermediate-range nuclear forces (INF). This agreement represented a substantive shift in Soviet policy. It also demonstrated the extent to which Gorbachev was prepared to compromise for the sake of reaching agreement. More generally, however, the INF treaty was important because it marked an important breakthrough in arms control.

The new flexibility in Soviet negotiating strategy became apparent when Gorbachev abandoned the linkage he had made between the INF treaty and SDI research and deployment, and between intermediate and strategic weapons. He also agreed to include SS-20s targeted on China as well as those deployed in the western part of the country. And he revoked the longstanding Soviet objection to on-site verification. It was this that made the INF treaty possible and it was also one of the reasons why it was a watershed in arms control. Numerically the treaty only reduced the total number of existing nuclear warheads by 4 per cent. It was the first agreement, however, to abolish an entire class of weapons. This was another reason why it represented a breakthrough in arms control.

Verification had been one of the most intractable problems of arms control negotiations since the war. The Soviet leadership had always rejected on-site verification on the grounds that the real intention was surveillance of other, unrelated military and economic developments. The deadlock was broken when satellite surveillance made it possible to use 'national technical means' of verification. But satellites could only detect stationary missiles with single warheads – once mobile missiles and multiple warheads were invented, intrusive means became the only way of checking that agreements were being honoured. In the middle of 1986 Gorbachev had reversed the traditional Soviet objection in connection with a series of confidence-building measures negotiated as part of the European Security and Cooperation (CSCE) process. By 1987 he was prepared to allow intrusive verification of the INF treaty. The United States then had to persuade its European allies to allow on-site inspection of the Cruise and Pershing-2 missile sites that would be abandoned as a result of the treaty.

The agreement in principle made by Reagan and Gorbachev that they would reduce strategic missiles by 50 per cent (START) and the difficulty of negotiating a total ban on chemical weapons indicated that intrusive verification did not resolve all the problems of checking that agreements were being kept. It was impossible to negotiate the details of START in time for it to provide a grand finale for the Reagan presidency. One reason was the difficulty of agreeing the mix of missiles that each side could keep. Another was working out how to verify mobile weapons. Abolishing a whole class of weapons, it turned out, was actually easier than simply reducing numbers.

Improved Soviet–American relations made cooperation possible in attempts to resolve a range of regional conflicts (see below). The improvement was maintained throughout the election campaign and until Regan actually retired. But American foreign policy remained in suspension for an inordinate length of time, as President Bush tried to decide what policy to adopt towards the Soviet Union. Gorbachev and his colleagues, meanwhile, turned their attention to the rest of the world, and particularly to Western Europe.

**Soviet Policy towards Western Europe**

Almost as soon as he became General Secretary, Gorbachev launched an active policy towards Western Europe. Many people in the West suspected him of wanting to drive a wedge between the United States and Europe and between individual West European states. In fact, European security is an old preoccupation of Soviet policy and the concept of interdependence has revived it and given it new content and a new name. Gorbachev talks of the 'common European house' (Gorbachev 1987, pp. 190–95) in promoting the kind of cooperation in Europe that he maintains will enhance security and enable closer contacts between the two blocs.

To begin with, Gorbachev probably hoped to use the good offices of the West Europeans to moderate the harshness of the American administration. The negative response of many West Europeans to the Reykjavik summit and the INF treaty must have indicated to him, however, that when they felt that their security was threatened, the West Europeans too could become hostile. He must have realised quite soon that successful arms control agreements (which he believes to be the *sine qua non* of security) would be far more difficult to achieve if there was too much disunity in NATO. Moreover, if the American nuclear umbrella ceased to protect Western Europe, there would almost certainly be greater European military integration, and possibly nuclear proliferation with, for example, Franco-German nuclear cooperation. Developments like these would decrease European security. Thus, while a certain amount of dissension in the Atlantic Alliance is undoubtedly beneficial to the Soviet Union, the chaos that would ensue if the United States withdrew from Europe (or, for that matter, if any of the larger European NATO members left the Alliance) and the threat to Soviet security that would result from closer West European military integration cannot further Soviet foreign policy aims. To dispel suspicion that the 'common European house' is directed against the United States, Soviet commentators have recently taken to extending the hospitality of the 'house' to America (Davydov, 1989).

Gorbachev's West European policy envisages more than just security. It is to West Europe that the Soviet Union and other reformist East European countries look to expand their foreign trade, to increase their technology imports and for partners for joint enterprises. Moreover, integration in the European Community (EC) has recently been recognised to be far more successful than integration within the Council for Mutual Economic Aid (CMEA) and a worthy model to be emulated (Dashichev *et al.*, *Problems of Communism*, XXXVII, no. 3–4, May–August 1988, p. 64). In 1988 an EC–CMEA treaty was concluded, enabling individual CMEA members to deal directly with the EC (Malcolm 1989). The fear that the Common Market in 1992 might undermine some of these gains has probably contributed to the campaign for a 'common European house'.

Gorbachev has also worked hard to establish better bilateral relations with individual European countries. At the beginning of his tenure of office he visited or received in Moscow a number of West European leaders, establishing in particular a good working relationship with British Prime Minister Margaret Thatcher, the senior European political figure and the leader whose view of the Soviet Union coincided most clearly with that of the Reagan administration. He arranged visits to Britain, West Germany, Italy and France (and a stopover in Ireland on his way to Cuba) during the lull in Soviet–American relations in 1989. However important the trade agreements signed with individual countries, the better political atmosphere in Europe and the opportunity to project the new Soviet image, relations with the United States continue to take priority over relations with Western Europe as a whole or relations with individual West European countries. Although their support and encouragement are welcome, Gorbachev needs the cooperation of the American administration in implementing his new policy regarding Third World conflict. It is to that policy that we now turn.

**Regional Conflict**

In theory the new Soviet technique for resolving regional conflict is not confined to conflicts in the Third World. In practice, however, this is where most conflicts occur currently and it is where the Soviet leadership has applied the theory. Since many regional conflicts were, before Gorbachev, called national liberation struggles which the Soviet Union supported, it is here in particular that substantive changes can be seen in Soviet foreign policy.

The priority of Soviet relations with the Third World had been falling even before Gorbachev came to power. This was associated with gradual disillusionment about the political reality and likely economic and social development of most less-developed countries, including those that called themselves socialist-orientated. But there had also been a growing awareness in the Soviet Union that Third World conflicts could not easily be resolved by military means and that there was an inevitable loss of prestige when Soviet clients could remain in power only with Soviet military aid. Moreover, the experience in Afghanistan proved that direct intervention incurred general opprobrium without necessarily achieving victory for those it was meant to help. It was not until Gorbachev came to power, however, that the logical conclusions were drawn and that Soviet policy was adjusted accordingly. The most dramatic result was the Soviet withdrawal from Afghanistan. During the negotiations that preceded the withdrawal, attempts were made to apply the new conflict-resolution techniques.

According to Soviet policymakers and theorists, regional conflict can be resolved through dialogue, national reconciliation and a willingness to share political power (Kovalev, *Vestnik MIDa*, no. 3, 10 October 1987, p. 11). The resolution will be effective as long as arms are not supplied to the conflicting parties and there is no external intervention. It will be even more stable if there is some kind of international or superpower guarantee of the process. In the case of Afghanistan, Babrak Karmal, the leader installed by the Soviet army in 1979, was persuaded to step down in favour of Dr Najibullah. A programme of national reconciliation was launched which involved abandoning the most unpopular reforms, encouraging non-Party participation in local government, declaring a ceasefire in the civil war and offering amnesty to returning refugees. The hope was that this would reduce support for the rebel Mujahideen, end the fighting and allow the Soviet army to leave with honour.

National reconciliation did not work in Afghanistan. Instead painstaking 'proxy' negotiations (since most of the parties involved in the dispute would not negotiate directly with one another) under the aegis of a representative of the Secretary General of the United Nations, Diego Cordovez, produced the Geneva Accords in April 1988 whch, while they also did not end the fighting, allowed the Soviet army to withdraw in a relatively orderly manner if not with honour (Saikal and Maley 1989). In other words, the civil war continued, but by February 1989 the Soviet army had withdrawn. The chief obstacle to achieving other important goals of Soviet foreign policy had, at last, been removed.

Similar conflict-resolution techniques have been adopted in Angola, but without direct Soviet involvement. Soviet encouragement of Cuban withdrawal and support for the political negotiations were nonetheless vital elements in the process. The Soviet Union is also not directly involved in the negotiations to withdraw Vietnamese troops from Kampuchea, although again Soviet support for the process can be assumed. The Ethiopian government had indicated that it is willing to negotiate over Eritrea and Tigray. The Soviet Union also supported the negotiated end to the Iran–Iraq war and it has been actively promoting a Middle East peace conference. Political settlements have been proposed for Nicaragua and South Africa.

At the United Nations in December 1988, Gorbachev outlined the Soviet view on Third World regional conflicts and the role that the Soviet Union now believes that the United Nations should play in resolving them (*Pravda*, 8 December 1988).

This does not mean, of course, that the Soviet Union has completely abandoned all its Third World allies and friends. High profile has been given to Soviet–Indian relations; Syria and Libya still get arms from the Soviet Union; Gorbachev visited Cuba in 1989 (but probably warned Castro against getting involved in other regional conflicts). Nonetheless, it is clear that no less-developed country, whether or not it is socialist-orientated, can now take for granted Soviet military aid. It is ironic, given that lack of revolutionary fervour was one of the accusations levelled by the Chinese against the Soviet Union at the start of the Sino-Soviet dispute, that the new policy on regional conflict has contributed most to bringing that dispute to an end.

## China

In May 1989 Gorbachev visited China for the first Sino-Soviet summit in 30 years. Brezhnev had begun trying to improve relations between the two countries in 1982. The Chinese stipulated three conditions that had to be fulfilled if relations were to be 'normalised': a reduction of Soviet troops on the Sino-Soviet border, the withdrawal of the Soviet army from Afghanistan and the withdrawal of Vietnamese troops from Kampuchea. The new policy towards regional conflict has fulfilled two of these conditions and Soviet arms reductions have fulfilled the third. Gorbachev has also unilaterally granted a fourth concession. In July 1986, in a speech he made in Vladivostok, he announced that the border between the two countries along the Amur river lay in the centre of the navigation channel rather than on the Chinese bank, as Russian and Soviet leaders had always maintained and Chinese had always denied.

In fact, the summit between Gorbachev and Deng Xiaoping was a symbolic climax to the steady improvement in relations which has been taking place over the past four years. There have been regular meetings at the level of deputy foreign minister; economic relations, including cross-border trade, have expanded rapidly; cultural and scientific exchanges have increased; and border talks have reopened. Each side believes that it can learn from the other's reforms. But both probably value good relations with the United States rather more than good relations with one another.

## Eastern Europe

In respect of Soviet relations with capitalist countries, more activity usually denotes better relations. It can be argued that with regard to Soviet relations with Eastern Europe, however, the less the activity the better the relations. And in some senses there has been very little activity in Soviet–East European relations. But this does not denote that there has been no change. Perhaps the greatest shifts concern first, the way in which past relations are being re-evaluated, and second, the degree of diversity which is being tolerated.

Some new politial thinkers believe that too much activity and direction from successive Soviet leaders in the past has caused 'deformations' both within the political and economic systems of the individual members of the Warsaw Treaty Organisation and in relations between them (Dashichev, *et al.*, *Problems of Communism*, XXXVII, no. 3–4, May–August 1988, pp. 60–64). They point to the paucity of contacts between individual East European countries, particularly at levels below the top echelons of Party and government, and to the way this undermined bureaucratic attempts to impose economic integration via CMEA. These views are not universally shared within the Soviet Union and they are certainly not held by all East European leaders. But that they can be expressed at all, especially in the pages of *Problems of Communism*, is an indication of the vast changes that are taking place.

In general Soviet relations with the countries of Eastern Europe are far less ideological now than they have ever been before. The great and growing diversity which can be observed concerns particularly the extent to which various countries are embracing reform. There has been no attempt to impose a pattern from Moscow, although impatience is obvious from time to time with those East European leaders who are clinging to old ways. Gorbachev has increased activity in one respect at least – greater efforts are made to inform and consult the leaders of other countries. In other words, the Warsaw Treaty Organisation is being treated more like an alliance, although the members are distinctly junior partners rather than equals. But the overwhelming impression is that Soviet leaders have considered their relations with Eastern Europe to be rather less important than the momentous events they have been promoting elsewhere.

A number of questions in relation to Eastern Europe remain unanswered. What role, for example, is envisaged for the socialist European countries in the 'common European house'? The most serious question is whether the Brezhnev Doctrine still applies. What would happen, for example, if an East European leader announced that he was withdrawing his country from the Warsaw Treaty Organisation? It is not just the fate of Eastern Europe that depends upon the answer to that question, but the future of Gorbachev's entire foreign policy and the seriousness with which it is regarded around the world.

## CONCLUSION

It is not only in relation to particular countries or areas that changes have been evident in Soviet policy. The Soviet Union has accorded far more importance to the United Nations in the last couple of years, for example, than ever before. It was at the United Nations that Gorbachev announced unilateral conventional arms reductions of 500 000 men and 10 000 tanks and the withdrawal from the front line of those weapons and units capable of launching a surprise attack. These cuts are connected with a review of Soviet strategy. Attempts are being made to work out what level of arms are required for 'reasonable sufficiency' and whether a strategy of 'defensive defence' can be made operational.

Gorbachev has also initiated schemes that have met with little success. His proposal for a 'Helsinki-type' process in the Asia–Pacific region, for example, was universally dismissed. Other proposals for nuclear-free zones have also not received much response. One thing that he has successfully demonstrated, however, is that he has a seemingly endless supply of offers. How seriously should we take them? How optimistic can we be about future prospects?

Perhaps one of the most hopeful things that has occurred in the last four years resulted from the discussion in the Soviet Union about verification. The discussion led to a consideration of the importance of trust in international relations. That in turn led Soviet theorists to examine their own past rhetoric and actions. The result was twofold. First, the baleful effect of *Soviet* actions and *Soviet* rhetoric on the perceptions of adversaries was recognised for the first time. And Soviet theorists and policy makers began to accept some responsibility for past events. Second, the fact that the use of 'enemy images' did not fit the desire for peaceful coexistence and a new cooperative world order became clear (Popov, *Lit. Gaz.*, 28 October 1987). The change in the tone used by most, but not all (Sanakoyev, *International Affairs (Moscow)*, no. 2/1988, pp. 75–85 provides a counter-example), Soviet writers about international relations was striking. If both sides in the East–West relationship understand how important perceptions are, and how much words affect them, both might adopt more temperate actions and words.

But understanding perceptions and moderating words will not carry the present momentum forward. It will require positive responses and positive initiatives from the West. And our willingness to initiate will depend upon our judgement of whether the Soviet Union will revert to old thinking and policy or whether the new policy is here to stay. The avowed aim of Gorbachev's foreign policy is primarily to make *perestroika* possible and successful. But the relationship works both ways. The ability to continue the new foreign policy will depend upon the success and continuation of *perestroika*. Future prospects, therefore, are largely a function of Soviet domestic reform.

# 11    The Arts

## JULIAN GRAFFY

### 1    INTRODUCTION

Initial responses to *glasnost* in culture largely took the form of comparisons with the Cultural Thaw under Khrushchev. Superficially these comparisons were very attractive. In both periods an extended period of cultural stagnation under a repressive leader (Stalin; Brezhnev) was followed by the death of that leader and years of political transition (the years before Khruchchev's emergence as the dominant ruler; the Andropov and Chernenko regimes) which culturally showed signs of preparation for liberalisation. This culminated in the hegemony of a new leader (Khrushchev; Gorbachev) who, as part of his consolidation of power, encouraged a degree of openness both in culture and in terms of historical analysis specifically directed at a revelation of the faults of his predecessor's regime. In addition, in 1986 a frequently repeated nostrum was that whereas the Thaw had come 'from below', *glasnost* had been 'imposed' from above.

In 1989 these comparisons look decidedly threadbare. In 1956 the Soviet Union was emerging from a lengthy period of total isolation from, and lack of information about, the West. By contrast Brezhnev's Soviet Union was far less isolated and less uninformed. On the contrary the country was welcoming more and more Western visitors and had an immeasurably better educated and more sophisticated public. Nor did its official culture present a picture of total bleakness. Despite Khrushchev's 'Secret Speech' the revelations of the truth of Soviet history produced during the Thaw remained tentative and meagre. One of the most exciting achievements of *glasnost* has been the sheer scale and vigour of its excavation of the Soviet past. Although the Thaw also produced a number of artistic landmarks, of which the most important was probably Solzhenitsyn's *One Day in the Life of Ivan Denisovich*, published by the journal *Novy mir* in 1962, and saw the start of the careers of young writers such as

Aksenov, Voznesensky and Evtushenko, major taboos remained including the publishing of émigrés. In the sphere of culture there is no doubt that the range and importance of the achievements of the last four years have utterly eclipsed those of the Thaw.

## 2 LITERATURE

### The Journals

There are two centres of power in the contemporary Soviet literary world, the Unions of Writers and the literary press. In addition to the Union of Soviet Writers, there are also unions for each of the Soviet republics and for Moscow. Despite the replacement of Georgy Markov as First Secretary of the Soviet Writers' Union by Vladimir Karpov in 1986, the unions remain a bastion of reaction and privilege. This is true especially of the Union for the Russian republic.

All the excitement in the literary world has been concentrated on publishing activity, in particular on the literary monthlies. (It is the practice in the Soviet Union for new publications to appear first in the journals and only then in book form.) Just as Tvardovsky's *Novy mir* became a symbol of the Thaw, so the journals and the press in general are now the standard-bearers of *glasnost*, but what is striking this time round is the enormous number of newspapers and journals involved in the process. Among the most celebrated are the monthly journals *Novy mir* and *Znamya*, the illustrated weekly magazine *Ogonek* and the weekly newspaper *Moscow News*, all of which acquired new editors (who then rejuvenated their editorial boards) in 1986. But several other Moscow and Leningrad journals have been just as ambitious in their recent publications policy, including *Oktyabr'*, *Druzhba narodov*, the young people's journal *Yunost*, the Leningrad journal *Neva*, and the theatrical journals *Teatr* and *Sovremennaya dramaturgiya*. Nor is this process confined to the centre. Such provincial journals as *Volga* (published in Saratov), *Podem* (published in Voronezh) and *Don* (published in Rostov) have also become compulsory reading. Some of the most exciting work is appearing in the other republics. (The remote Republican press has a long tradition of daring in these matters.) It is surely no coincidence that such Baltic journals as *Daugava* and *Rodnik* (published in Riga) and *Raduga* (published in Tallinn) are currently among the most interesting of all.

Clearly these changes are finding an enthusiastic response among readers. Circulation of *Ogonek* has doubled to well over 3 000 000 since 1987 and almost all the print run is now sold on subscription. *Novy mir*, printing 496 000 in December 1987, is now printing 1 629 000; the figures for *Druzhba narodov* over the same period show a leap from 150 000 to 1 170 000. The 1989 print run for *Yunost* was 3 100 000. Subscription to the Soviet press as a whole rose by 18 000 000 in 1988. In late 1988, a plan to hold down journal circulation in 1989 led to an outcry. Compromises were made, but it seems certain that the liberal press could sell considerably more copies were it able to print them.

There are, however, notable exceptions to the general euphoric espousals of the new openness. Both *Nash sovremennik*, a journal closely associated with Russian nationalism, and *Molodaya gvardiya*, officially a publication of the Komsomol, make regular attacks on the liberals and their publishing policy. *Moskva*, an organ of the Writers' Union of the Russian Republic, takes a more equivocal position, despite the conservative stance of its editor, Mikhail Alekseev.

## Russian Writers

The term 'literary journals' as widely applied to the Soviet monthly press requires some elaboration, for their contents are by no means confined to literary matters. Nevertheless a majority of their pages are devoted to the publication of fiction, poetry and plays.

The number of twentieth-century writers who have had works published for the first time (or for the first time in several decades) in the Soviet press during the last four years in enormous. Writers who began their careers in the period of Russian Modernism, from 1890 to 1930, are now being presented to readers in a far fuller way. Notable among this group are the cases of Akhmatova, Mandelshtam, Gumilev (whose work had not appeared since he was shot in 1921), Pilnyak, Platonov, Kharms and Bulgakov. (The number of publications of Bulgakov's works, of letters, of memoirs and of literary criticism leaves no doubt that he is now the most genuinely popular of twentieth-century Russian writers.)

The publication of writers from the first wave of emigration has not only marked a relaxation of attitudes to their individual fates, but has also, by the very fact of bringing them within the orbit of official Soviet publication, required a reassessment of literary history. Zamyatin's anti-uptopian novel *We* finally appeared in the country in which it was written in 1988 (*Znamya*, nos 4–5). Several Nabokov novels, including *The Defence*, *Laughter in the Dark*, *Invitation to a Beheading*, *The Gift*, *Mary*, *Despair and Pnin* have already been published in the journals, while others, including, remarkably, *Lolita*, have appeared in book form.

The most important body of work to appear in the journals since 1985 consists of fiction, drama and poetry written by established Soviet writers of this and later generations who did not emigrate (and many of whom are now dead) concerned with the examination and true remembrance of periods of Soviet history from the revolution through collectivisation, the purges, the war, to late Stalinism and beyond. This is entirely consistent with the general concern of *glasnost* with memory (*pamyat*), with managing at last to tell the truth (and the many contradictory truths) of Soviet experience and to expose the falsifications of the hitherto unchallengeable official version. Some of these works were already widely known in the West, including Pasternak's *Dr Zhivago* (*Novy mir*, nos 1–4, 1988), Akhmatova's poem of the purges *Requiem* (*Oktyabr*, no. 3, 1987, and *Neva*, no. 6, 1987), Vasily Grossman's *Life and Fate* (Oktyabr, nos 1–4, 1988), Dombrovsky's *The Faculty of Unnecessary Things* (*Novy mir*, nos 8–11, 1988), Lidiya Chukovskaya's *Sofia Petrovna*, (*The Deserted House*, *Neva*, no. 2, 1988) and Tvardovsky's collectivisation poem *By the Right of Memory* (*Znamya*, no. 2, 1987 and *Novy mir*, no. 3, 1987). Notable new publications have included Rybakov's *Children of the Arbat* (*Druzhba narodov*, nos 4–6, 1987) and its sequel *The Year 1935 and Others* currently being serialised in the same journal; Anatoly Pristavkin's *A Golden Cloud at Night* (*Znamya*, nos. 3–4, 1987, on the fate of the displaced peoples); the second book of Boris Mozhaev's *Peasants and their Women* (*Don*, nos 1–3, 1987, on collectivisation) and Mikhail Shatrov's plays about Lenin. This list could be greatly extended.

Another group of writers, who had been excluded from Soviet publication for sending their work abroad, including Yuli Daniel, Vladimir Kornilov and several contributors to the banned *Metropol* collection of 1979, have all now found their way back to their Soviet readers. A work long since justly admired in the West, Venedikt Erofeev's *Moscow-Petushki* appeared in 1989.

With all this concentration on the recuperation of the literary past, it remains difficult for young writers to find space in the journals (the literary tastes of whose editors, usually men of a certain age, are often at odds with theirs). Two celebrated exceptions are Sergei

Kaledin, whose story set among gravediggers, *A Humble Cemetery*, appeared in *Novy mir*, (no. 5, 1987) and the short-story writer Tatyana Tolstaya. Tolstaya's collection *On the Golden Porch* appeared in Britain in 1989, and a translation of *A Humble Cemetery* will appear soon.

It was obvious during the first stages of *glasnost* that the work of the so called 'third wave' émigrés was being approached with the utmost caution by the literary magazines. Most of these writers were not safely dead, like Zamyatin and Khodasevich, and were observing developments in their country with enthusiastic but sceptical attention. During most of 1987, despite an obvious softening of attitudes to the general phenomenon of emigration, repeated rumours of the imminent publication of this or that émigré writer turned out to be unfounded. Then, in December of 1987, it was appropriately *Novy mir* that broke this further taboo by publishing a small selection of the poems of Iosif Brodsky. (It had been announced on 22 October that Bordsky was that year's winner of the Nobel Prize for Literature, an event which increased speculation about his possible publication in his homeland, and to the great credit of *Novy mir* their plans turned out to be already far advanced.)

The *Novy mir* publication was followed by several other selections of Brodsky's poetry in a variety of journals, and 1988 turned out to be the 'year of the third-wave émigrés' in the Soviet press, as more and more of them became beneficiaries of the new daring. First among them were the poet and song-writer Aleksandr Galich, who had died in 1977, and the novelist and short-story writer Viktor Nekrasov, whose death in 1987 has been sympathetically reported in sections of the Soviet press (itself a breakthrough). By the autumn other living émigrés, including the novelist Sasha Sokolov and the poets Naum Korzhavin and Yury Kublanovsky, were published. December saw two symbolic publications, the beginning of serialisation of Vladimir Voinovich's *The Life and Extraordinary Adventures of Private Ivan Chonkin*, (*Yunost*, no. 12, 1988–2, 1989) and, in *Novy mir*, Yuz Aleshkovsky's widely-loved, but definitively 'unpublishable' satirical poem *Comrade Stalin, You're a Great Scholar*. At the beginning of 1989 Andrei Sinyavsky returned to Russia for the first time since his emigration and was interviewed in a number of Soviet newspapers and journals. In February *Znamya* published Georgy Vladimov's story of the adventures of a labour-camp guard-dog *Faithful Ruslan*, and the February and March issues of the journal *Inostrannaya literatura* put questions to, among others, Sinyavsky, Voinovich,

Vladimov, Aksenov and (another until recently 'unimaginable' name) Aleksandr Zinovev. In August, *Moscow News* carried an interview with Eduard Limonov. The number of major living émigré writers who have to some degree returned to Soviet print has reached double figures. Of course it is certain that much of the work of these writers still remains beyond the bounds of what a Soviet editor would see fit to print. But the implications of this process, in terms of the changed attitude to the very phenomenon of a Soviet artist choosing to live abroad, the fact that this no longer automatically makes him an artistic pariah, should not be underestimated. It is yet another way in which pluralism of viewpoint has entered the Soviet press.

Not all major émigré writers, it seems, are being welcomed back with alacrity. The publication, in the first issue of *Krokodil* for 1988, of an extract from Vasily Aksenov's *In Search of Melancholy Baby* seems in retrospect to have been calculated to provoke the irate letters from outraged pensioners that duly followed in issues 7, 9, 11, and 19. No further publications of Aksenov followed until 1989, when *Yunost* published *Our Golden Ironburg* (nos 6 and 7). Vladimir Maksimov, the editor of the Paris-based *Kontinent*, whose frequent contributions to a range of émigré publications cast a critical eye over current developments has, also unsurprisingly, not been slated for republication.

The most famous of the émigré writers is, of course, Aleksandr Solzhenitsyn, and it is around his name that most speculation has centred. Stories appeared in the Western press in March 1987 announcing imminent publication, but were soon denied. Later that year Anatoly Strelyany, a member of the *Novy mir* editorial board, insisted that the journal would publish Solzhenitsyn. Instead, Strelyany left the board. In June 1988, Vladimir Karpov, the head of the writers' union, said at a press conference that he had heard rumours that *Novy mir* was to publish *The Cancer Ward*, and in July a German radio station affirmed that Mr Gorbachev had written two letters to Solzhenitsyn in support of publication. All this was categorically denied by the writer's wife. In August, the newspaper *Knizhnoe obozrenie* carried a succession of materials insisting that Solzhenitsyn be given back his Soviet citizenship and reminding its readers that in 1969 he had written to the Union of Writers in support of 'Glasnost, full and honest *glasnost*'. The campaign around Solzhenitsyn's name was still at its height when, as widely reported in the Western and émigré press, the October 1988 issue of *Novy mir* printed on its back cover an announcement that serialisation of *The Gulag Archipelago* would begin in 1989. News of this caused a call 'from the very top' to the printers and a new cover, with no mention of *Gulag*, was substituted. Apparently, however, copies had already gone on sale in Kiev, which perhaps explains the extraordinary appearance, on 18 October, in *Rabochee Slovo*, the Kiev newspaper of the southwestern section of the Soviet railway network, of Solzhenitsyn's 1974 appeal *Live not by Lies*. In a number of speeches in November 1988 Vadim Medvedev, a secretary of the CPSU Central Committee, insisted that Solzhenitsyn would not be published. Nevertheless the campaign for publication of his writings continued and in March 1989 the Latvian Russian language monthly *Rodnik* published the speech Solzhenitsyn made in Zurich on 31 May 1974, three months after his expulsion from the USSR, on receiving a prize from Italian journalists. In the summer of 1989, *Ogonek* (nos 23 and 24) published Solzhenitsyn's early story, *Matrena's House*, which had first appeared in *Novy mir* in 1963. In August 1989, serialisation at last began, appropriately in *Novy mir*, the journal with which Solzhenitsyn had made his debut with *One Day in the Life of Ivan Denisovich*, of *The Gulag Archipelago*, the most symbolic of all the publications of hitherto forbidden works, and the most definitive sign yet of the determination to tell the truth about the past. Large-scale plans to publish Solzhenitsyn in both book and journal form were being laid in the summer of 1989.

## Western Writers

It is not only Russian writers who have suddenly found the path to Soviet publication opened. Several Western works have at last appeared in Soviet journals. The publication of Zamyatin's *We* has been accompanied by that of a number of works by Western authors that share its scepticism over utopias: Orwell's *1984* and *Animal Farm*, Huxley's *Brave New World* and Arthur Koestler's *Darkness at Noon*. Kafka's *The Castle* has appeared in two different translations. Joyce's *Ulysses* was serialised throughout 1989 by *Inostrannaya literatura*. Fans of Western thriller-writers are getting a heady diet of Hammett and Chandler. The Alma Ata journal *Prostor* which broke off publication of Frederick Forsyth's *The Day of the Jackal* in February 1974, resumed publication of it in December 1988. It has announced John le Carré's *The Looking Glass War* for 1989. Other popular Western works brought to Russian readers in 1988 ranged from *The Name of the Rose* to *The Growing Pains of Adrian Mole*.

**Literary Criticism**

Another important section of the literary journals is made up of the
pages given over to literary criticism, and to surveys of the material
being printed by their rivals. As reactions to the torrent of hitherto
unknown work continue, the very picture of what is valued by Soviet
critics and readers is changed out of recognition. 'Soviet classics',
force-fed to generations of students, are quietly being dropped
overboard. Literary scholars are also making good use of the
opportunity they now have to reveal the 'blank spots' of Soviet
literary history. There have been detailed analyses of the persecu-
tions of Meierkhold, Zoshchenko, Zabolotsky, Pasternak, Sinyavsky
and Daniel, Brodsky, Lyubimov and many others. Controversy has
raged throughout 1987 and 1988 over the hounding of Aleksandr
Tvardovsky and his journal *Novy mir* in the late 1960s. Many of the
participants in that struggle, from both sides, are still active in the
literary world today. Contributors to such liberal journals as
*Oktyabr*, *Ogonek*, *Moscow News* and *Daugava* have taken great
pleasure in revealing how such vociferous opponents of the new order
as Mikhail Alekseev, Sergei Vikulov and Anatoly Ivanov, current
editors of *Moskva*, *Nash Sovremennik* and *Molodaya gvardiya*,
respectively, and Petr Proskurin, a powerful member of the board of
the Russian Writers' Union, were among the eleven signatories of an
infamous letter of July 1969 attacking Tvardovsky. In their turn
*Moskva*, *Nash Sovremennik* and *Molodaya gvardiya* carry detailed
assaults on the liberal version of events and widen them to include
condemnation of the current policy of *Ogonek*'s editor, Vitaly
Korotich, and others. This case shows eloquently the use to which
'literary criticism' can be put in Soviet journals. The fight over the
past is also a fight over the present.

**Book Publishing**

Though Soviet book publishing has not yet been revolutionised to the
extent of the literary journals, there are now a number of signs that
the so-called 'book hunger' is being addressed. Hardhitting articles
have pointed to the ludicrously large editions devoted to the works of
powerful but unpopular (and sometimes unreadable) writers, and to
other shortcomings of the industry. The newspaper *Knizhnoe obozrenie*, published by the State Committee for Publishing, Printing and
the Book Trade, has commissioned several surveys of readers' tastes.

This has led to the institution of a system of 'express publication', which has substantially cut the gap between journal and hardcover publication for works that are in great demand. Publishing houses are playing more aggressively to market forces, producing several rival editions of popular works and often pricing above the usual rate, a development that has provoked lively debate. There have been attempts to introduce cooperative publishing houses in many major cities, but so far these seem to have faltered, in part through the unwillingness of official publishing houses to cooperate.

### The Unofficial Press

It might have been imagined that the removal of constraints from the official press would be a signal that *samizdat*, the unofficial press, had outlived its usefulness. On the contrary, the period of *glasnost* has seen a remarkable boldness and vigour in the parallel press. Some of these journals, such as *Chasy*, *37*, *Obvodny kanal*, *Mitin zhurnal* and *Predlog*, are explicitly concerned with literature. Others, such as *Glasnost* and *Referendum*, regularly publish material on cultural matters. There have been three meetings of the editors of the parallel press, the first in Leningrad in October 1987, the second in Moscow in May 1988. The third meeting, held in Moscow in November 1988, was attended by representatives of fifty-three publications, appearing in Moscow, Leningrad, Lvov, Tbilisi, Pskov, Riga, Sverdlovsk, Vilnius and Baku, which gives some idea of the current strength of the unofficial press. The role of these publications seems to be that of a vanguard, going further and faster in directions in which parts of the official press then follow. In addition, some journalists are now finding it possible to contribute regularly to both the official and the unofficial press, and some official journals, such as the Riga-based, *Rodnik* and *Daugava*, have published materials from and about the unofficial press.

For a fuller analysis of developments in the literary world, see *Graffy*, 1989.

## 3  CINEMA

### The Fifth Congress of the Union of Cinematographers

1986 was the crucial year for setting in motion the equally far-reaching changes that have taken place in the Soviet cinema. On 4 April of that year a meeting of the Komsomol branch at VGIK, the country's leading film school, to which Elem Klimov among others was invited, was called to express dissatisfaction with the way the 72-year-old rector, Vitaly Zhdan, had been running the school since 1973. The ensuing campaign to oust Zhdan succeeded in the autumn, but attempts to replace him with the young film director Sergei Solovev were frustrated. Eventually, in June 1987, his deputy, 59-year-old Aleksandr Novikov, was appointed to the post of rector. This was anything but a victory for the radicals, but the shortcomings of the film school were widely aired in the press in 1986 and must have been in the minds of delegates to the Fifth Congress of the Union of Cinematographers, held in the Kremlin's Palace of Congresses in May of that year. Some of them will also have been uncomfortably aware of the financial crisis facing their industry. According to figures quoted in *Cahiers du Cinéma* (May–June 1987), 50 per cent of Soviet films were attracting fewer than 5 000 000 viewers, whereas, because of artificially low seat-prices and high production costs caused by inefficiently lengthy shooting, a figure of 17 000 000 was needed for the average film to break even. Each year subventions to the industry were costing the state 78 000 000 rubles. Audiences were choosing bought-in foreign films rather than Soviet product. Thus although cinema attendance remained considerably higher than in the United States, let alone Britain, the industry was neither financially nor artistically healthy. Later figures showed a striking fall in attendances from 4 thousand million in 1986, to only 3½ thousand million in 1987.

The Union of Cinematographers was founded in 1965, and in 1986 membership, comprised of a wide range of cinematic professions including scriptwriters, critics and historians as well as those directly involved in the making of films, stood at about 6500. There was a board of fifty people. The congress turned out to be perhaps the single most breathtaking manifestation of cultural *glasnost*. Two-thirds of the members of the board were replaced, including the First Secretary, Lev Kulidzhanov, and such powerful directors as Sergei Bondarchuk and Nikita Mikhalkov. The new First Secretary was Elem Klimov, five of whose six films, including *Agony*, *Farewell* and *Come and See*, had been subjected to bannings and delays. Other new board members included the directors Andrei Smirnov, Eldar Shengelaya and Vadim Abdrashitov, maker of a series of films fiercely critical of Soviet society, and the *Pravda* film critic Andrei Plakhov.

The speeches and decisions of the Fifth Congress were published in the October 1986 issue of the film monthly *Iskusstvo kino*. It was formally admitted that there was a crisis in Soviet film criticism and in the film press. The old Board and Secretariat were accused of utterly failing to influence the creative process in a positive way, despite a 1984 Party directive. In particular they were found to have shown indifference to the problems of the distribution system, and not to have encouraged talented young people to succeed in the industry. Nineteen decisions were appended to the report of the proceedings, including the reorganisation of the editorial boards of the magazines *Iskusstvo kino* and *Sovetsky ekran*; an insistence that the quality of the materials used, especially film, should be improved; and a requirement that young people should be helped to make careers in the cinema, in particular through improvement of the young people's experimental group at Mosfilm. The most immediately influential of their decisions was the one to set up the so-called *Conflict Commission*, whose brief would be to view all the films that had been shelved and, if they were considered fit for showing, to ask Goskino, the State Cinema Organisation, to help arrange for their distribution.

## The Conflict Commission and Unshelving

So far, according to Andrei Plakhov, chairman of the Conflict Commission, over a hundred films have been unshelved, a sufficient number for the reasons for their banning to become clear. Unorthodox interpretation of history was clearly, as with literature, a major factor. Klimov's own *Agony*, made in 1972, had not been shown in the Soviet Union until 1985 because its picture of the Tsar and his family was thought to be too sympathetic. The most important case under this rubric is that of Aleksei German (b. 1938), son of the writer Yury German, all three of whose films have been devoted to historical subjects and all of which have been the victims of harassment, delays, threats and shelving. German is now one of the stars of cinematic *glasnost*, but as he has pointed out in recent interviews, the fact that each of his films provoked vitriolic attacks, an official 'severe reprimand', threats to sack him and endless delays in setting up his next project has taken its toll. He has frequently described himself as too 'washed out' to take on a new film.

German's first film, made in 1971 as *Operation Happy New Year* from a story by his father, was finally released, under the title *Roadcheck*, in 1986. It describes the partisans' battle against the

Nazis without false heroics, and treats its hero, Lazarev, who had previously been in German imprisonment and would therefore be officially considered a deserter, with understanding and sympathy. The film ends with Lazarev dying bravely with the partisans. This unorthodox treatment of an ideologically sensitive subject provoked the wrath of Goskino and was promptly banned. Lenfilm had to repay the entire cost of making it. German was told to 'go away and have some fun' for a few years. His next film, *Twenty Days without War*, was based on a story by Konstantin Simonov about a war correspondent's leave from the front in Tashkent. This film was delayed, threatened, described as 'the shame of Lenfilm', but eventually shown in 1977 and widely admired.

*My Friend Ivan Lapshin*, German's third film, again from a story by his father, was first planned in 1969, filmed in 1979, and finally shown in 1984. It is an absolutely remarkable work, shot with considerable ambition and assurance, that is now regularly chosen as one of the best Soviet films of all time. Though *My Friend Ivan Lapshin* did not have to wait for the setting up of the Conflict Commission to get a release, an examination of its fate is instructive, for again it is the treatment of history that caused all its problems. Set in the provincial town of 'Unchansk' in 1935, the film traces the adventures of its eponymous hero, a local police investigator, and the other inhabitants of his communal apartment. At the beginning, in a scene that takes place during Lapshin's fortieth birthday party, there are songs, jokes and revolutionary enthusiasm. Subtly and chillingly, the reality behind this surface jollity is exposed and the film becomes permeated with threats, hysteria and hints of death and imprisonment in the camps or on the White Sea Canal. Only at the very end does the face of Stalin appear on the front of a tram carrying the band whose martial music has provided the film's stirring soundtrack. This excellent film provides an ambiguous and devastating picture of the 1930s quite at odds with earlier cinematic versions.

Other major films that surfaced after the Conflict Commission had begun its work had also been shelved because of their unacceptable presentation of Soviet history. The most famous of these is the Georgian director Tengiz Abuladze's *Repentance*, made in late 1983 and early 1984, but not shown until October 1986, apparently at the urging of Raisa Gorbacheva, Eduard Shevardnadze and Egor Ligachev. The most powerful scenes in this film echo directly the horrific and absurd experience of the Stalinist purges – the heroine and her mother standing in a queue to find out whether they will be allowed to send anything to her arrested father; a confession by one of the characters that he has been involved in a plot to dig a tunnel from Bombay to London; and a scene in which the women search in vain for the father's name on logs sent down river from where they have been felled by prisoners. History, too, clearly caused the banning of such films as Irakli Kvirikadze's *The Swimmer*, also partly set in the Stalin years, and *The Beginning of an Unknown Era*, set during the Civil War, of which two parts, directed by Larisa Shepitko and Andrei Smirnov, have now been shown.

Another remarkable film devoted to the Civil War, Aleksandr Askoldov's *The Commissar*, made in 1967, was shelved largely because of its sympathetic portrayal of its Jewish characters and its flashes-forward to the Holocaust, something the authorities in charge of Goskino were unable to countenance. Askoldov has described how the Goskino chairman, Romanov, summoned him and said: 'I have two proposals for the salvation of your artistic career. First, you must cut the scene where the Jews are herded into gas chambers. Secondly, let's think about turning this Jewish family into a family of some other nationality...'. Askoldov's unwillingness to agree to these proposals led to the film's banning, to his dismissal as 'professionally incompetent', and to his explusion from the Party. His career was comprehensively ruined. Even the Conflict Commission does not seem to have been able to intervene for this film. It took an impassioned tirade from Askoldov at the Moscow Film Festival in 1987, after Klimov told a Brazilian journalist who had enquired about the working of the Commission, 'Yes, in short, everything's been done ... everything's fine ...' finally to secure its release.

It would be erroneous to suggest that history was the only cause for a film to end up shelved. The work of German and Abuladze, Shepitko and Smirnov, Kvirikadze and Askoldov, is as subversive aesthetically as it is historically.

Kira Muratova, another hugely talented director whose career was in ruins until the intervention of the Commission, makes films about the ordinary, unrhetorical lives of ordinary people, yet her work, including *Short Meetings* (1967) and her masterpiece *A Long Farewell* (1971), the story of the relationship of a slightly feckless divorced middle-aged woman and her sixteen-year-old son, ended up on the shelf. 'Ordinary' life too was apparently a subject where ideological 'guidance' was needed and ideological orthodoxy had to be observed. Muratova was told that her characters were not 'jolly enough', that their lives were not sufficiently well organized, that they danced the wrong way, that her film was 'not socialist realism, it's bourgeois realism'. Suddenly, with the release of a number of her films at once, another hitherto submerged career has surfaced.

The fate of Aleksandr Sokurov (b. 1951) offers another major example of a career lived on the shelf. Sokurov, now recognised as the leading exponent of Soviet art cinema, was clearly aesthetically unpalatable, and until the intervention of the Commission, which not only recommended that his work be released but also arranged for his belated acceptance into the union, none of his many films had been officially shown. Sokurov's *The Solitary Voice of Man*, made for 4000 rubles in fifteen days from the same Platonov story from which the émigré Andrei Konchalovsky made *Maria's Lovers*, is film-making of intense poetry and vision.

The release of the films of German, Askoldov, Muratova, Sokurov and many others has rewritten the cinematic history of the last twenty years.

## Current Developments

Andrei Plakhov has recently identified two key strands in the work of the post-unshelving period: sociological and authorial, poetic cinema.

In the area of sociology, documentarists have been quick to take advantage of the new freedoms, with several films devoted to social issues and in particular the lives of young people. Juris Podnieks's *Is it Easy to be Young?* (1986) the most famous of them, includes a report on the trial of seven young people accused of wrecking a train carriage after a rock concert, and footage about soldiers who have returned from Afghanistan. In *Supreme Court*, another Latvian documentarist, the veteran director Herz Frank, follows a young man from his trial for murder to his execution in November 1987; Georgy Gavrilov's *Confession, Chronicle of Alienation* (1988) observes three years in the life of a young Soviet drug-addict, with all his anger, pain and degradation. Iosif Pasternak's *The Black Square* (1988) combines startling visual and documentary material on the lives and work of the nonconformist artists of the 1960s to the 1980s with analysis of the attitude of the authorities to art throughout the Soviet period. Marina Goldovskaya's *Solovki Power* (1988) uses archival material, including a film made in 1928 on the orders of the secret police, and interviews with survivors to give a chilling portrait of the notorious prison island. These remarkable films and many others bear witness to the immense energy and ambition of Soviet documentarists, a phenomenon also evident at the first festival of documentary cinema, held in Sverdlovsk in 1988, at which the major prizewinner was Frank's *Supreme Court*.

In the area of feature films, a number of recent successes have also been concerned with giving a truer picture of the lives of the young, notably *Little Vera* (1988), the first film of Vasily Pichul. Set in a drab provincial town, *Little Vera* charts the tensions and limited aspirations of a working class family. Vera's father is a drunk, her mother numbed by overwork. Her ostensibly successful brother has escaped to Moscow where his marriage has failed. Faced with the prospect of a ghastly job, Vera prefers marriage to a feckless, cyncial student, who moves into the family's cramped flat. Though its assessment of Soviet life is cheerless, *Little Vera*'s bracing truthfulness has made it one of the major successes of the *glasnost* period.

Feature film-makers can also now address history with a new directness. Set in 1937, Evgeny Tsymbal's first feature, *Defence Counsel Sedov* (1988), from a story of Ilya Zverev, tells of attempts by a Muscovite lawyer to save the lives of four agronomists, already sentenced to death on an absurd charge of sabotage. Though his dogged persistence seems to bring success, the authorities are not to be so easily denied their prey, as the film's devastating climax reveals. Tsymbal's film, a work of great aesthetic daring and maturity, seamlessly incorporates archival material from the period, including a speech made by Mikoyan for the 'glorious' twentieth anniversary of the security organs. *Defence Counsel Sedov* captures the texture of life during the purges with horrifying precision.

A group of young Leningrad film-makers associated with Aleksandr Sokurov are also attracting considerable attention. The prolific Sokurov has just finished *Save and Preserve*, a version of *Madame Bovary* shot in the Caucasus, while Konstantin Lopushansky's *Letters from a Dead Man* (1986) imagines the world after a nuclear war.

All the films mentioned in this survey, both those unshelved and those made under the new conditions, have elicited much praise and won major prizes at Western film festivals. Two new festivals have also been inaugurated within the Soviet Union. The *Golden Duke*, held in Odessa and devoted to popular cinema, attracted eighty-four films from eighteen countries to its first festival in September 1988. That same month, the far more ambitious *Arsenal* festival, held in Riga, showed over two hundred avant-garde and independent films from the Soviet Union and abroad at its first session.

From the evidence recorded above the Soviet cinema would appear to be experiencing a renaissance. Yet interviewed in October 1988 about the current situation (*Ogonek*, no. 44, 1988), the director Andrei Smirnov, who has been Acting First Secretary of the Union of Cinematographers while Klimov has been away making a film, struck a surprisingly pessimistic note: 'I wish everyone interested to know that now, in October 1988, nothing has changed either in the production or in the distribution of Soviet films – the same plan, the same output norms, the same antediluvian technical base, the same shocking film and equipment ... the same rates of pay.' He went on to make a telling point that is as germane to the other arts as it is to the cinema. Removal of the former constraints will not of itself produce works of genius. Genius will remain as rare as ever. Certainly the newly-completed document for the restructuring (*perestroika*) of the Soviet cinema industry, to which Smirnov also alludes, gives some indication of the ambiguities of the current situation. The new cinema, we learn, will be based on four principles: social and state control of cinematography; the independence of the cinema as a branch of state culture; the full economic and artistic independence of the newly founded studios; and economic self-financing (*khozraschet*). The unexamined tensions between state control and artistic independence, and between the economic and artistic independence of studios and economic self-financing will surely not take long to surface. Certainly when he spoke in London in July 1988 Aleksandr Sokurov was aware of the harm the *khozraschet* system might do to Soviet art cinema, prized in the West since the 1920s, but not necessarily well-equipped to survive in the market place.

For a full survey of developments in Soviet cinema, see Christie, 1989.


## 4  THE THEATRE

The theatre has extended its thematic boundaries in both political and social terms in the last three years. The plays of Mikhail Shatrov, in particular *The Peace of Brest-Litovsk*, have been widely appreciated for affording a fuller discussion of Soviet history and for letting such long-unmentionable figures as Bukharin and Trotsky on to the Soviet stage. In social terms, Aleksandr Galin's play *Stars in the Morning Sky*, which concerns a group of prostitutes expelled from Moscow during the Olympic Games in 1980, displays an interest in and sympathy for the real lives of ordinary citizens that parallels developments in the cinema and in literature.

The most significant change in Soviet theatre has been the replacement of the old union, in 1986, by the new *Union of Theatre Workers*. One of their most effective initiatives has been the encouragement of experimental new 'Creative Studios', among whose productions have been a dramatisation of Gogol's story *The Nose*, and a version of Chekhov's *Ward Six* transposed to the Soviet period, which was much admired in Paris in 1988 and in Glasgow in 1989.

Of particular interest is the 'Poets' Evening' produced by the *Almanakh* group at the Pushkin Theatre in Moscow. The poets Dmitry Prigov, Lev Rubinshtein, Timur Kibirov, Mikhail Aizenberg, Sergei Gandlevsky, Denis Novikov and Viktor Koval, and the singer Andrei Lipsky offer an evening that is wideranging in theme and tone, extending from lyricism to daring parody of official Soviet language and values. So far their work has hardly appeared in the official press – it is no coincidence that their work is being performed under the auspices of the Union of Theatre Workers – though they are widely published in émigré journals. Their performances at the Institute of Contemporary Arts in London in March 1989 were greeted with acclaim.


5 ART


At the seventh congress of the Union of Soviet Artists, in January 1988, the 63-year-old painter, Andrei Vasnetsov, replaced Nikolai Ponomarev, who had headed the board of the union since 1973. Despite this change, the union, like its literary equivalent, remains a stronghold of conservatism. The radical developments in Soviet art are taking place elsewhere. The main art journals, as well as sections of the general press, are devoting space to hitherto unacceptable painters from the early twentieth-century avant-garde. *Ogonek*, for example, has run a well-illustrated series called 'A Collection of Twentieth-Century Russian Art'. There have been major exhibitions in Moscow and Leningrad of such masters as Malevich, Kandinsky, Chagal and Filonov, accompanied by excellent catalogues.

Moscow also saw major showings of Dali and Francis Bacon in 1988, signs of a widening of the range of what is acceptable in Western painting. Equally welcome is the new tolerance shown to previously harassed nonconformist Soviet painters. Ilya Kabakov described the consequences of thirty years of attacks on unofficial art in an article in *Literaturnaya gazeta* (19 August 1987). Now 'unofficial' artists are being exhibited in the Soviet Union and at galleries in Europe and North America that have always encouraged their work but now find a particularly enthusiastic market for it. Another sign of this huge Western interest is the auction of Russian avant-garde and contemporary Soviet painting held by Sotheby's in Moscow on 7 July 1988.

## 6 CONCLUSIONS

In their different ways, the worlds of literature, cinema, theatre and painting have been enlivened to a degree almost unhoped for in the course of the last four years. The official face of Soviet culture is transformed. But another significant phenomenon of the Gorbachev years has been the encouragement of informal groups in all areas of Soviet life. This development has been paralleled in the arts – groups and individuals who have been existing underground have suddenly surfaced. Many of them participate simultaneously in both official and unofficial culture. The flourishing of a 'parallel culture' is in large part connected with the evolution of the taste of young people. Rock music, the popularity of which among Soviet youth is increasingly apparent and acknowledged, cannot be smoothly accommodated into official cultural channels, despite, for example, the journals' attempts to woo young readers with series called 'An A–Z of Western Rock Music' (*V mire knig*) *or* 'Rock in the USSR' (*Rodnik*). (Full-colour pinups in the 'literary' journals of such luminaries as Boy George are one of the more bizarre consequences of cultural *glasnost*.) In addition to this development, avant-garde composers of classical music are also finding it easier to get a hearing for their work. (For a survey of developments in Soviet music, see Rice, 1989.)

In the world of cinema, the same 'paralleling' is now apparent. In addition to the official cinematic press there is an unofficial journal, *Ciné-fantôme*, run by the brothers Igor and Gleb Aleinikov, both still in their twenties. Avant-garde films are now being shot 'in parallel' by a number of film-makers in Moscow and Leningrad. Some of them were shown in 1988 at the first Riga film festival. Connections could be drawn betwen the Aleinikov brothers' short film *Tractor*, in which a seemingly orthodox Soviet documentary degenerates into absurdity and obscenity, and the play with Soviet language, ideology and aesthetics by members of the *Almanakh* group such as Prigov and Rubinshtein.

It is clearly not possible to predict how long such experiments will be able to flourish. Nevertheless, what has been achieved already can be seen as the beginning of the breakdown of the hegemony of the state version of Soviet culture, the beginning of a return to diversity. In 1921, at the start of the period of official control of culture by the state, the writer Evgeny Zamyatin ironically compared the Soviet Union to the *Paradise* in which 'you have only monophony, only rejoicing, only light, only a unanimous *Te Deum*' (Zamyatin, 1970, p. 59). What we are witnessing now (and what the publication of Zamyatin's novel *We* has been both a consequence of and a stimulus to), is the reassertion of a long-awaited and heady polyphony.

# Bibliography

AGANBEGYAN, Abel, *The Challenge: Economics of Perestroika* (London, Hutchinson 1988).

ANDREEV, Sergei, 'Struktura vlasti i zadachi obshchestva', *Neva*, no. 1/ 1989, pp. 144–73.

ANTIC, Oxana, 'A New Phase in the Struggle Against Religious Communists', RL Research Bulletin, RL 18/87, 14 January 1987.

BARBER, J. D., 'Children of the Arbat' *Detente* no. 11/1988.

BAUMAN, Z., 'Officialdom and Class' in F. Parkin (ed.), *The Social Analysis of Class Structure* (London, Tavistock Publications 1974).

BAUMAN, Z., *Berkeley–Duke Occasional Papers on the Second Economy in the USSR*, no. 10, April 1987.

BERLINER, Joseph, 'Organisational Restructuring of the Soviet Economy' in *Gorbachev's Economic Plans*, Vol. 1, (Washington, DC, USGPO, 1987), pp. 70–83.

BOVIN, A., 'Mirnoe sosuchchestvovanie i mirovaya sistema sotsialisma', *Mirovaya ekonomika i mezhdunarodnie otnosheniya* (MEMO), no. 7, 1988, pp. 5–15.

BUCK, Trevor and John COLE, *Modern Soviet Economic Performance* (Oxford, Blackwell, 1987).

BUNGS, Dzintra, 'Cultural Leaders Call for Greater National Sovereignty', *Radio Free Europe Research (Baltic Area SR/7)*, 13 July 1988.

BUTENKO, Anatoly. 'Protivorechiya razvitiya sotsializma kak obshchestvennogo stroya', *Voprosy Filosofii*, no. 10/1982, pp. 16–29.

BUZGALIN, A. 'Protivorechiya sotsialisticheskoi ekonomiki na sovremennon etape', *Voprosy Ekonomiki*, no. 5/1987, pp. 28–9.

CHRISTIE, I. 'The Cinema', in Julian Graffy and Geoffrey Hosking (eds), *Culture and the Media in the USSR Today* (London, Macmillan, 1989), pp. 43–77.

COOK, C., *The Soviet Livestock Sector*, (USDA, Foreign Agricultural Economic Research, no. 235) (Washington, DC, June 1988).

DAHM, Helmut, *Sozialistische Krisentheorie. Die sowjetische Wende – ein Trugbild* (Munich, Erich Wewel Verlag 1987).

DASHICHEV, V., 'Vostok – zapad: poisk novykh otnoshenii', *Liternaturnaya Gazeta*, 18 May 1988.

DASHICHEV, V., et al. 'East-West Relations and Eastern Europe... The Soviet Perspective', *Problems of Communism*, no. 3–4, May–August 1988, pp. 60–70.

DAVIES, R. W., 'Soviet History in the Gorbachev Revolution', *Socialist Register 1988* (London, Merlin Press, 1988) pp. 37–78.

DAVYDOV, Yu., 'The Soviet Vision of a Common European House', Unpublished paper presented to the BISA–ISA Conference, London, 1989.

DAWISHA, K. and J. VALDEZ, 'Socialist Internationalism in Eastern Europe', *Problems of Communism*, no. 2, March–April 1988, pp. 1–14.

DEUTCH, Shelley, 'The Soviet Weapons Industry: An Overview' in *Gorbachev's Economic Plans*. Vol. 1 (Washington DC, USGPO, 1987, pp. 405–30.

DYKER, David, *The Future of the Soviet Economic Planning System* (London, Croom Helm 1985).

EUROPEAN STRATEGY GROUP, *The Gorbachev Challenge and European Security*, forthcoming.

FEDOSEEV, P. N., 'Dialektika internatsionalnogo i natsionalnogo v sotsialisticheskom obraze zhizni', *Voprosy Filosofii*, no. 12/1981, pp. 24–36.

GIRNIUS, Saulius, 'Lithuania in 1988', Radio Free Europe *Background Report*, 16 December 1988.

GLICKHAM, C., 'New Directions for Soviet Foreign Policy', Radio Liberty Research Bulletin, RL Supplement no. 2/86, 1986.

GOMULKA, Stanislaw, *Growth, Innovation and Reform in Eastern Europe* (Brighton, Wheatsheaf, 1986).

GORBACHEV, M. S., *19th All-Union Conference of the CPSU: Report by Mikhail Gorbachev, Moscow, Kremlin Palace of Congresses, June 28, 1988, Documents and Materials* (Moscow, Novosti, 1988).

GORBACHEV, M. S., *Perestroika: New Thinking for Our Country and the World* (London, Collins, 1987).

GRAFFY, Julian, 'The Literary Press', in Julian Graffy and Geoffrey Hosking (eds), *Culture and the Media in the USSR Today* (London, Macmillan, 1989), pp. 107–57.

GRANICK, David, *Job Rights in the Soviet Union: Their Consequences* (Cambridge, Cambridge University Press, 1987a).

GRANCIK, David, 'Commentary' in *Gorbachev's Economic Plans*, Vol. 2 (Washington DC, USGPO, 1987b), pp. 336–43.

GREGORY, Paul and Robert STUART, *Soviet Economic Structure and Performance*, 3rd edition (New York, Harper and Row, 1986).

GREGORY, Paul and Robert STUART, *Gorbachev's Economic Plans*, Vol. 1, and Vol. 2, Joint Economic Committee (Washington DC, USGPO, 1987).

HALLIDAY, F., *The Making of the Second Cold War* (London, Verso, 1983).

HANSON, Philip, *Trade and Technology in Soviet-Western Relations* (London, Macmillan, 1981).

HANSON, Philip, 'The Soviet Economic Stake in European Detente', in H. Gelman (ed.), *The Future of Soviet Policy Toward Western Europe* (Santa Monica, CA, Rand, 1985), pp. 29–51.

HANSON, Philip and Keith PAVITT, *The Comparative Economics of Research, Development and Innovation in East and West: A Survey*, (London, Harwood Academic Publishers, 1987).

HANSON, Philip and Elizabeth TEAGUE, 'Has Party Membership Begun to Fall?', Radio Liberty, *Report on the USSR*, 3 April 1989.

HARRISON, M., 'Stalinist Industrialisation and the Test of War', unpublished report of work in progress, Department of Economics, University of Warwick, 5 May 1988.

HAUSLOHNER, Peter, 'Gorbachev's Social Contract', *Soviet Economy*, Vol. 3, no. 1 (January 1987), pp. 54–89 (1987a).

HAUSLOHNER, Peter, 'Commentary' in *Gorbachev's Economic Plans*, Vol. 2 (Washington DC, USGPO, 1987b), pp. 344–52.

HECHT, L., *The Soviet Union Through its Laws* (New York, Praeger, 1983).

HEWETT, Ed., *Reforming the Soviet Economy* (Washington DC, Brookings 1988a).

HEWETT, Ed., 'Economic Reform in the Wake of the XIX Party Conference', *PlanEcon Report*, Vol. 4, no. 29 (22 July 1988) (1988b).

HOSKING, G. A., 'At Last an Exorcism' *The Times Literary Supplement*, 9–15 October 1987.

ILVES, Toomas, 'A Scathing Attack on Language Policy', *Radio Free Europe Research (Baltic Area SR/5)*, 17 July 1987a.

ILVES, Toomas, 'Conformist Communists Propose Turning Estonia into Closed Economic Zone', *Radio Free Europe Research (Baltic Area SR/7)*, 28 October 1987b.

ILVES, Toomas, 'Protest Letter from Cultural Unions', *Radio Free Europe Research* (Baltic Area SR/1), 21 January 1988a.

ILVES, Toomas, 'Cultural Unions Adopt Resolution on Nationality Reforms', *Radio Free Europe Research (Baltic Area SR/6)*, 3 June 1988b.

JOWETT, Ken, 'Soviet Neotraditionalism: the Political Corruption of a Leninist Regime', *Soviet Studies*, Vol. 35, no. 3 (July 1983), pp. 275–97.

JOZSA, Gyula, *Das Reformproject Gorbatschows im Rahmen des politburokratischen Systems*, Teil I: *Sowjetburokratie im selbstkritischen Lichte der Glasnost*, Berichte des Bundesinstituts fur ostwissenschaftliche und internationale Studien, Cologne, no. 43/1988.

JOZSA, Gyula, *Das Reformproject Gorbatschows im Rahmen des politburokratischen Systems*, Teil II: *Dysfunktionen des Systems Motive, Probleme und Widerspruche der Perestroika*, Berichte des Bundesinstituts for ostwissenschaftliche und internationale Probleme, Cologne, no. 6/1989.

KOSTAKOV, Vladimir, 'Zanyatost: defitsit ili izbytok', *Kommunist*, no. 2/1987, pp. 78–89. Translated as 'Employment: Scarcity or Surplus', *Problems of Economics*, Vol. 30, no. 3 (July 1987) (1987a).

KOSTAKOV, Vladimir, 'Polnaya zanyatost. Kak my ee ponimaem?', *Kommunist*, no. 14/1987 pp. 16–25 (1987b). Translated as 'Full Employment: how do we understand it?, *Problems of Economics*, Vol. 30, no. 10 (February 1988).

KOSTIN, L., 'Perestroika sistemy oplaty truda', *Voprosy ekonomiki*, no. 11/1987, pp. 41–51. Translated as 'Restructuring the System of Payment of Labor', *Problems of Economics*, Vol. 31, no. 3 (July 1988) pp. 62–80.

KOVALEV, A. G., 'Sdelat perestroiku glavnym predmetom nashei zhizni', *Vestnik Ministerstva inostrannykh del SSSR (MIDa)*, no. 3/10, October 1988, pp. 9–13.

KUBALKOVA, V. and A. A., CRUICKSHANK, *A Time to Think New: Soviet 'New Thinking' on International Relations* (Berkeley, CA, University of California Press, 1989).

KULIKOV, Vsevold V., 'Protivorechiya ekonomicheskoi sistemy sotsializ-ma kak istochnik ee razvitiya', *Voprosy Filosofii*, no. 1/1986, pp. 117–28.

LANE, David (ed.), *Labour and Employment in the USSR* (Brighton, Wheatsheaf, 1986).

LIGHT, M., 'The Study of International Relations in the Soviet Union', *Millennium: Journal of International Studies*, 16/2, 1987, pp. 287–96.

LLOYD, D., *The Idea of Law* (Harmondsworth, Penguin, 1981).

McAULEY, Alastair, *Economic Welfare in the Soviet Union* (Madison, Wisconsin University Press, 1979).

McAULEY, Alastair, *Women's Work and Wages in the Soviet Union* (London, Allen & Unwin, 1981).

McCAULEY, Martin (ed.), *The Soviet Union under Gorbachev* (London, Macmillan, 1987).

MALCOLM, N., *Soviet Policy Perspectives on Western Europe* (London, RIIA/Routledge, 1989).

MANN, Dawn, *Paradoxes of Soviet Reform: The Nineteenth Communist Party Conference* (Center for Strategic and International Studies, Washington, DC), 1988.

MANN, Dawn, 'Elections to the Congress of People's Deputies Nearly Over', Radio Liberty, *Report on the USSR*, 3 April 1989.

MARX, Karl, *The Eighteenth Brumaire of Louis Napoleon* (London, 1943, first published 1843).

MIRONOV, N. P., 'Vosstanovlenie i razvitie leninskihk printsipov sotsialis-ticheskoi zakonnosti (1953–1963)', *Voprosy Istorii KPSS*, no. 2/1964 pp. 17–29.

MIRSKY, G., 'Sotsialisticheskaya orientatsiya v 'tretem mire' (Nekotorye problemy issledovaniya)', *Rabochii klass i sovremenny mir*, no. 4/1988, pp. 118–29.

*NARODNOE KHOZYAISTVO SSSR* (various years).

NAHAYLO, Bohdan, 'Nationalities', in Martin McCauley (ed.) *The Soviet Union under Gorbachev* (London, Macmillan 1987), pp. 73–96.

NAHAYLO, Bodhan, 'Concern Voiced about Six Million Ukrainians Con-demned to "Denationalisation"', *Radio Liberty Research Bulletin*, RL92/88, 27 February 1988a.

NAHAYLO, Bohdan, 'Ukrainians Object to Moscow Patriarchiate's Depic-tion of Millennium as Solely "Russian" Affair', *Radio Liberty Research Bulletin*, RL476/88, 12 October 1988b.

NAHAYLO, Bohdan, 'Representatives of Non-Russian National Move-ments Establish Coordinating Committee', *Radio Liberty Research Bulle-tin*, RL283/88, 22 June 1988c.

NEUMANN, F., *The Democratic and the Authoritarian State* (London, Free Press of Clencoe, 1957.

PERELYGIN, V. N., *'Nekotorye voprosy . . .'*, *Rol prava v realizatsii pro-dovolstvennoi programmy SSSR* (Moscow, 1986).

PETROVSKY, V., 'Doverie i vyzhivaniye chelovechestva', *MEMO*, no. 11/1987, pp. 15–26.

POPOV, N., 'Amerikantsy i my'., *Literaturnaya Gazeta*, 28 October 1987.

POSHKUS, B. I., *Organizatsiya ekonomicheskoi raboty v khozyaistve* (Mos-cow, 1988).

RAHR, Alexander, 'Restructuring the Kremlin Leadership', Radio Liberty Research Bulletin, RL no. 423/88, 1988.

RAHR, Alexander, 'Gorbachev Changes Party Structure', Radio Liberty Research Bulletin, RL 519/88, 30 November 1988.

RAHR, Alexander, 'Gorbachev Battles With Opposition', Radio Liberty, *Report on the USSR*, 26 January 1989.

REES, E. A., *State Control in Soviet Russia: the Rise and Fall of the Workers' and Peasants' Inspectorate, 1920–34* (London, Macmillan, 1987).

RICE, C., 'Soviet Music in the Era of *Perestroika*', in Julian Graffy and Geoffrey Hosking (eds), *Culture and the Media in the USSR Today* (London, Macmillan, 1989), pp. 88–105.

RIGBY, T. H., *Lenin's Government: Sovnarkom 1917–1922* (Cambridge, Cambridge University Press, 1979).

SAIKAL, A. and W. MALEY (eds), *The Soviet Union Withdrawal from Afghanistan* (Cambridge, Cambridge University Press, 1989).

SANAKOYEV, Sh., 'Peraceful Coexistence in the Context of Military–Strategic Parity', *International Affairs* (Moscow), no. 2/1988, pp. 75–85.

SAUER, Thomas, *Paradigmenwechsel in der Politischen Okonomie des Sozialismus? Zu einigen Grundlinien des neueren gesellschaftswissenschaftlichen Denkens in der UdSSR*, Berichte des Bundesinstituts fur ostwissenschaftliche und internationale Studien, Cologne, no. 46/1988.

SCANLAN, James P., 'Reforms and Civil Society in the USSR', *Problems of Communism*, March–April 1988, pp. 41–6.

SCHAPIRO, Leonard, 'The Party and the State', *Survey*, October 1961, pp. 111–16.

SHAPRIO, J. C., 'Shatrov and his Critics: on the Debate over *Dalshe... dalshe... dalshe!*, unpublished working paper presented to Soviet Industrialisation Project Seminar, CREES, University of Birmingham May 1988.

SHEEHY, Ann, 'Slav Elected First Secretary of Tashkent City Party Committee', RL 333/85, 3 October 1985.

SHEEHY, Ann, 'Slav Presence Increased in Uzbek Party Buro and Secretariat', RL 94/86, 26 February 1986.

SHEEHY, Ann, 'The First Stage of Gorbachev's Reform of the Political System and the Non-Russian Republics', *Radio Liberty Research Bulletin*, RL520/88, 7 December 1988.

SHEVARDNADZE, E., 'V Ministerstve inostrannykh del SSSR', *Vestnik MIDa* no. 2/1987, pp. 30–34.

SHEVARDNADZE, E., 'Nauchno-prakticheskaya konferentsiya MID SSSR Doklad E. A. Shevardnadze', *Vestnik MIDa*, no. 15/1988, pp. 27–46.

SHMELEV. G. I., *Semya beret podryad* (Moscow 1987a).

SHMELEV. G. I., *Semya v sfere proizvodstva* (Moscow, 1987b).

SHMELEV, G. I. and S. I. ZAVYALOV (eds), *Puti povysheniya ispolzovaniya trudovogo selskoi semi* (Moscow 1987).

SHMELEV, Nikolai, 'Novye trevogi', *Novyi Mir*, no. 4/1988, pp. 160–75.

SOLCHANYK, Roman, 'A Letter to Gorbachev: Belorussian Intellectuals on the Language Question', *Radio Liberty Research Bulletin*, RL 142/87, 20 April 1987a.

SOLCHANYK, Roman, 'Catastrophic Language Situation in Major Ukrainian Cities', *Radio Liberty Research Bulletin*, RL286/87, 15 July 1987b.

SOLCHANYK, Roman. 'Statistical *Glasnost*: Data on Language and Education in the Ukraine', *Radio Liberty Research Bulletin*, RL152/87, 15 April 1987c.

SOLOMON, P. H. 'The case of the vanishing acquittal: informal norms and the practice of Soviet criminal justice', *Soviet Studies*, Vol. 39, no. 4, October 1987, pp. 531–55.

SOPER, John, 'Problems in the Kazakh Educational System', *Radio Liberty Research Bulletin*, RL 488/87, 2 December 1987.

SOPER, John, 'Kirgiz and Uzbek Writers Express their Views in Connection with Party Conference', *Radio Liberty Research Bulletin*, RL309/88, 12 July 1988.

*SSSR V TSIFRAKH V 1987 GODU* (Moscow, 1988).

*STATISTICHESKII EZHEGODNIK STRAN-CHLENOV SOVETA EKONOMICHESKOI VZAIMOPOMOSHCHI* (Moscow, 1987).

TATU, Michel, '19th Party Conference', *Problems of Communism* May–August 1988, pp. 1–15.

TEAGUE, Elizabeth, 'Gorbachev's "Human Factor" Policies' in *Gorbachev's Economic Plans*, Vol. 2 (Washington DC, USGPO, 1987), pp. 224–39.

TEAGUE, Elizabeth, *Solidarity and the Soviet Worker* (London, Croom Helm, 1988).

TEAGUE, Elizabeth, 'The Twenty-seventh Party Congress: Personnel Changes in the Politburo and the Secretariat', Radio Liberty Research Bulletin, RL no. 111/86, 1986.

TREML, Vladimir, 'Gorbachev's Anti-Drinking Campaign: A "Noble Experiment" or a Costly Exercise in Futility?' in *Gorbachev's Economic Plans*, Vol. 2 (Washington DC, USGPO, 1987), pp. 297–311.

TROFIMENKO, G., 'Towards a New Quality of Soviet–American relations', *International Affairs* (Moscow), no. 12/1988, pp. 13–25.

VALKENIER, E. K., *The Soviet Union and the Third World: An Economic Bind* (New York, Praeger, 1983).

WADEKIN, Karl-Eugen, *The Private Sector in Soviet Agriculture* (Berkeley, Los Angeles and London, 1973).

WEBER, Max, *The Theory of Social and Economic Organisations* (New York, Free Press, 1947).

WHEATCROFT, S. G., 'Unleashing the Energy of History, Mentioning the Unmentionable and Reconstructuring Soviet Historical Awareness: Moscow 1987', *Australian Slavonic and East European Studies*, Vol. 1, no. 1/ 1987, pp. 85–132 (1987a).

WHEATCROFT, S. G., 'Steadying the Energy of History and Probing the Limits of *Glasnost*; Moscow July to December 1987', *Australian Slavonic and East European Studies*, Vol. 1, no. 2/1987, pp. 57–114 (1987b).

WINIECKI, Jan, *Economic Prospects – East and West: a View from the East* (London, Centre for Research into Communist Economies 1987).

YASMANN, Victor, 'The Soviets and the Leading Role of the Party: From a "State" Party to a "Party" state', Radio Liberty Research Bulletin, 14 July 1988.

*ZAKON SOYUZA SOVETSKIKH SOTSIALISTICHESKIKH RESPUB-*

*LIK 'O KOOPERATSII V SSSR'* (draft), (Moscow, Izdatelstvo Izvestiya Narodnykh Deputatov SSSR, 1988).

ZAMYATIN, E., *A Soviet Heretic: Essays by Yevgeny Zamyatin*, Edited and translated by Mirra Ginsburg (Chicago and London, University of Chicago Press, 1970).

ZHURKIN, V., S., KARAGONOV and A. KORTUNOV. 'Vyzovy bezopasnosti – starye i novye', *Kommunist*, no. 1/1988, pp. 42–50.

# Index

# DATE DUE